CONVERTIBLE CONVERSATIONS

by Paul Gray

ENDORSEMENTS for

CONVERTIBLE CONVERSATIONS

"In *Convertible Conversations*, Paul Gray has brought us into the Perichoretic Circle of life, love and even laughter in the midst of a world that often drags us through loss and grief. As young Jack moves through the loss of his parents and into a new world, readers will find themselves releasing their grip on a past they may have held sacred and being introduced to a new and different world of grace that exceeds what none can imagine who haven't traveled the same road of death and discovery. This book will encourage you, entertain you and most of all, equip you to live the life you were created to know and enjoy. We have a Papa who guides us into deeper truth than we have known. Walk with Him through this book and be transformed."
Dr. Steve McVey
President, Grace Walk Ministries
Vice-President, Global Grace Seminary

"I read *Convertible Conversations* on a flight from Tulsa to Anchorage. Normally I don't read a lot on planes because I fall asleep and I don't like to sleep when I'm riding with someone! Wasn't a problem with this book. Paul did a great job of keeping me riveted to the story line. Felt like I was right there with Fred, Nana, Jack and Mikey! I felt God's unconditional love on every page. Can't wait to share it with my friends and family."
Brett Neil
President, Sparks Construction, Bixby, Oklahoma

"Paul Gray's writing reflects a man of many talents and experiences, supported by a fundamental confidence through his relationship with God. A showman and a preacher, Gray also tells

a sentimental story about unconditional love in *Convertible Conversations*. It is the kind of book you would enjoy talking about with someone else."
Clenece Hills, Retired teacher

"Like Paul Gray, I have come to believe that until we get the foundational lens right... God is a loving Father... all our theology will eventually miss the mark. Though I might not agree with all of his conclusion or characterizations of the church I believe he is lifting up an important conversation. A conversation like this will eventually get us to new heights and a better understanding of who God is, how much we are loved and what He wants to do through us in this life."
Tom Bassford
President "Significant Matters" Kansas City

"Convertible Conversations" is very much written in a conversational tone, which seems natural and allows for good story flow. A lot of really good questions are raised in these conversations and Paul provides some good answers or food for additional thought. He includes a really insightful picture of the Trinity from a musician's perspective. It is an excellent book for anyone who is uncomfortable with some of the traditional church teachings on judgement and punishment."
Wayne McDaniel, CFP®, CLU, ChFC, CAP®

MOTIVATION CHAMPS PUBLISHING

All rights reserved, including the right to reproduce this book or portions thereof in any form whatsoever.

For publishing information, please contact www.motivationchamps.com ISBN:978-0-9981194-7-2 / Ebook ISBN: 978-9981194-9-6

Convertible Conversations/ Paul Gray

Manufactured in the United States of America For information about special discounts for bulk orders or speaking engagements, please contact gal22021@gmail.com

Contents

Part 1 Once in A Thousand Years _____ 1
    Confirmed _____ 6
    The End of the Beginning _____ 7
    The 'Hellish Darkness' _____ 10
    Taking Care of Business _____ 15
    Letters from the Dead _____ 15
    God is Never Mad at You _____ 17
    Making Plans _____ 19
    Playing Hardball and Cheap Religious Platitudes _____ 22
    Recalling Inappropriate Funerals _____ 27
    Prelude to the Celebration of Life _____ 28
    The Celebration of Life _____ 30
    The Receiving Line _____ 34
    The Leaving Process _____ 35
    Moving Day _____ 36
    BBQ and the Yellow Rose of Texas _____ 37
    Everyone Has a Story _____ 40
    Confession and "The Fire" _____ 44
    "The Grace Uh God" _____ 49
    Heading to Kansas _____ 51
    The Flint Hills of Kansas _____ 54

Part 2 No, No! Swim, Dad! _____ 55
    The "Really Is" _____ 58
    The Trusting Axe _____ 59
    The First Convertible Conversation _____ 62
    America's Favorite Pastime and the Sin of Certainty _____ 68
    First Day of Fifth Grade _____ 79

- Blue Jays and Groundhogs 83
- The Second Day of School 89
- So, What Do You Teach? 90
- Answered Prayers 95
- Trumpet Lessons and Respect 95
- The '10-10-10-70 Plan' 97

Part 3 Close Up Horror 102
- Payback or Putback 114
- Rumors, Gossip, and Malicious Mischief 123
- Behind Bars and Broken 125
- God's Will 131
- An Unpleasant Incident 133
- Nothing 136
- Grace in Real Time 139
- Squirrely 141
- When I Destroy My Enemy, I Make Him My Friend. 145
- Playing the "General" Card 148
- The Spectrum 151
- An Invitation 154
- A New Friend 157

Part 4 Grace Community 159
- New Insight on An Old Story 162
- Religious Pain 166
- Angry as Hell 169
- Fearing The Worst 174
- Where Do Lies and Evil Come From? 176
- The Poison We Drink Hoping the Other Person Will Die 179
- A Helluva Number 182

Part 5 Autumn in Kansas 188

Out Home ... 191
Turning Eleven ... 197
Chocolate Covered Faces ... 199
Uncovering Fake News– The Biggest Lie of All Time ... 203
All Good Things Come From God ... 212
Old Mack Donald ... 213

Part 6 An Unlikely Minister ... 216
Transitions ... 216
What Did You Do Today? ... 221
Evening Information ... 224
God Works All Things Together ... 226
'Stupid'… Again ... 229
Summer Time ... 239

Section 7 The Unforced Rhythms of Grace ... 240
Instrumental Change ... 240
Christmas is Coming ... 244
Back to Texas ... 246
A Bouquet for Clara ... 253
'Til We Meet Again ... 255
Spring Semester ... 259
Long Distance Relationship and Trinity Trio ... 262
The Divine Triune Circle Dance ... 264
Music, Music, I Hear the Music ... 271

Part 8 Ultimate Reconciliation ... 274
What's Next? ... 274
So Long, Good Friend ... 287
Grace: Unconditional Love in Action ... 290
New Old Clothes and Freddie's Last Letter ... 302

Part 9 End of One Era and Beginning Of Another ... 308

    Gallivanting in Galveston 309
    The Next Day 320
    Afternoon Fun 320
    What God Requires, God Provides 326
    Dinner and an Invitation 330
    The Honeymoon's Over 331
    Bearing Down at Baylor 333
Part 10 The Last Convertible Conversation 335
Section 11 Remembering Pops 342
    Celebration of Life 343

Part 1
Once in A Thousand Years

News of Hurricane Harvey consumed everyone in Conroe, Texas and the rest of the country. The "once every 1,000 years disaster" of late August 2017 changed the lives of over two million people in the Gulf Coast and outlying areas.

People lost homes, cars, pets, and businesses: many lost all their worldly goods and personal possessions, barely escaping the flood waters with their lives.

Over 70 people lost their lives. Freddie and Rachel Miller, their only son, Jack, and his grandparents instantly had their lives changed in the most horrible of ways.

Jack's parents, both public school music teachers and leaders of a grace-centered community, started helping those in need as soon as the hurricane slammed the greater Houston area.

Grandparents Fred Sr. and Susie Miller, both 70 years old, arrived from Kansas to Conroe a few days before the hurricane. As was their custom, they made the trip every year to enjoy the Labor Day weekend with their only son and his family. But this trip was to be like no other.

They had a couple days of family fun before Hurricane Harvey slammed Corpus Christi, Dickinson, Rockport and surrounding coastal towns. Grateful to have their son's grandparents staying with him, Freddie and Rachel knew that God was calling them to help others in harm's way. They responded to the call for volunteers without hesitation.

At the end of their second long day of helping stranded families atop their flooded homes, Freddie and Rachel mesmerized their family with stories of average locals joining volunteers from parts of Texas and even other states, who came together to help people in harm's way.

They learned of a large mattress store opening its doors to displaced people to give them a place to sleep. They heard about closed grocery stores and restaurants giving away food and other necessities. They were fascinated by accounts of people in little row boats and those in huge luxury boats with cabins and sleeping quarters teaming together to rescue people from their attics and the tops of their homes.

Exhausted, they all went to bed around midnight, and Jack's parents hoped to sleep in a little before again heading down Highway 45 in their truck to meet other volunteers at a Red Cross staging area; however, urgent messages on their cell phones prompted them to leave earlier than anticipated.

Anticipating another day of her son and Rachel, the daughter she never had, going to help those in need, Susie Miller rose before dawn and had a hearty breakfast ready as the others awoke. The five Millers ate hurriedly as they watched news reports about the ever-spreading flood damage and heard totals of thousands of people left homeless, many of them now residing in shelters, and a growing number of lives lost.

Without verbalizing it, they all hoped that the waters wouldn't get to their neighborhood in Conroe. Little did they know that soon they would be part of those statistics.

Waving goodbye to Rachel and Freddie, Jack and his grandparents settled into another day of watching the continual reports of Harvey's devastation, gasping as they saw yet another familiar Houston area landmark partially– or totally– submerged.

They were transfixed as a reporter told them that Harvey was much more than a hurricane or a tropical storm. He said that it's the result of perfect weather conditions that may only happen once every thousand years. They realized they were watching a historical event that would be talked about for generations.

"The storm is generating an amount of rain that would normally be seen only once in just over 1,000 years," said Edmond Russo, a deputy district engineer for the Army Corps of Engineers. "The worst is probably yet to come; Houston is expected to receive more rainfall."

"Reservoirs designed to control flooding in the greater Houston area are full and flood waters are starting to flow over the top. Hours after the Addicks Reservoir was overtopped, officials in Brazoria County, just south of Houston, warned that a levee at Columbia Lakes had been breached by floodwaters and urged any residents who had not already evacuated the area to leave immediately, warning: 'GET OUT NOW!'

"The worst is not over yet. All the rainfall north of Houston has to go somewhere. Hurricane Harvey is truly one for the history books."

Not wanting to worry Jack, Fred Sr., and Susie did their best not to show their concern about their son and his wife's safety, but neither had a good feeling about this particular day. They made another trip in the continuous rain to the grocery store and joined the lines of people stocking up in anticipation of not having food or drinkable water available if their area flooded as the nearby towns already had.

After returning home, a friend came and invited Jack to join him and some friends at one of their houses to play video games while his grandparents tried to come up with emergency plans for their family's safety should floodwaters reach even their elevated neighborhood.

They had dinner together, and going against their long-standing tradition of not having tv on during meals, they watched the news as they ate.

"Look!" they all three said in unison as they saw Freddie and Rachel being interviewed by a reporter. The couple was standing next to their truck in water over their knees.

"I'm speaking with Freddie and Rachel Miller from Conroe. This is the third day they've been here rescuing people with their monster truck. Tell me what you'd be doing if we didn't have this disaster."

"We're both public school music teachers, so we'd be directing bands, getting ready for the first football game." Freddie replied.

"Are you here on your own or with a group?"

The pretty young woman wearing an Astro's cap with her blonde ponytail sticking out through back responded, "We're involved in a grace community, a small group that practices grace– God's unconditional love perpetually in action, helping people in a variety of ways."

"You've certainly been doing that by bringing in group after group of people with white sheets hanging out their second floor windows– some even on their roofs. How many would you estimate you've brought to safety?"

"Oh, gosh," Freddie said. "I'd say we've made 40 trips or so– about one every fifteen minutes for the last ten hours and we usually bring back three to five people each time… and some pets," he grinned.

"That's about 150 people just today… and this is your third day?"

"That's right." Rachel responded. Her winsome good looks and perpetual smile seemed to light up the screen. "But it's not just us. Our whole group from Conroe is here, and we get paired up with other volunteers whom we've never met. It's been a great experience helping people."

"I'll let you folks get back to your work. Thanks for your service!"

The reporter continued, "Thousands of volunteers like Freddie and Rachel have selflessly gone back into harm's way over and over again here in the Hurricane impact zone. They, along with the police and fire department, are truly Houston's finest. They are volunteer first responders that are saving lives and rescuing people that otherwise might be swept away by these raging waters.

"I want to remind all our viewers to stay inside. Don't attempt to drive or walk in these flood waters– they can be much deeper than they appear, and sudden currents that come when a levee or reservoir is breeched can sweep you away in an instant. Unfortunately we have reports already of people drowning when their vehicle was washed away."

The Millers talked excitedly with each other about seeing Freddie and Rachel on the news and were extremely proud of them, and more than a little worried as well.

They played a game of Monopoly, and waited the return of Jack's parents from another day of rescue activities. Expecting their arrival around 10 p.m. as they had the previous two days, they all showed their concern when 11 p.m. and then midnight came and went.

Assuring Jack that things would be all right, his grandparents convinced him to go to bed, promising to wake him when his parents arrived. With his constant companion, a golden Labrador named Mikey, snuggled next to him, he finally dozed off.

The elder couple slept fitfully on recliners in the living room, the sound muted on the tv. Periodically, they would awake as strong rain and wind gusts hammered the house. Their concern grew as the clock changed hour by hour.

Eventually they both fell sound asleep and were startled to hear Jack calling, "Pops, Nana, did my folks come home and leave already? Why didn't you wake me?"

Still groggy, his grandfather awoke to the gravity of the situation.

"They aren't home, yet, Jack. They must have needed to help all night. I'm sure they'll be home soon or they'll call us."

A general uneasiness descended over the three as the day wore on. Constant news reports about the rising toll of missing and confirmed dead seemed to increase the darkening pall that enveloped the household.

Watching the news prompted Jack to ask a myriad of questions. "Do you think Mom and Dad might be in one of those houses rescuing people from their attic? What happens to people in a car that gets swept away underwater? Could they be in a hospital? Why don't they call?" There were no good answers.

Under the guise of running an errand, Fred left the house and drove under dismal rain clouds to the County Sheriff's office a block off of 1st Street at the 336 East Loop exit. The area was teeming with local, state, and federal emergency personnel and their vehicles. The National Guard had trailers conveying huge rescue boats, Blackhawk helicopters were taking off and landing, tv cameras, radio station mics, and print reporter's cell phones were involved in an array of interviews and updates.

After several inquiries, Fred made his way to the appropriate place to report missing persons. The gentleman in charge, Lieutenant Davis, a compassionate middle-aged man, listened intently to Fred and took down all the pertinent information. He sent out an email, checked some sites on his data base, then excused himself to go to another room to make some calls.

"Well, the good news is that we don't have any record of them in a hospital…or, uh… having had a fatal accident. The bad news is the same; we just don't have any record of them. I'll put out an APB with their names and a copy of the picture you provided me. We'll do our best to find them quickly… but you know with all the chaos and emergencies, I can't honestly tell you when that might be."

Fred exhaled slowly, looked at the floor, and eventually said, "Thanks, Lt. I know you have a very hard job. I'll look forward to hearing from you."

He drove back to his son's home with a sinking feeling in his chest.

Arriving at the Miller home, he told his wife and their 10-year-old grandson where he'd been and the situation. He then gathered the three of them on the living room couch and prayed, "Jesus, we don't know what to do and we're really worried. But You know what's going on and we trust You. Thank You for taking care of all of us."

Tears welled in their eyes as they bravely hugged each other and tried to put on a good front. Jack went to his room, pulled out his sketch book, and began to draw.

Fred and Susie held hands as they sat in silence looking at news reports, hoping to catch a glimpse of Freddie and Rachel. They checked their cell phones often to make sure they were on and had plenty of battery power in case they called.

Confirmed

After two more gut-wrenching days of no contact from their kids or the sheriff's office, Fred and Susie Miller, now 70 years old, really began to show their age. Bags were visible under puffy eyes. Their normal smiles were nowhere to be seen. They found themselves irritable with each other, the dog, the weather, and most anything.

Since Freddie and Rachel didn't have a land line, and had their cell phones with them, any friends who missed them had no one to call. Most were on rescue teams themselves, and had no reason to think anything might be amiss with their friends.

Reluctant to sleep lest they miss a call, they spent the nights on recliners in the living room– except for periodic trips to Jack's room to answer his tearful calls or comfort him after a nightmare.

During the days, Jack spent most of his time in his room with Mikey. He spent his time sketching and crying.

Fred and Susie did their best to keep each other's spirits up and to give Jack hope, but with each passing hour, the task became harder and harder. After two days and three nights of not knowing where their son and his wife were, they had another dinner in relative silence and watched the news as the darkness of night covered Conroe.

Their spirits quickly soared as they looked through the living room picture window and saw the lights of a car pull into the driveway. Just as quickly, their heart sank as they saw that it was a police car. Lieutenant Davis and a woman in civilian clothes made their way to the front door.

Fred, Susie, and Jack Miller sat in stunned silence as the Lt. softly informed them that their loved one's bodies had been identified after washing up in an overflowed residential area in Houston.

The End of the Beginning

The unexplainable loss of those two lives meant that 10-year-old Jack Miller's life would never be the same. He would never again wake up to his mom sweetly singing, "It's time to get up, time to get up, time to get up this morrrrning!"

Never again would he feel his dad's strong hand tousling his uncombed hair at the breakfast table as he said, "How's my best boy today?"

Never again.

Never again would Jack's grandparent's lives be the same.

As the three heard the police officer's surreal statement, they gasped and slumped against each other. They listened to his report, but it seemed like a dream... a nightmare. Fred and Susie silently prayed that they would wake up and be assured it wasn't real– except it was.

Jack sobbed and buried his head in his hands. Mikey sat by his side, whimpered sympathetically, and gently raised a paw which he rested on Jack's thigh.

The compassionate Lt. explained that he had no information about what happened, and that unless someone whom they were serving with came forward, they might never know what happened.

He assured them that Freddie and Rachel's service to those in need was deeply appreciated by the community, and then introduced them to his companion, Miss Amy Winters, from their bereavement section. He informed them that she could stay with them for a while, as needed, while he went back to his duties. Fred, feeling the need to be strong for his wife and grandson, declined the offer.

Susie, however, in a rare instance of "overriding" her husband, quickly said, "I'd like that, if you don't mind."

"Miss Amy has unique skills– a gift you could say– to help people in situations like this. You're in especially good hands with her. We'll send a car to pick her up when she's ready."

Susie Miller excused herself to the kitchen to make coffee. Her hands trembled so much that she made several messes before she finally got the coffee to brew.

Her husband of close to 50 years sat dazed and almost trance-like, barely mumbling responses to Miss Amy's compassionate remarks. The slender, middle-aged, African American woman with slightly greying hair, wearing blue jeans and a Houston Astros' tee shirt, had been in similar situations many times before, especially the past two days during the flooding.

Knowing just what to do, and without saying a word, Miss Amy walked to the kitchen and gave Susie Miller a warm and genuine hug. Then taking her hands in hers, she looked her in the eye and said, "I'm so, so sorry."

Helping her bring coffee into the living room, Miss Amy sat in between a stunned little boy and his grandmother. Without a word, Fred slipped out of the room and into the rain-soaked back yard.

"GOD! WHY? WHY!" He yelled at the sky, shaking his fists and gritting his teeth. "What have I done? How could you let this happen? Why? WHY?" He picked up a rock and with all his might, angrily threw it at the backyard fence. Then he threw another, and others.

Soon, he was pounding his fists against the side of the house– alternating between sobbing and raging in anger. Terrible words came from deep in his belly, words he had sometimes thought, but had not said out loud since his early days in the army a half-century before. Now he was screaming those words at the sky.

As lights came on in the neighboring houses, Fred's strength waned and he slumped to the ground, now harboring shame and condemnation that compounded the grief that was swirling in his mind.

The *'Hellish Darkness'* as he would be calling it seemed to envelope Fred in its grotesque, horrible distortion of existence. He felt himself slipping into inconsolable anguish.

Momentarily forgetting where he was, he was shocked back to reality by the gentle touch and soothing voice of Miss Amy kneeling by his side with her arm around him.

"Go ahead and let it out, Mr. Miller. Holding it all in doesn't impress God or me or anyone else."

"Oh, my boy… My Freddie… Oh, God…WHY?" He rocked back and forth, Miss Amy rocking with him and gently holding him in her surprisingly strong arms.

A few moments had passed when he muttered, "Susie… I need to go help Susie."

Miss Amy helped him up and the two went back into the living room where Fred saw his wife slumped over, head in her hands, weeping softly. The *'Hellish Darkness'* had been attacking her as well. He sat beside her, and holding her, they both wept for several minutes.

Then, excusing herself to get more coffee, Susie went to the kitchen.

Suddenly, Fred found himself again overcome with rage. Growling and gnashing his teeth, he picked up a coffee table book, tried to rip it apart, then threw it at a wall, hitting a picture that sent it crashing to the floor.

The sound shocked Mikey, and his barks seemed to shock Fred back to his senses. He quickly went to the pooch, said some soothing words and ushered him back to Jack's side. Jack just stared. He, too, felt like throwing things, but he didn't.

This was to be the worst day of their collective lives.

The 'Hellish Darkness'

Eventually, the gravity and ramifications of the news sent Jack's young mind racing.

"You mean I'll never see my mom and dad again?" The little boy wailed, alternating between hyperventilating, sobbing uncontrollably, and beating on the side of the couch before he wore himself out and slumped into his grandmother's arms.

All the older couple could do was hold him and sob with him. They wanted to be strong for him, to be his source of strength in his greatest time of need, but at the moment, they were all three in need of strength from a source beyond themselves to overcome The *'Hellish Darkness'*.

Fred Sr. and Susie summoned all the courage and supernatural power they could to hold their lives together for the sake of their now-permanent charge. They wanted to help Jack as best they could, even while they were experiencing the devastation of losing their treasured, only child, and their daughter-in-law, whom they adored.

The usually rambunctious Labrador, Mikey, sensed the mood and lay on the floor next to Jack's feet and nuzzled him.

Eventually, the tears stopped, or rather, took the first of many intermissions, and the three awkwardly tried to determine what to do next.

Miss Amy Winters assured them that she would stay through the morning and help them any way she could.

After talking some more, Susie brought some blankets to Miss Amy to use on the couch. They put Jack to bed, and the three Millers all had very fitful nights of attempted sleep. Each woke up at various times thinking they'd had a nightmare, only to once again realize they weren't dreaming.

In the morning, Fred and Jack took their showers while Suzie fixed some breakfast. Miss Amy kept her company. The Millers were in shock and a myriad of thoughts flooded their minds.

Fear seemed to grip Jack in a ferocious head-lock and refused to let go. He found himself shaking in the shower, even with the water pretty hot. Fred heard a familiar, soothing voice deep in his soul saying: *Don't be afraid. Jack is really scared. I want you to be My voice to let him know there's nothing to fear because of Me. This is your assignment now.*

He hurriedly finished showering, dried off, got dressed, then went to Jack's room where he found him shaking and sitting on the side of his bed, still wet, with a towel partially draped around him.

Fred quickly got another towel, wrapped it around his grandson and held him close. He didn't speak for a while. Finally, he said, "Jack, this is awful. It doesn't get any worse than this. I know you're scared, and Nana and I are saddened beyond belief. There's no getting around any of that. And even though you're scared, I want you to know that we can trust God. He loves us and…"

Jack interjected, "God!? God took Mom and Dad away from me. It's not fair! I don't want to hear about God… ever. I hate Him."

Still holding his grandson tightly, the older man didn't say anything immediately.

"Jack, I felt the same thoughts last night. I yelled at God in the back yard. I beat my hands on the side of the house." He showed his grandson the scrapes and swelling.

"You can trust us. Nana and I love you, and we're here for you. We will take care of you. It won't be the same, but we'll make it, the three of us. We'll be there for each other. We won't let anything happen to you." Silently, he wondered if he could keep those promises.

"And Jack, even though we get mad at God… He's not mad at us."

They rocked back and forth for a while before Fred told Jack to take his time getting dressed and then come out to eat breakfast.

Susie had hot coffee with a lot of cream ready for her husband and for their welcome companion, Miss Amy. The Millers sat at the kitchen table and held hands, waiting for their grandson.

The sound of Jack pounding on his bedroom door and

screaming, "I hate You!" startled them and they both jumped up to intervene, but Miss Amy stepped between them and the door.

"If I may, I'd suggest that you let him be for a while. You can fix the door and put Band-Aids on his knuckles. He needs to let out some steam and know that he's not in trouble."

Against their will, they sat back down. After some time the 'Hellish Darkness' released its grip on Jack and the pounding and screaming tapered off. After a while, Jack, eyes and nose reddened, right fist covered with a wet washcloth, came in and sat down at the table.

"Think you can eat, or should we take a look at those knuckles first?" his grandfather asked. Without speaking, Jack removed the washcloth to reveal some skinned-up, puffy-red fingers.

"Can you make a fist?" Fred asked as he demonstrated. Jack opened and closed his hand a few times without wincing.

"How's that feel?"

"Sore, but not too bad."

"I know how you feel," he said, holding his hands out to remind Jack of his own emotional venting. "Let's go ahead and eat and if we need to afterwards, we'll get us some ointment and Band-Aids."

Fred realized that he really wasn't able to thank God for their food. He didn't feel very thankful.

There was little conversation at breakfast. Afterward, Miss Amy helped Susie with the dishes as Fred sat at the kitchen table, his mind swirling with a myriad of thoughts. Jack disappeared into his room, grabbed his sketchbook, and painfully, because both his hand and his heart hurt, began to draw.

The walls of his room contained the usual things for a boy about to go into 5th grade: sports posters, school banners, and action heroes. Jack's walls also had a plethora of black and white pencil sketches. He'd started drawing at an early age and had the unique ability to transfer feelings to pictures.

By mid-morning, people started to come by. The hardest interactions were with people who didn't yet know what had happened−some friends hoping to get together, one sales person, and someone from the police department.

The first call they received came on Fred's cell phone. "Mr.

Miller, Sergeant Ramsey from the sheriff's office. I'm so sorry about the accident."

"Thank you, Sergeant."

"As you instructed Lt. Davis who came to your house last evening, we arranged for the funeral home closest to your residence to retrieve the... bodies, and I want to give you their contact information so that you can, uh, proceed."

He took down the information and asked if they found his son's truck. After a pause, Sgt. Ramsey said, "Our forensic team will analyze it to see if they can determine the cause of the damage, but it appears it was swept up in the floodwaters. It's badly beat up and full of mud and debris. It's been impounded and it will likely be weeks before we have time to look at it. When we're finished, we can dispose of it for you and we'll let your insurance company know about it being totaled."

"Oh..." Imagining what that could have meant about the fate of his son and daughter-in-law, Fred pounded his fist against the wall several times and wailed, "Oh, God...no..."

He ignored Sgt. Ramsey's, "Sir... Sir... Mr. Miller..." and eventually dropped the phone and collapsed on the couch.

As they all rushed to him, Susie asked, "What is it, honey?"

"I, uh... they...oh, I can't say... I'll tell you later." He got up and went out the back door and began pacing around the yard.

Miss Amy gently said to Jack and his grandmother, "This is so hard... for each of you. Don't be surprised if you don't know what to say or do at times. It's okay. It's okay."

They appreciated her words, but each knew it was anything *but* okay.

After several minutes of pacing, cursing, doubting, being anxiety ridden and knowing he was not in control of himself, Fred went back into the house and said, "I'm so sorry... I should be the strong one here... I'm even a pastor...but I just... can't."

Miss Amy took him by the arm and sat next to him at the kitchen table. She motioned for his wife and grandson to join them.

"Mr. Miller, there's no regulation that says you or anyone needs to be strong right now. Doesn't the Good Book say somewhere that there's a time for grieving and a time to be happy, or something like that?"

Without waiting for an answer, she continued, "This is as hard as it gets. Don't kid yourself or try to be something you aren't. No one expects you to be God here. As a matter of fact, I think God wants to help you in your weakness. He wants to do that with each of you."

She was so glad to know that this family was spiritually oriented and that she could openly talk about God with them.

They sat in silence for a bit, then after thanking Miss Amy, Fred excused himself again to the back yard, and called the funeral home. As he was dialing, he noticed a big oak tree in the corner of the lot. He remembered that as a boy, when he was really upset, he would vent his anger by chopping on a big tree. He wished he had an axe.

The young woman on the phone from the funeral home delicately told him that the bodies were badly bruised and bloated and it would take time for them to be prepared for viewing.

Fred stopped her from explaining further. He couldn't handle the details. He made an appointment to meet with the funeral director later that afternoon and proceeded to walk around the block before going back inside.

The sun was out and the rain had stopped temporarily, and a couple of Jack's friends– not knowing what happened– came over to play. Miss Amy met them at the door and stayed outside with them. She asked the boys for their parent's names and phone numbers and asked them to return home and ask their parents what had happened. Then she called all the parents and informed them of the situation. She knew from experience that it was best for a child's parents to relay sensitive information, rather than have them hear it from a stranger.

Fred explained that they would need to go to the funeral home later that afternoon. Miss Amy listened compassionately and, without saying much, frequently offered comforting touches and hugs as were appropriate.

Eventually, Amy Winters' time with the Millers came to an end for the day. They all had a sense that God had prepared her and sent her at just the right moment to help them in their greatest time of need. She embraced them both, telling them she would arrange her schedule so that she could come over each day as long as they needed. She left her card with them and made her way to the patrol car that had been sent to collect her.

Thanks and long hugs were more than enough reward for Miss Amy. As she rode away, she had a deep sense of God's very real presence with her, and with the Millers.

Contrary to how she often felt in similar circumstances, she was at peace as she left to re-enter her world as part-time police department employee and full-time wife, mother and grandmother who provided care and nurturing for three generations in her home.

Taking Care of Business

Since they had already been asked to take care of Jack "in case anything ever happened," their signatures were on file at the bank and they had a key to the younger Miller's safe deposit box. They also knew where the "important papers" file box was in Freddy's home office.

Fred started on the uncomfortable task of seeing what was in the box while Susie did her best to help Jack comprehend what was now going to transpire.

He lifted the lid of the aluminum box and found a bible verse taped inside: We know that the love of God causes everything to mutually contribute to our advantage. Romans 8:28.

He leaned back, sighed and whispered, "Jesus, I can't see any advantage to this tragedy. I just can't. I need your faith now more than ever."

He was assured as he felt the thought *"You have it, Fred."*

Letters from the Dead

Fred waded through the dozen or so file folders neatly color coded in the aluminum box.

"READ THIS FIRST" appeared in big letters on the manila envelope in the first folder. It contained a single, typewritten letter with the heading: "Final Instructions 1.10" and was addressed, "Dear Mom and Dad."

"Since you're reading this, something must have happened to Rachel and me. While I can only imagine your grief, we all know that she and I are now enjoying the best meal we've ever had at the banquet table with Jesus, Papa and Sarayu that you talked about so often, so no tears for us! We know that you two and Jack will be here celebrating with us at just the right time."

Fred Jr., along with his wife, parents, and many others, liked to use the Native American word, 'Sarayu' meaning "spirit or wind" in referring to the Holy Spirit.

"Speaking of Jack, I can only ask that you raise him just like you did me: spending time with him; loving him unconditionally; having fun with him; giving him opportunities; encouraging him; and when he messes up, always making sure he knows he's not bad, but that he's just temporarily made a poor choice; and most of all– teaching him about the only true God, Jesus's Papa who loves him unconditionally and is totally for him. You and I both know the lies that bad religion will attempt to foist off on him, so stay the course, as you did with me!

"This is the 10th version of this document. I've done a new one each year since Jack was born. In this box, you'll find a copy of our will, financial and investment information, people and institutions to notify, and instructions on insurance policies that will provide funds for you to take care of Jack very well through college and not put a financial burden on you. You have a key to our safe deposit box and it contains titles, CD's, etc., as well as a video of the interior of the house, values of items and information about jewelry, etc.

"There are separate, more personal letters to each of you from Rachel and me in the folder labeled 'family.' There are also two letters from us to Jack. Please give him the first one as soon as you think is right, and give him the other one on his 18th birthday.

"We know that you continually listen to God, and you'll know what to do now in every situation, so no worries!"

It was signed: *"Love you both, Freddie,"* with the following hand-written verse: *"In that day you will know that just as I am in my Father, you are in me and I am in you!"* John 14:20

"P.S. Dad, please read my letter to you before you do anything else."

God is Never Mad at You

The 70-year-old, grief-stricken man sensed a bit of strength and inner fortitude after reading his son's letter addressed specifically to him. He started proceeding to the next folder, but was interrupted by a soft, "Hey, Pops…"

"Oh, hey Jack."

"What are you doing, Pops?"

"Just going over some papers your dad left for me, but they can wait. Want to go for a walk?"

Without responding, Jack grabbed his Astros baseball cap and started towards the front door.

When they came to visit, Fred often took Jack for walks in their neighborhood, just as they did when Jack came to Kansas to visit his grandparents.

Without articulating it, each knew that an invitation to go for a walk was code for, "Let's go hang out, explore, and talk about things we wouldn't talk about in front of other people, especially women because they don't always understand boys." It was really an invitation into deeper community.

Neither the older man nor the young boy spoke for the first couple of blocks. As they approached the neighborhood elementary school where Jack would have started fifth grade this week if it weren't for the hurricane, the boy said, "Pops, what will happen to me now?"

Not fully able to answer that question, Fred Sr., as was his habit, silently prayed, "Jesus, I can't do this. I'm on empty. But you live in me. You know how to answer Jack. You know what You want to say and what Jack needs to hear. So, as always, would You answer him?"

Taking in a deep breath, then slowly exhaling, as a physical reminder that he was letting go of being in charge of the situation and letting Jesus in him do His thing, Fred heard himself saying, "Son, God knows exactly what's going on right now. He is as sad as we are. But He's not worried. Even right now He's working this whole situation out for your good– to your advantage. We may not be able to see what all that means, but we can trust Him. He loves you and Nana and me. He's with us in everything we do."

"But He must be mad at me. I said I hated Him. I don't think He loves me anymore."

Stopping and kneeling down so he could look Jack in the eyes, Fred said, "Jack, God loves you unconditionally no matter what. He adores you. You are His special child. There is nothing you can ever do to cause Him to love you any less. He loves you as much as is possible to love someone!"

"Even if I got mad at Him?"

"Unconditional love means love with *no* conditions. None! I got really mad at God last night, and again this morning. Fortunately, God knows it's because we don't understand. Even though it doesn't feel like it sometimes, He really is good. And He really loves you. Never ever worry that you have offended Him or made Him mad at you or caused Him not to love you. You don't have to be afraid of Him."

The older man was saying these words as much for himself as for his grandson. He needed to hear them.

"He wants you to know how much He loves you and to never fear Him. There are absolutely *no* conditions to His love. That's the real truth, Jack!"

"Whew…" Jack's sigh of relief said it all. In addition to overwhelming grief, evil had heaped a heavy layer of guilt on the young boy's mind and heart, and on his grandfather's, too.

Hearing words of truth about his Heavenly Father's love for him pulverized the guilt, at least for now, as it did with Fred.

Jack threw his arms around his kneeling grandfather, and hugged him for all he was worth. He held his head a little higher and had a bit more spring to his step as they continued walking.

"I know you're wondering about what will happen in the near future. I would think that after a few days of taking care of things here, the three of us will go back to Kansas. Nana and I will get to enjoy being with you every day instead of just a few times a year."

"But what about my friends? My school? The guys on my baseball team? What about Mikey?"

"We'll take Mikey with us, Jack. He'll do just fine in Kansas," Fred said confidently, all the while knowing that Susie said years ago there would be "absolutely no more pets!"

"I know you'll miss your friends and your school, but your dad knew that nice people and good schools reside in Kansas, too."

Neither spoke for a while and eventually when they came to the end of the school's sports complex, Jack picked up a rock and threw it with all his might towards the outfield where, just a few days ago, he'd practiced catching fly balls that his dad hit to him.

His grandfather threw one too. Then, taking turns throwing and releasing pent-up emotion, the two shared another of what would become many times of releasing energy that demanded to be let out.

It was a good release for pent-up anger and a host of unidentifiable emotions that would now be coming their way on a regular basis.

They walked for another half hour without speaking.

Making Plans

Mikey, oblivious to the gravity of the situation, boisterously met the two as they opened the door to the only home Jack had known. They could smell bacon frying as Nana called them in to lunch.

She was glad to have had some time by herself where she could actually scream, yell, and say things she would never say in front of others. Condemnation was flooding her mind, but she used all her strength to keep her husband and grandson from further worry.

She motioned for Fred to join her in sitting across from Jack, so as to not take his dad's place.

She said, "I hope Mikey's not disappointed that there won't be any scraps left for him. I'm so hungry, I could hardly wait 'til you boys got back to get started. Anyway, there'll be lots for him when he gets to Kansas." Noticing Fred's obvious sense of relief, she gave him a knowing smile that he had come to love over the years.

Fred was again unable to give thanks to God for their food. His customary prayer of, "Thank you for our food and for all the good things you do for us and for always taking care of us," didn't seem appropriate. Jesus understood.

Nana was right, there were no leftovers. She pretended not to notice as Jack handed bits of bacon and toast to Mikey under the table.

After cleaning the dishes and making a couple of phone calls, the three piled into Jack's mom's car and drove to the funeral home.

Jack had never been in such a setting. Fred and Susie and been in similar places all too often. They were met by a staff member who spoke softly and didn't appear to be relational. She led them to a private room.

Viewing the two bodies was the hardest thing any of them had ever done. Fred and Susie's own parents had graduated to the life-after some years ago, but their deaths were expected. Nothing compares to losing a child prematurely.

They each alternated between soft tears and outright sobbing. They took turns making their way from one casket to the other. This was the first time Jack had felt the cold clamminess of a dead body.

He winced and moved his hand away with a sick, sinking feeling because this was nothing like the warm arms of his parents who hugged him when he was scared.

Fred and Susie attempted to comfort and help Jack, but their own grief made it almost impossible. The best they could do was embrace each other in periodic group hugs.

Complying with Freddie and Rachel's wishes, the senior Millers gave instructions for cremation and the knowledgeable and compassionate funeral director suggested that each of the three have a time to be alone with the bodies and say their goodbyes. Fred and Susie went to the adjoining room, leaving Jack with his parents for the last time.

They took care of details with the director and made plans for Fred to lead the service two days later. Mr. Richardson, the funeral home director, attempted to gently persuade Fred Sr. to have one of their chaplains officiate the service rather than for Fred to do it himself. Firm in his resolve, Fred wouldn't relent. Susie knew his reasoning and nodded ascent.

After making all the arrangements and trusting the funeral

home to make the proper notifications, the new family threesome made their way to a nearby hotel to tentatively reserve rooms for family and friends they assumed would be arriving soon. However, because of the flood, they learned there were no rooms available within a hundred miles, and that the airports were still closed.

None of the three talked much as they drove home.

The evening was a blur of phone calls, texts, emails, and Facebook posts where they both informed people of the tragedy and let them know they couldn't come to the funeral. There was also a steady stream of neighbors dropping by with food, condolences, and questions. They ate a meal that neighbors had provided, then some of Jack's buddies came by. After receiving assurance from their parents, Fred and Susie agreed to let the boys (and Mikey) go to the school fields and attempt to play on the synthetic turf that was hopefully dry. They were grateful for Jack to have a divergence and they also needed some time together with just the two of them.

When there was a lull between calls and visitors, Fred held Susie in his arms and the two sobbed and hugged for a long time before any words could come.

"I knew from being with some of our friends through the years, that nothing could be harder than losing a child prematurely… but to lose them both so suddenly… and now to have to help Jack make it through this… and to raise him… oh, honey. How can we do this?"

Wiping away ever-flowing tears as they sat on the couch, Fred continued to hold the hands of his bride and said, "We can't. We just can't. If we try to do it by our own strength and understanding, it will be a mess.

"You saw had badly I lost it last night… and this morning..."

Squeezing his hand, she replied, "And fortunately you didn't hear the words I screamed this morning while you and Jack went for your walk. I was so embarrassed afterwards. The 'Hellish Darkness' was doing a number on me."

"Me too," he said. "But we've got to remember not to beat ourselves up over this, honey. I sure was thinking plenty of awful things. I guess I just didn't have the energy to do them. I do know that Jesus has always come through for us, and I guess all those previous times have given us good reason to trust Him now, right?"

"Yes, and Jack will certainly have the opportunity to experience His love and help as well."

They were interrupted by simultaneous phone and doorbell rings. There were more brief visits, condolences, and food from a number of people. Miss Amy called and arranged to come for a late breakfast the next day.

Jack was exhausted when he arrived home at dusk after playing with his friends.

"How'd it go?"

"Okay," he said.

"I bet it helped to be with your friends."

"Yeah. They didn't know what to say, and neither did I. One of them really made me feel good though."

"How's that?"

"Well, she hugged me for a long time and told me how sorry she was and how she would always be there for me."

"Oh, how nice." Susie said. The word "she" wasn't lost on either of his grandparents, but they didn't ask questions.

Later, Jack took a shower, scarfed down some cake that a neighbor had brought, and said goodnight to his grandparents.

A short while after Fred and Susie dozed off in the guest bedroom down the hall from their grandson, they were awakened by a blood-curdling scream. "Dad… Swim! Swim, Dad!" Mikey barked as they bolted out of bed and ran to Jack's room. He was still asleep, but obviously in torment from a bad dream.

Susie lovingly caressed his cheeks as she and Fred each prayed silently, thanking Jesus for being with Jack and calming him. Eventually, they settled in for a somewhat fitful sleep.

Playing Hardball and Cheap Religious Platitudes

They all slept in the next morning, but were up and ready for the breakfast Miss Amy brought them at 10:00 a.m.

The three related to her as sort of a "priest holding confession" as they lamented their bursts of anger and conveyed their doubts and fears. She was an excellent listener and comforter. After a while, they all seemed to feel somewhat better.

She stayed for a couple of hours and managed to have brief, personal conversations with each of them. Miss Amy was an angel in disguise.

After she left, Fred helped Jack begin deciding what he would be bringing with him to Kansas, and the boy started to understand that much of what was so familiar to him would no longer be in his life. This further exacerbated his growing sense of loss and he became withdrawn.

Not wanting to casually throw cheap platitudes at the deep and devastating loss, Fred let Jack process his own thoughts and emotions while continually praying that Christ in him would tell him what to say and when.

No out of town relatives or friends would be able to get into the area due to the flood, which was a bittersweet blessing. The Millers wanted family to be there, but also felt so drained that the thought of answering questions and rehashing their loss repeatedly was not appealing.

Susie fixed a picnic dinner from the plethora of food that had already been brought by friends and neighbors. The three, along with Mikey, left the house early that afternoon and drove to a small town a few miles away where there hadn't been any flooding. They found a nice city park where Mikey could run and they could get away for a while.

The adults both turned off their cell phones, Nana started setting up for their picnic and Fred said "I brought the bag of baseball stuff that was in the garage. You want to play catch?"

"Yeah, I guess," Jack said, although he wasn't really feeling much into doing anything.

Fred got out two gloves. The first was an older one that he remembered buying for Freddie years earlier in high school when he played American Legion ball then used in college and beyond in recreational fast-pitch softball. The other was a brand-new glove just right for a 10-year-old boy.

They tossed the ball around as well as they could with Mikey wanting to play too.

Throwing harder and harder seemed to be a good outlet to

release pent-up emotion for Jack, and although he would like to have done the same, age and the desire not to hurt his grandson both limited the velocity of Fred's throws.

Playing catch and the change of scenery did them all good. After they cleaned up, Susie said, "Jack, how are you doing with all the people coming by and all of these things?"

"Most of them I don't know. I want to be nice to them, but I really don't know what to say sometimes, especially when they say weird things."

"Give us an example, honey," Nana said gently, having a good idea of what she was about to hear.

"Well, one old lady with bad breath and hair on her chin kneeled down and got close to my face. She pinched both my cheeks at the same time and said, 'The Good Lord musta needed your Momma and Daddy a lot more than you did. He has a special place for them in Gloooory..'" Without trying to be funny, Jack did a pretty good imitation of the elderly woman's voice.

"Ummm. Anything else?"

"Several people said, 'They're in a better place now, don't you worry'– or something like that. Some also said, 'We know how you feel.' But they don't. They DON'T! How can they know how I feel!?" he shouted.

After he regained his composure, Jack continued, "And this one guy said 'God is good… all the time. And the Lord giveth and the Lord taketh away.'

"God may be 'good', but, taking away my parents, that doesn't seem good to me. How can it be good if it's not good for us?

"This other lady told me that maybe God was doing this to teach me something and I needed to really pay attention. Is that true? Is this my fault?"

By now Jack was visibly shaken. He continued, "She waved her finger at me and said, 'I sure hope your folks were saved! The fires of hell are awful and they last for an awful long time.' Are my mom and dad on fire right now?"

Susie moved next to him and wrapped him in her arms as they rocked back and forth. She said, "No. No! A thousand times no. And this is not your fault. God does not work that way, ever.

Never!

"Those are nice, well-meaning people, Jack. They think they're helping, but they are very misinformed. Actually, none of those things are true.

"Even though it doesn't seem like it to us right now, I know that God is good. There is nothing bad in God. Nothing. God is all good, always. That means than whenever something bad happens, it's not God causing it to happen. He simply doesn't cause bad things to happen. When they do, He works, even in the bad things, to bring about something good."

Fred interjected, "The key for us is to learn to ask Him how He sees the situation and to tell us what He wants us to know and do. That's the only way we can see what really is, to see what good God is doing in something that seems so awful."

"Then who does cause bad things to happen? Who caused the hurricane, Pops?"

"That's just nature, Jack. God doesn't cause hurricanes to happen. That's just a product of the planet we live on. Sometimes people cause bad things to happen, but not always intentionally. Sometimes we don't even know we're doing it. For example, we don't know what happened with your dad's truck.

"Any number of things could have happened with a storm this violent and strong. Perhaps something blew off a rooftop and knocked them underwater or a fallen tree being swept along in a strong current hit them..

"They could have seen someone in dire need and thought they could get to them, but found out the water was too deep.

"Or it could have been someone who was making their truck at the factory wasn't paying attention and made a bad part that just wore out at that time. Whatever it was, and we may never know, you can be confident that God didn't cause it. He didn't plan it. God loves you, and everybody. He's for you, and everybody. He doesn't cause anything bad to happen to us."

"It sure seems like it sometimes," the boy lamented.

"We know," his grandmother replied softly. "We know."

"And you're right, Jack, none of those people who talked to you know how you feel. They may have had a loved one die, but they aren't you and they can't really put themselves in your situation. None of those people who said these things are bad people, Jack. They just don't know. They've heard other people say similar things and they repeat them, thinking they're helpful, but they're not.

"God doesn't need anything. He doesn't need your parents to be with Him in Heaven. He was always with them here on earth! Yes, they're in a better place in the sense that there's no evil in heaven, everything's good there, people don't get sick and their bodies never wear out. People don't hurt each other there.

"While your mom and dad miss you immensely, they are extremely happy there– partly because they know that one day you'll be with them forever. But knowing that doesn't really take away our pain or make us feel any better, because we're *here* and we miss them. It doesn't help someone to tell them their loved ones are in a better place.

"And Jack… you need never worry about your parents being in hell. People have a lot of wrong ideas about hell anyway, but you need never worry about that."

"But how can Mom and Dad be happy in heaven without us?"

Susie gently said, "We don't know everything and exactly how all this works, son, but we do know that God is good and He loves us and He's for us. My guess would be that somehow God is able to show your mom and dad that we're ok, and even let them know exactly when we'll be joining them in Heaven.".

"But that will be a long time from now, won't it? At least for me?"

As Fred and Susie smiled, Jack realized how he had unintentionally classified them as old and with not much time left. "Oh, I didn't mean…"

"No worries, kid!" Jack laughed for the first time in days. "We're well aware that we're not as young as we used to be! You know, with God, and in Heaven, there's no time. It's not like here with 24 hours a day. Heaven lasts forever. It never ends, and time is not part of the picture. There's no night and day, it's bright sunlight all the time. We can't comprehend that now, but one day we will.

"So, I believe your mom and dad know exactly when we'll be joining them and even though they miss us, the fact that they are with Jesus and experiencing and understanding His love for them in a whole new way means that it's not a problem to be apart for what is a brief time compared to eternity.

"Maybe it's sort of like them going to work in the morning while you're at school. They know you're okay and they look forward to seeing you in the evening."

Jack seemed satisfied with that explanation.

Nana asked, "Jack, did any of these folks say anything that was helpful?"

After thinking for a moment, the boy replied, "One guy just said, 'I'm sorry, son.' And he sat there by me for a while and didn't say anything else. I could tell by the way he looked that he was good."

"Jack, I've found that's about the best we can do. Just being with someone is the most important thing. We don't really need to say much more than, 'I'm sorry.' You may hear more of that tomorrow evening at the reception and even more the next day at the celebration of your folk's lives.

"Remember the people aren't bad. They're just not well-informed. They're in the dark. So, here's what you can do. Just tell Jesus that you know He loves you and that He loves all those well-meaning people. Tell Him you don't always know what to say, and ask Him to say and do whatever He wants through you and as you. Then just let Him. Whatever He does will be perfect!"

"Is that what you and Nana are gonna do?"

"Oh, honey, we've been doing that since the night your folks didn't come home," Susie said. "Sometimes I forget and try to say what I think is the right thing or I try to tell the other person how they're wrong, and that never works very well," she laughed. "Thankfully, God's grace covers all those things."

Just then, Mikey barked at a squirrel and they realized they needed to make their way to the car and return home.

Recalling Inappropriate Funerals

The blur continued the next day with a seemingly endless stream of interruptions of questions and decisions that had to be made.

All the while, Fred made a conscious attempt to let Jesus live as him both in relating to the ever-expanding group of mourners and well-wishers, and especially with Jack. He and Susie frequently checked with him and made sure he was involved and included.

Fred had a vague sense of being part of a bigger event with everything still happening all around them in the aftermath of the hurricane. Other lives had been lost. Tens of thousands were living in homeless shelters. Hundreds of thousands were living with friend and relatives or had left the area. Many had lost all their worldly possessions.

Still, his family's loss was *personal*… not something they saw on the news.

Fred insisted on leading the celebration of life services for Freddie and Rachel primarily because he felt it was his duty and that God might somehow be displeased with him if he didn't. He knew and taught others that God doesn't relate to us that way, but old habits and indoctrinations are hard to break.

Finding an appropriate time, he went to a nearby coffee shop and clarified his notes for the service the next day.

Prelude to the Celebration of Life

Floral arrangements of all shapes and colors filled the front of the room, which was jam-packed with people even in the midst of the ongoing flood rescue operations in the area. Freddie and Rachel were gregarious, inclusive, non-judgmental, positive people whom everyone liked and gravitated to. Friends, co-workers, neighbors, members of their grace group of spiritual seekers, and Jack's teachers and friends all filled the room. Attendants quickly opened accordion doors to expand the seating capacity.

Recorded music from Mercy Me's *Welcome to the New* CD played, to the great enjoyment of some and apparent disdain of some of the more staid attenders.

As they waited, people read the funeral program which contained the usual information and some bible verses with the descriptive 'NKJV' meaning New King James Version and "MB indicating the Mirror Bible.

Susie sat next to Jack at the far left of the front row as others filled the rows close to them. She let Jack bring a sketchbook with him, understanding that drawing was like a security blanket to him, and hoping it would keep him occupied when necessary.

She purposely didn't leave room for anyone to sit next to Jack, as she wanted to protect him from possibly being cornered by someone who might inadvertently contribute negatively to his emotional state.

Neither of his parents had siblings. Rachel's father died of a heart attack before Jack was born and her mother, with whom Rachel never had a close relationship, soon remarried, moved to another country, and rarely communicated to her daughter or grandson. She sent a floral arrangement and a note saying she was sorry that she couldn't get a flight into Houston.

Nana gently rubbed Jack's shoulder as they waited for the service to begin. Jesus was showing her that a myriad of thoughts, questions, and emotions were running through Jack's mind and heart.

Although virtually overcome with deep sadness herself, Susie, none-the-less, had a deep-seated peace over knowing the total love surrounding her son and his wife, knowing they would one day all be together, and knowing that the Holy Spirit of Christ in her was also with Freddie and Rachel and in Jack and Fred in this time and place. She realized that there were really no words to convey this to someone who had yet to experience it.

She became the conveyer of a continual supply of tissues to Jack and was surprised by the unspeakable gratitude of joy that God had given her the privilege of actually "being Christ" to this dear, vulnerable boy whose world would never again be what it had been just days ago. Helping Jack also took her mind off of her personal grief.

The voice inside her, whom she had grown to hear, trust, love and delight in, whispered: *I've got Jack. You can trust Me with him and you can trust Me to say and do the right things through you. Relax. Rest. Trust Me.*

The Celebration of Life

After seeing the nod from the funeral home director, Fred took his notebook and made his way to the oak lectern in the front of the room. Although he had spoken in a variety of churches and presided at numerous weddings and funerals, Fred never liked being behind a pulpit. He wanted to avoid the impression of separation, exclusivity and hierarchy that he felt most pulpits conveyed. And he had never officiated a service for his own child.

After welcoming the group, he read the obituaries word for word. They included Freddie and Rachel's career achievements, hobbies, love of family and friends –the usual expected information. He briefly related how the two met, spoke of their courtship, and told some humorous stories about their early years of marriage.

Then he stepped out from the pulpit, walked to the center of the room in front of the aisle, looked around, and continued, "I would not be wrong in telling you how proud I am of this couple, nor would it be wrong to ask any of you to speak about them, but I would imagine that would keep us here well into the night.

"I also may be in a better position than most to tell you about the many accomplishments and achievements they earned during their all-too-brief life. But I'm not gonna do those things."

Looking around, he continued, "Some of you think I'm speaking because I want to save money and not have to pay a hired speaker…" That got the chuckles he anticipated to lighten the mood.

"First of all, Freddie and Rachel don't want anyone here to feel like you're saying 'goodbye' to them. You'll see why in a few moments.

"What I was asked to do from my son, who left me explicit instructions, was to tell you all– and especially his son Jack– some very important things."

Upon hearing those words, Jack closed his sketchbook, carefully laid it on the floor under his chair, and his mind locked in like radar on an approaching airplane, focusing intently on what Pops was saying. It was like the grief, sadness, and despair of the past few days were all on hold as he was hearing words of ultimate significance for him. The Holy Spirit of Christ was revealing His Truth to Jack, and to others.

"Freddie and Rachel had a revelation from God about how God loves everyone, made everyone in His likeness and image, is for everyone, has forgiven everyone, accepted and included everyone, and is for everyone. Much to their surprise– and mine, too– God actually likes us all… and He likes being with us.

"God is good, even though in regional tragedies like Hurricane Harvey and personal tragedies like with our family, it doesn't always seem like God is good.

"Scripture tells us that everything good comes from God. That means to me, that when we see people doing good things in some way or another, it is God motivating them. That has never been more apparent in my lifetime than in these last several days in the Houston area.

"The truth that God loves everyone and is for everyone has been reinforced to me in a huge way as I, like most of you, watched the continuing news of the flood relief efforts. Just a few miles from here, many of you in this room, along with Freddie and Rachel, did innumerable good things for people whom you didn't know, and most likely will never see again.

"Freddie and Rachel left our house for the third day in a row, to do whatever was needed."

Choking up, he had to pause, blow his nose– which seemed overly loud coming through the lavalier mic just inches away. The noise and accompanying grins helped him compose himself and continue.

"I've seen news reports of a mattress store owner opening his doors so that displaced people could stay there. I've seen people from this area and further away show up at impact zones with pickup trucks and RV's loaded with bottled water and other supplies that they gave to those in need. I've seen restaurants and grocery stores giving away food and needed items to people. I've seen construction men with bull dozers going into neighborhoods and clearing people's driveways for them at no charge.

"I've seen people from near and far bringing boats to the area and simply going where people needed them… looking for white sheets and towels hanging out windows… then going in, sometimes at great risk to themselves… and rescuing people.

"Like some of you, we saw Freddie and Rachel being interviewed on TV just after they brought more people in whom they rescued.

"And I've noticed that race, religion, ethnic background, socioeconomic status, age, education are not in play. Over and over I've seen good things, acts of kindness, performed by good people with no expectation of anything in return, and no need for recognition.

"The first responders have been tremendous, as were Lt. Davis and Miss Amy Winters from the sheriff's department who served us so well.

"But from what I've seen, the real first responders have been neighbors, people from all backgrounds who have come together to help people who are in harm's way.

"I want to read you the short phrases that are listed on the back page of your program. The truth in these words are what God used to make Freddie and Rachel the kind of people that drew you all to them. I think the truths in these phrases were never more evident than they have been in people in the Houston area these past few days."

He proceeded to expand a bit on each of the following points:

- God is love *in relationship.*
- Jesus, His Father, and the Holy Spirit have included everyone in that relationship.
- Grace is God's love in action continually poured out on you.
- God is totally good and God is totally for you.
- You need never fear God.
- Jesus did everything to take care of everyone's relationship with God forever.
- God is in the process of revealing what His love means to you, and He will continue as long as it takes.

"You can also find words that Freddie asked me to convey to you on your program.*

"In wrapping things up, I want to mention a national news report I heard a couple of days ago on the news. Reporter Kelly Wright was covering the president and several cabinet members who were in a church not too far from here in Rockport. The church was a staging place for the Red Cross.

"The reporter interviewed Rockport Mayor C.J. Wax, who thanked all the agencies and departments and volunteers, then he got choked up.

"The reporter said something like 'I can hear your heart breaking and your sadness and I can assure you that God is with you. Be not dismayed, He will be with you all the way through. Stay Texas strong. Stay God strong. Texans are known for that. Keep the faith alive.'

"Those remarks touched me and reminded me of something Jesus said the night before He died, just before He prepared a room for His Holy Spirit to live in each of our hearts, and ascended back to the Father, where they are seated around a huge banquet table right now with Freddie and Rachel rejoicing about each of you, because they know you are all in their family: John 14:20 NKJV says, 'In that day you will know that just as I am in my Father, you are in Me and I am in you!'

"Just as you Texans are known for being 'God strong,' a day will come, if it hasn't already for you, when you will know that you are in Christ and Christ is in you. Freddie, Rachel, Jesus and His Father all hope that for everyone here, that day comes soon– the day that you realize that Jesus, His Father, and the Holy Spirit are in you, not out there or up there or over there, but *in* you– closer than the air you breathe–and that you are in them.

"Knowing that they will one day be with all of you again, rather than you thinking you're here to say 'goodbye' to them, they are saying: 'til we meet again!'"

Taking Fred's cue, a technician in the side room started the song *Welcome To The New*.

Fred walked to the end of the front row and sat on the other side of Jack. Experiencing a sense of peace and well-being that he had missed the past several days, the 10-year-old softly asked his Grandfather, "Pops, that's true, we're gonna be with them again, right?"

"Yes, Jack. You can absolutely count on that."

The Receiving Line

Fred, Susie, and Jack greeted Freddie and Rachel's friends for over an hour, most of which was very uncomfortable for Jack. But he was very grateful for his own friend's hugs and their assurance that they'd come to Kansas to visit and vice versa. Fred and Susie smiled as they saw Jack hug a cute little freckled face girl.

Some people were unable to speak, but bravely shook hands and gave hugs.

After an hour or so, Fred started to tire. His age and the exhaustion of the previous days combined to wear him down.

Several people commented on Fred's remarks and mentioned that they had never heard God portrayed as Fred described. He offered each of them a card, and said, "I'd be glad to visit more with you about God. He's especially fond of you. Here's my card. Contact me anytime."

He knew from experience that some people would contact him, and he loved helping them. However, he was starting to wish the line would end very soon.

Gratefully, he noticed with relief that there were just a few more people in the line.

The last person seemed unusually distraught. He would be easy to spot in any crowd, as he was about 6'5" and had very curly red hair. He was a young, twenty-something man who appeared to have been affected very deeply by the loss of Freddie and Rachel.

He was gaunt-faced and looked as if he hadn't slept in days. Fred assumed that he had been helping in the relief effort as had many others.

The young man took Fred's hand with both of his and sobbed, "I'm so sorry… so sorry… so sorry." His voice was unusually high pitched and nasally, sounding much like a cartoon character.

Fred asked if he taught school with his son, and the man shook his head no. He asked if Freddy had been his band director, and again the man shook his head no. He wasn't able to say anything else.

Reaching in his pocket, Fred took one of his last cards, placed it in the man's hands, and said, "If you ever want to talk, please call me."

Greeting Susie and Jack with the same words and sobs, the young man left and as the three Millers shared a hug, Susie prayed out loud, "Dear Papa, we need You so much. Thanks for being here with us in all of this."

Fred asked the funeral home attendant to please take the flowers to a retirement center or someplace where they would be enjoyed, and they made their way back to Jack's home.

The Leaving Process

Since the local schools were closed indefinitely, and with daily necessities still in short supply, Fred and Susie decided it would be best to get back to Kansas as soon as possible. Having to make a sudden decision about what to do with an entire household of furniture, appliances, clothing, and a lifetime's accumulation of personal items is not something a person can really train or prepare for. Yet, that's the task that faced Fred and Susie Miller regarding their now-deceased son and daughter-in-law's worldly possessions.

Recently retired, the elder Millers still lived in their family home of many years in Eastern Kansas. They, too, had a home full of furniture and personal items, including an assortment of Freddie's things that had seemed destined to remain there until someday far in the future when he would inherit his mom and dad's home and belongings.

Fate, however, had reversed the roles.

Miss Amy helped them by contacting some people in need who had lost things in the flood. After helping those folks, they gave many other items to the Salvation Army.

They would take Jack's things and a limited amount of important family items back to Kansas in a trailer pulled by Rachel's car, and then rent the furnished home through a local agency that Amy recommended. It was immediately available and non-flood damaged housing was already at a premium. The home would prove to be a great source of on-going income for Jack in his college and early adult years, as well as a long-term connection with memories of his parents and his youth.

Susie secretly packed two of her son's suits and several other clothes in one of Freddy and Rachel's suitcases and set it aside from the other clothes to be donated.

The Millers, with the help of some of Freddie and Rachel's friends, worked together on the moving project for a couple of days, and were fortunate to get a ticket on one of the first flights available after the airport reopened.

Moving Day

After breakfast, Jack sat on their front porch sketching, and rubbing Mikey's ears.

He was quiet and guarded as they finished loading the trailer and his Mom's car. His grandparents made sure he had ample time to go throughout the only home he had known, think about memories of things that transpired in each room, and have time alone with Mikey.

Miss Amy brought them pastries for breakfast and left them with assurances that they could call her for help when needed.

Finally, it was time for the three Millers and the black lab to pile into the car and drive away. Some of Jack's buddies were there to see them off with promises of staying in touch and visiting. Tears were flowing amongst the three and even Mikey seemed subdued.

No one spoke for several blocks.

After dropping Susie off at George Bush Intercontinental Airport so she could get home to get groceries and prepare their house for this new, completely unexpected, stage of their life, Fred, Jack, and Mikey made their way out of the metropolis.

Seeing standing water in many neighborhoods off the freeway as they left only provided a sad reminder of the reason why they were leaving.

Soon, Jack started sketching.

Fred's mind ran from one scenario to another in his anticipated, new schedule. Eventually they came to the north side of Dallas where they checked into a pet-friendly motel.

Flying somewhere above them on her trip back to Kansas, Susie was periodically attacked by The 'Hellish Darkness' and then comforted by Sarayu. Finally she lapsed into a fitful sleep.

BBQ and the Yellow Rose of Texas

"What do you feel like eating?" Fred asked his grandson.
"Pops, I saw a sign for a barbeque restaurant just before we got to the motel. Could we go there?"
"Good idea, son. Maybe we can even bring back some bones for Mikey!" he smiled.
After inquiring at the front desk, they found it was easily within walking distance. Making sure Mikey had plenty of water and was secure in the motel, the two set off on what was now to become their thing– walking and talking.
"I wonder if the Rangers are at home tonight, Pops. Dad and I watched them play the Astros in inter-league play sometimes."
"Don't know, Jack. Wherever they are, if they're playing, we can watch after dinner, unless you want to go swimming first."
"Oh, yeah! That would be great!"
"And I promise you I'll take you to Royals games in Kansas City. You may even come to like them as much as the 'Stros."
"No way!"
The two walked a few blocks and then made their way into a scene from the past—a mom and pop barbeque joint with one large room housing a myriad of tables with red and white checkered tablecloths and rolls of brown butcher paper to be used as napkins. It appeared to have had the same furniture and decorations for several decades. Only a few tables had customers since it was still a little early for the dinner crowd.

They both enjoyed the rather talkative, middle-aged waitress with dish-water blond hair piled high in a 1950's beehive. She wore a little too much makeup, but otherwise fit the nametag pinned on her checkered apron: Rose.

"Hi boys. I'm Rose, the original Yeller Rose of Texas. Have

y'all been here before?"

"This is our first time, Rose. What do you have that an old man and his 10-year-old grandson would like for dinner? We're pretty hungry after driving up from Houston today."

"Houston! That's where I grew up!" She smiled. "Wish I'd never left, but that's another story for another day. At least I missed the big hurricane. What brings you to Dallas?"

Realizing this was the first of ordinary questions that would require great wisdom in answering so as to not put Jack in an awkward situation, Fred replied, "We're just passing through–heading home to Kansas."

"That's nice. A boy and his Grandpa on a road trip! Bet you'll be glad to get home and see your mom and dad, won't you, son?"

The smile that had been on Jack's young face left instantly and his eyes welled up with big tears as he turned to look away from the well-meaning server.

"Actually, Rose, he's coming to live with his grandmother and me. His parents died helping rescue flood victims." Now the tears came to the older man as well. It was just all too recent and too raw.

"Oh, uh… you boys take your time with the menu and I'll be back to get your order in a while. Help yourself at the salad bar. It's included with every meal and you can get your own choice of drink at the pop machine over there." Embarrassed, she quickly made her way to the lady's room to touch up the makeup that was now lined with her own tears.

"Excuse me, Jack. I have to go to the restroom."

Hating to leave his grandson, but knowing he was about to let his emotions overcome him, Fred Miller made his way to the far end of the restaurant and was relieved to see that no one else was in the men's room. He quickly locked the door.

Leaning against a concrete wall, Fred pounded his fists so hard that they soon were hurting. He resisted the urge to scream, but still said loudly, "Freddie! Freddie! Why? Oh, God, why?"

After a couple of minutes, he composed himself, washed his face, unlocked the bathroom door, and found his grandson waiting on him.

"You okay, Pops? I was worried."

"I'm okay, Jack. I just miss your dad and mom. Come on, let's check out the salad bar, ok? We'd better not get too much so we can save room for the ribs and be sure to get some bones to take to Mikey."

As they were silently eating their salad, Fred was fighting off guilt and condemnation for being weak with his grandson. Rose came back and asked if she could sit down for a moment. He stood to pull back a chair for her and she started talking as she sat.

"I told you boys that I was from Houston, too. My mom and dad split up when I was just starting high school. He always drank too much and she finally said enough. One night he was there, and when I woke up the next day, he was gone and I never saw him again."

Fred was used to strangers opening up and relating their life story to him, but this seemed strange to the 10-year-old.

"Mom couldn't make ends meet for me and my little sister, so we all came to Dallas and moved in with my grandparents. A couple of years later, Mom got cancer. She fought it, but…" Her voice trailed off as a far-away look glazed her eyes.

Coming back to the present, Rose continued, "Anyway, Sis and I stayed with Gramps and Grandma Shirley. They raised us well and taught us everything we needed to know, especially hard work," she smiled.

"See that man at the cash register?" They looked and saw an elderly man wearing a cowboy hat, sitting on a stool behind the register, visiting with some customers.

"That's my Gramps. He started this place over 50 years ago. Grandma Shirley and him were the only help to begin with. Then it grew and he ended up hiring a bunch of local kids over the years to be servers and work in the kitchen. He always cooked up 'til a few years ago.

"I worked here in high school and then, after fifteen years of a bad marriage, with no place to go, really, I came back to live with them. I help take care of Grandma now and bring Gramps to work every day before lunch, and we go home together when the dinner crowd thins out. They mean the world to me and my sis.

"Anyways, young man, I wanted you to know how lucky I

was... am... to have grandparents who loved me and raised me and taught me and took care of me, twice now. I can see that you're in good hands, too, and even though the world might stink right now, the good Lord's watching out for you and He's working everything out for you. You can believe Ol' Rose."

Jack and Pops were riveted to every word their server-turned-friend said as she told them about the many loyal customers they had and how many had become family to them. She related how her grandfather sponsored youth baseball teams and took left-over food to a homeless shelter every evening.

"Your grandpa sounds wonderful, Rose. Did, uh... how did he and your grandmother handle their daughter dying, and the other sad things?" Fred asked.

"I don't want to lie to you, it was hard. Sometimes he'd drink a little too much after the restaurant closed and he'd have really bad dreams—they both did. They tried to help me, but it was hard for them. I guess they did as good as they could, you know?"

Fred nodded and looked down at the table.

"Look, mister, I don't know you or nothin', but if you think you got to suck it up and be perfect and never show any sadness or anger or feelings or stuff, you got to get over that shi... uh, stuff. That will eat you up. Be real. It's okay. I know."

Eventually, many more customers showed up and she needed to serve them. She took Fred and Jack's order, and soon brought them a mound of ribs accompanied with a grocery sack for taking leftovers and bones back to the motel.

Everyone Has a Story

As they chowed down, Fred said, "Everyone has a story, Jack."

"What do you mean, Pops?"

"Well, you remember the lady that checked us in at the motel? And the couple unloading their car at the room next to ours? And see that guy sitting by himself at the table over there?"

As Jack nodded, he continued, "They all have a story. They may look rich or just ordinary. They may be friendly and outgoing or not say much. They might be the owner of the business you're in or someone who works there part time. But they all have a story."

"We have a story now, too, don't we?" Jack responded.

"Yeah, we do. And right now, I don't like how the story is going very much."

"Me neither."

"I guess everyone has had something happen in their life that had a tremendous effect on who they are now and where they are now. Most everyone has had some disappointment somewhere. Some more than others, it seems.

"I do know this. Every single person is hard-wired by God to crave unconditional love, genuine acceptance, and to know that they have value in some way. We all work hard to get people to love and accept us, and we work to earn value so we can feel like we deserve to be liked and loved.

"But things happen. We mess up. And even the best human beings aren't perfect. Many times, we end up hurting the people we love the most, and they don't feel loved or accepted or they feel like they're not worth much. We may not even know we hurt them, but they're hurt, just the same."

"Pops, I think my other grandma… I think she hurt my mom. We hardly ever heard from them and sometimes I heard Mom talking to Dad and wondering what she did to make her mom like that…"

"Son, your other grandma has a story too. I know your mom's heart was broken about all that. But your other grandma's not a bad person. She has a story. And God's working in her too, even though she may not know it. One day He will make everything right and your Mom and her will be together again.

"'Til we meet again, right?" Jack asked.

"Yep! See, Jack, some people had a real tough time growing up. Some people have made mistakes that really cost them. Others just never had the opportunity to do what they really wanted to do. Illness, like cancer with Rose's mom, has affected some people or their family members. When your other grandpa died, that must have really hurt your grandma.

"Many people have lost loved ones, like Rose did, and like we have.

"At the same time, maybe some of those same people, or others that you run into, had a coach or teacher or relative that encouraged them and saw to it that they got some opportunities that really helped them.

"And everyone has had unexplainable things happen that they might call a break or good fortune that has also greatly affected them. I believe a lot of those things come from God, but most people don't know it.

"My point is, everyone has a story. Something good, something bad, a win, some losses, usually a combination of things that have come together to affect where they are now and who they are now.

"Only when we make the effort to listen and ask questions can God really start to show us what's going on with another person. Then we can better relate to them and experience something good that otherwise we'd miss.

"And, Jack, most importantly, only God can perfectly give us unconditional love, genuine never-ending acceptance, and help us understand that we have immense value to Him. Since He's God, and is the most important person in the universe, once we know how much He loves us, that He's accepted us and will never reject or leave us, and that we matter to Him more than anything, then we can make it through whatever story life throws our way.

"Once we know how much we matter to God, then we can quit trying to impress people and quit worrying about how they feel about us, and we can instead focus on helping other people.

"I've found that when we listen, Jesus will reveal things about someone else to us that will then move us to say or do something that will lead to a conversation that will bless the other person and us. I call them 'God moments.'"

"Do you think Rose did that, Pops? Did Jesus tell her to come over and visit with us?"

"He sure could have, Jack. That's the kinda thing He does all the time. You'll find that out more and more as you learn to listen to Him. Sometimes you'll just feel like something is the right thing to do. You might not actually hear from God, but later you realize it was Him nudging you to do something that otherwise you wouldn't have done."

As usual, Fred benefitted from hearing these words of truth he had learned over the years, as much as did those hearing them.

The two used up a large amount of butcher paper to take care of grease and barbeque sauce they got all over their hands as they scarfed down a Texas-size dinner. Rose brought them some wet wipes with their cherry pie and left them a page torn from her order pad where she had scribbled, "Two ribs, two desserts." She told them they could pay at the cash register.

Not knowing the total, but guessing it to be around $40, Fred put a $20 bill on the table for their tip.

"Twenty dollars?" Jack asked. "I thought a tip was supposed to be ten percent or something like that."

"You're pretty quick with your math, Jack! There's no set rule, but I always give 20% or more, even if the service is bad. You never know what's going on in a person's life, and I want to bless them however I can. God has provided for me financially, and I want to be someone He can use to help other people too. Waitresses don't make a lot of money and they depend on tips to help them get by."

"Sort of like everybody has a story, right?" Jack asked.

"Right, partner. You never know how much a generous tip might bless someone and they will eventually know that it was Jesus who was taking care of them just when they needed it. Rose is a special person, and I just wanted to bless her. Ok, let's take those bones and get 'em back to Mikey."

They stopped at the cash register and got a good look at the wrinkled old gentleman under the 10 gallon hat, whom they now knew was the owner, Rose's Grandpa.

"The ribs were great, sir. Best we've ever had. You have a wonderful place here. How much do we owe you?"

"On the house, boys! It's been my pleasure to serve you and see a grandpa and his grandson have a nice meal together."

Fred suddenly remembered seeing Rose visit with the old man while they were eating. He realized now that she was telling Gramps their story. Not wanting to rob the old man from the blessing he was giving them, Fred didn't try to talk him out of it.

"Well... that's a special treat, what do you say, Jack?"

Looking at the old gentleman and not missing a beat, Jack immediately said, "Did Jesus tell you our story?"

Laughing, Gramps said, "I guess He did, son. I guess He did."

Once they were outside, Jack asked, "What does 'on the house' mean, Pops?"

"It's another word for grace. It means that nice man didn't charge us for our meal. We didn't do anything to earn it or work for it, and he just decided to give it to us for free, just because that's the kinda guy he is."

It was a sweet moment for everyone, including Rose, with a twenty-dollar bill in her hand as she watched them through a restaurant window. Then she went to the lady's room to touch up her make-up once again.

Confession and "The Fire"

Mikey tore into the bones with delighted fervor. A few were big enough for Fred to play fetch with the bouncing lab while also watching Jack enjoy a game of Marco Polo with some other kids at the swimming pool.

The Astros returned home for their first games after the hurricane and their double header with the Mets was on TV when the two were finally finished swimming and ready to settle down for the night. They each had a queen bed and Mikey was snuggled in his basket-bed on the floor between the two.

Jack told his grandfather about different Astros games he'd been to with his parents earlier in the summer, and after remarking about several calls that the umpires seemed to have blown, Jack said, "Pops, do you think it hurt? Like, were they in pain for a long time?"

Realizing Jack was talking about his parent's death, he muted the sound on the TV and gently said, "I don't know, Jack. We're assuming that they drowned, and that can happen in just a few minutes."

"Oh. Pops?"

"Yes."

"Then what happened?"

"Then, Jack, they were immediately with Jesus. In the next second they were face to face with the One who is love and has always loved them. It's hard for us to really know, because we haven't been there, but as best as I can tell, Jesus surrounded them with pure, white, dazzling light. It's like He radiates light, kind of like the sun lights up the sky.

"And Jesus is all good. All good! There is nothing bad or dark at all in Him or with Him. His love is like this white-hot, fiery, river of love and goodness that flows out of Him to everyone. When you're right in front of Him, it just consumes everything about you. It's so pure, and warm, and good."

"Does it hurt? That fire?"

"Well, it can, Jack, but not like if you stick your hand in a fire and get burned. It's totally different. Let's see if I can describe it. Uh… Jack, did you ever do something bad and then your dad found out about it and had a talk with you?"

Hanging his head and wanting to lie, Jack nevertheless found himself saying "Uh, yes… I, uh… really wanted a new ball glove, but dad said my old one was good enough for this year. One day after our first game, when we were getting ready to go home, a kid forgot to take his glove. It was just like what I wanted. I knew it belonged to a kid on the other team which was from a different part of town. So, uh… I took it. I was hoping dad would never notice it."

"And he did?"

"Oh, yeah. The next day when we were gonna play catch in the back yard, I was gonna use my old glove, but he found the new one and asked me where I got it."

"Then what?"

"I told him."

"And?"

"He got a real sad look on his face. He told me that some other boy was really sad because he lost his glove, and that maybe that boy's dad even gave him a spanking for losing it. He told me it was wrong and that I should have given the glove to our coach and told him where I found it."

"How did you feel, Jack?"

"Oh, terrible. I knew it was wrong. I knew I was bad for taking it. I know my dad was disappointed. I was really hurting."

"Ok, Jack, we'll come back to that in a minute, but for right now, I want you to know that when God's white-hot, fiery love comes at us when we see Jesus face to face, it will burn up any and everything like that… that we haven't already dealt with God about.

"For example, let's say that the night your folks died, your dad might have gotten irritated with your mom about something while they were helping people. And let's say he said something not real nice to her, and he felt bad about it right away, but he never apologized. Then when He saw Jesus, that white-hot, fiery love, would have just consumed that−burned it up. Your dad might have had a little twinge of remembering how bad it felt for not apologizing, just like you felt bad when you knew you did the wrong thing in taking the glove.

"God's pure, unconditional love, like a consuming fire, will burn all those things up real quickly and then you'll be perfect and none of those things will ever happen again in heaven!"

"But what about hell, Pops? What is that like and how do you keep from going there?"

"What have people told you about hell, Jack?"

"One of the guys on the baseball team, Barry, said that his brother is real mean to him. He beats him up all the time and takes his allowance money and blames Barry for everything. He lies and tells their parents that Barry did things when it was really him.

"Barry said he hopes his brother dies and burns in hell forever so God can pay him back for all the bad things he's done. Barry says his brother deserves to be tortured in hell. Barry says that the Bible says God burns bad people there forever."

Fred let out a long breath, asked for Jesus to speak as him, and continued, "Jack, because we humans think other people deserve to be tortured in hell, some people came up with the idea that God feels the same way. But He doesn't.

"God is totally different than us. He's way better than we can ever imagine. He still loves us no matter what we've ever done. Of course, it hurts Him when He sees us do bad things that hurt us and other people, but it never affects how He feels about us. We're all His children and He loves us no matter what. He doesn't keep any record of wrong things we do! Can you imagine that? The Bible tells us that He chooses not to remember our sins or even bring them up to us!

"So, Jack, here's what I understand happens. Let's take Barry's brother for example. When he dies, he's gonna come face to face with Jesus, just like your mom and dad. And Jesus's bright light is going to expose… bring to the light, show this boy… all the bad ways that he treated his brother. He may have even thought it was okay to treat Barry that way, but Jesus's light will expose that for the evil that it is.

"Then, Jack, what happens next will be heaven, or hell, for that boy. If he accepts that what he did was wrong and feels the hurt that he caused Barry, and Jesus, then Jesus's love will burn that all up, and restore that boy to the way Jesus made him.

"However, if that boy digs in his heels and says, 'No, Jesus. I was right. Barry deserved all that, I'd do it again. You can't tell me what to do. I want to do it my way.' Well, Jesus is gonna stay right there with that boy and continue to love him, and continue to let him know that Jesus's way is the right way.

"As long as that boy resists and refuses to accept Jesus's love, he's gonna feel awful. Jesus's light will continue to expose the boy's bad thoughts. He'll be mad and angry and maybe even hate Jesus… and all the while Jesus will be saying, 'That's okay. I still love you. I'm still here, and we're not going anywhere, either one of us.'

"That will feel awful for that boy. It will be terrible. There's nowhere for him to go to get away from Jesus and His love. So as long as he refuses to accept Jesus's love, that white-hot, consuming fire is going to spotlight the boy's bad attitude and bad actions and it's gonna feel horribly painful to him, not painful like an actual burn, but painful in his mind and in his heart. Do you know what I mean?"

"I think so, Pops. When Dad asked me about where I got the glove, I felt really bad. I wanted to run away. I didn't want to be with him. But he never yelled at me, he never told me I was bad, he just stayed there with me and waited for me to talk. Finally, I blurted it all out and cried and told Dad how sorry I was and what a bad kid I was."

"Then what?"

"Dad told me how much he loved me and he made sure I knew

I wasn't a bad kid, but I had just made a poor choice that hurt someone else, hurt Dad, and actually hurt me. He reminded me that he and Mom loved me and that they weren't mad at me, but now I needed to go with him to my coach's house and give him the glove and tell him what happened.

"How'd you feel about all that, son?"

"Awful, until it was over. Then I felt a lot better because I knew the other kid would get his glove back and I knew Mom and Dad loved me and I was okay with them."

"How do you think you would have felt if you refused to tell your dad the truth and resisted him?"

"I know I would have felt awful."

"That's how people feel when they resist Jesus, Jack. Here on earth we can sometimes get to where it doesn't seem to bother us much That's called having a hard heart. But in the next life, when we see Jesus face to face, we can resist Him and refuse to accept His love and His acceptance of us, and He won't go anywhere. He will stay right there We'll be in His presence and that light will continue to expose our darkness, and it will be really painful–that's what hell is. It's never God punishing us, it's our own sin, our wrong actions and attitudes that are punishing us."

"Barry's brother… if that happens to him, he won't keep on resisting Jesus, will he? I mean, after a while he'll stop resisting and accept Jesus's love, won't he? I don't want him to suffer like that forever!"

"Jack, you have Jesus's heart… just like your dad! I remember when he and I talked about this very thing. He actually helped me understand because I used to believe lies about God punishing people in hell. Your dad helped me see the truth.

"We don't know for sure, because none of us has ever been there, but we know that nothing can ever separate us from God's love. We know that God's love never fails and it lasts forever. We know that God is patient. We know that God is good and there is no bad in God. We know that God is not willing that any one perish, or stay in that state of rejection, but His will is that everyone change their mind and accept the love God has for them.

"I believe that Jesus will stay right there with Barry's brother, and every person, pouring out His love and forgiveness and acceptance and inclusion on them, and I can't for the life of me believe that any person could reject that forever. Technically, I guess it's possible. But it's like believing the unbelievably ridiculous to believe that someone, anyone, could resist that kind of love forever.

"Since I believe that, I don't worry about Barry's brother or anyone else. I believe that Jesus's love will ultimately win out with everyone."

Jack let out a little sigh of relief and said, "That's good news, Pops."

"Oh, Jack, you don't know the ultimate truth of what you just said! That is really good news for everyone!"

Jack opened his sketchbook, signaling that the discussion was over, at least for now. Fred watched some more of the game as Jack filled a page with a drawing, and eventually they both fell asleep. Even Mikey was snoring lightly. Eventually, Fred turned off the set and told Jesus how grateful he was to have this very special time with his grandson when he was really needed.

Jack didn't seem to have any nightmares that night.

"The Grace Uh God"

Always an early riser, Fred got up early the next morning, let Mikey out to do his business, then took his shower before waking Jack.

Taking their seats in the motel café, Fred explained to Jack that they could do the breakfast buffet or order from the menu and both agreed the buffet was more appealing. A nice lady, maybe a little older than their waitress the previous evening, came by to see them and said, "How you boys doing this morning?"

"Doing well, Ma'am. How 'bout you?" Fred responded.

"By the grace uh God I'm here, I guess… sure beats the alternative, don't it? Y'all want to do the buffet? Just help yourselves."

She agreed to bring coffee for Fred and orange juice for Jack as they each overflowed their plates with fried potatoes, bacon, scrambled eggs, toast, and fresh fruit.

"What's the 'grace uh God', Pops?"

"It means a lot of different things to different people, Jack, but it's way, way better and has more meanings than we'll ever understand.

"Last night when that nice old man at the barbeque place didn't charge us for our dinner– he gave us something good that we didn't deserve and didn't earn. That was grace. That's what God does.

"And I was also thinking about grace last night when you were telling me about the baseball glove you found.

"What did you think your dad was gonna do when he found out what happened?"

"Oh, I was afraid he might really punish me… like ground me and tell me I couldn't play baseball anymore. Maybe even something worse!"

"But he didn't punish you, did he?"

"No sir! I had to take the glove to my coach and tell him what I did, and that was hard, but it didn't feel like punishment."

"Right. When you do something wrong that you could get punished for, but the person in charge doesn't punish you, that's called 'mercy'–not getting what you deserve. Do you see that?"

"Sure, Pops. I deserved something bad, but Dad didn't do anything bad to me. But what does that have to do with grace? What's grace?"

"Grace is getting something really good when you don't even deserve it. Mercy is one thing– not punishing you, not giving you what you actually deserve. But to go a step further, when someone turns around and gives you something good, even when you don't deserve it, that's called grace!"

"My Dad did that!"

"After hearing your story last night, I remember that when we played catch the other day, you had a brand new glove. Did your Dad get that for you?"

"Yeah! A couple of days after I took the glove back and apologized to Coach Loneski, we had our next practice. About a half hour before practice, Dad asked if I wanted to play catch. I said sure, and he told me to go get our gloves and a ball.

"When I looked in the bag, there was a brand new glove just

like I'd wanted earlier in the summer. I didn't know how it got there and I was afraid maybe I'd done something else wrong and forgot about it. I didn't know what to do. So, I took it to Dad and said, 'This new glove was in the bag, but I didn't take it from anyone. I swear, Dad. I don't know where it came from.'

"He smiled real big and lifted me up and hugged me like he didn't want to let me go and he said, 'I know, Pardner… I just decided to get it for you.'

"Pops, I asked him why and he said, 'Just 'cause I love you. Now let's play catch.'"

"You know, Jack, after you told me the glove story last night and I remembered that you had a new glove, I thought something like that might have happened. That's grace.

"You actually deserved punishment, but your dad didn't give you what you deserved. Remember, that's mercy. Then he gave you a new glove, something you didn't deserve at all, just because he loves you. That's grace, real grace!"

"What made you think he might have done that, Pops?"

"Memories. Let's just say that your dad got a new glove, or something like that, a few times when he was a kid!"

"Really? My dad did something bad?"

"We all do, Jack. We try not to, but none of us are perfect. And if God didn't love us unconditionally and give us grace over and over, this old world would be pretty miserable. God never punishes us. Most of the time, the things that we do wrong punish us or other people punish us, but God never does. He only loves and gives grace. There's nothing like it—nothing like Him!"

About that time, the waitress came by with their check, and looking at the 10-year-old, she said, "You get enough to eat, young man?"

"By the grace uh God, I did, Ma'am!" Jack smiled.

Heading to Kansas

As they headed north, Fred would periodically relate stories to his grandson about towns they passed, frequently pointed out farmers, truckers, and others whom they saw, always relating how they each have great value to God.

They drove around Wichita to the far East exit and stopped at a nice mom and pop diner filled with pictures of airplanes from the Boeing and Cessna plants where many of the country's military and commercial planes were designed and built.

Realizing they had some time to spare after lunch, Fred drove them about a mile to the massive Beech Aircraft plant and airfield.

Fred told Jack that Cessna and Boeing once employed more than 40,000 people in Wichita. Those companies and all the supporting businesses for them were responsible for Wichita being called the Air Capital of the World.

On this day there was a smattering of small and medium planes taking off and landing. Fred reminisced about coming there as a boy and seeing numerous huge planes with thousands of people working.

He said rather wistfully, "You know, Jack, God has orchestrated this wonderful world so that each person has something wonderful to contribute to the whole. And most of the time they each do something they enjoy, something they're excited and passionate about.

"Have you ever thought about a game you wanted to play or something you wanted to do with your buddies, and you imagined where it would be, what it would look like, and what you needed to do it—then you called the guys and got together and did it?"

"Yeah! Last year I thought it would be cool to make a student newspaper. I thought we could write about lots of stuff. Colin likes to take pictures and Grayson likes to write. Erwin draws cool graphic things and I like to sketch. We even had a girl on the team. Clara's dad has an office in their home and he has a humongous printer that he let us use!" Jack got more and more excited as he related his story to Pops.

"Dad taught me how to do some Photoshop and Microsoft Publisher stuff, so I could almost see in my mind what it would look like before we did it! We ended up doing it every month and the rest of the class really liked it, especially when we wrote about them!"

"That's wonderful, Jack! I bet you can do something like that in

Kansas, too!

"Just like you could picture in your mind what the paper would end up looking like, God can do that too. God knows everything. God knows what it takes to make everything work. They– Jesus, Papa… and Sarayu actually dreamed up all the people that would ever live before they made the first one!

"They knew you, Jack, before creation! And They loved you before They ever made you! They knew just what you would look like, act like, and when you would be born and everything… and They were excited about you being in Their family!"

"They know everything?"

"Yep."

"Even the bad things I've done?"

"Yep."

"And They still love me?"

"Yep! Hard to imagine, isn't it? We don't even like ourselves sometimes because of bad things we do, but nothing we do can make Them stop loving us! Remember, They don't keep a list or record of our bad deeds, and They don't even bring them up to us. They choose to not even remember them. That's called grace. They continue to give us Their love even when we think we deserve for Them to dislike us and punish us.

"Now, Jack, what I want you to see is that God loves everyone. God knows all about every one, and everyone is in God's family. God delights in working things out so they all come together for our good, just like you delighted in coming up with your paper and choosing the right guys and girl to draw, take pictures, write, publish, and print. By the way, is Clara the girl that came to your folks service with your friends?"

"Yeah."

"She's cute!"

"Pops!" Jack's face flushed as he grinned and looked away. Eventually, he said, "You talk about God a lot, Pops."

"I guess I do. I'm just excited about how good God is and I want to make sure you know that too!"

"Oh, Okay."

The Flint Hills of Kansas

The landscape changed as soon as they entered the Flint Hills. There were large, rolling hills with few trees, some herds of cattle, occasional groups of horses, and views for miles in every direction with no sign of civilization. Jack was fascinated with wind farms−huge, silver turbines standing on top of hills.

"Pops, last year when my teacher found out that my Dad was from Kansas, she laughed and said something about everything being flat there. This isn't flat at all!"

"Great observation! Some parts of Kansas are very flat – you can see for miles – and there's not much to see! But the Flint Hills are like the beautiful places you see in old western movies, without the mountains, of course!

"Where we live in Lawrence, it's very much like Missouri, Illinois and the rest of the Midwest. There are hills, valleys, a ton of trees, rivers…you'll like it."

While he was still speaking, Fred heard soft snoring and realized that Jack had fallen asleep just past Emporia and Fred used the last part of the trip to think about what lay ahead of them now that he and Susie were no longer empty-nesters.

After an hour or so, they came into the city limits of Lawrence, Kansas, home of the Jayhawks and the Millers– Fred, Susie, and now Jack Miller.

Part 2
No, No! Swim, Dad!

There were still a couple hours of sunlight left when Fred and Jack drove onto the winding lane that led up to the spacious, older home nestled in the edge of a wooded area that transitioned into the city nature park.

When Fred's parents first bought the property in the early 1950's, it included about 80 acres of woods, a winding creek, and some pasture that was good for grazing cattle. It had been considerably outside of the city limits.

Over time, they sold off portions of the property and even formed a small development company that converted much of the land into a nice residential area. But they wisely kept a few acres around their big 1940's farm home. Fred grew up in this home and then returned to it with his young family years later.

The original barn had been converted into a four-car garage, tool shed, and work room with plenty of storage. It even had a second story man-cave that Freddie Jr. had used as a special hangout place for him and his buddies.

There was enough room for them to drive Rachel's car and the trailer inside the garage and they decided they would wait to unload them until the next day.

Susie had fried chicken, gravy, mashed potatoes, corn, fresh tomatoes, a cherry pie, and her ever-present sweet tea all ready for them. Mikey made himself right at home and was instantly ready for whatever food scraps were indiscreetly passed to him by the men. Susie pretended not to notice.

She had checked two large suitcases on the plane− one filled with clothes, including some of her late sons which would be saved until Jack grew to the same size, and the second packed with things for Jack's room.

The latter included some of his stuffed "guys" that he liked to sleep with: a Stay Puft Marshmallow Man, Orbit (the Houston Astro's mascot, a lime-green outer-space creature wearing an Astro's jersey with baseball antennae), and a very well-worn sock monkey that seemed to make the cut every year even as other more "childish" items were discarded.

Susie remembered that her son had similar "guys" that made the cut until some of his junior high buddies started razzing him about them. She smiled as she figured this current group might make it one more year.

In addition, she carefully packed about 20 sketches that had been tacked onto the walls of Jack's room in Texas. She would rather have things framed and hung nicely, but decided to let her grandson put these, and future, sketches up with tacks as he wished. Sheetrock could easily be filled or replaced. Memories... not so easily.

She'd prepared a blanket bed for Mikey right next to Jack's new bed, which had been his dads for many years.

Jack adjusted quickly to his new room. It was where he slept on their twice-a-year visits, and having his "guys" and Mikey there with him made it even more comfortable.

But it wasn't home, and his mom and dad weren't in the guest room as they'd always been.

Some of the sketches from home found their way to the walls, along with a couple from the trip to Kansas. Others were carefully placed under his new bed.

He finally drifted off to sleep after about an hour, his pillow and "guys" damp from tears.

Fred and Susie relaxed with a glass of wine and had their first really private conversation in days. "Well, my dear, things are going to be a little different now, aren't they?"

"Yep" Susie replied. No more line dancing every Tuesday night at the Elks club."

Playing along with her obviously tongue-in-cheek antithesis, Fred interjected "And certainly no more running marathons every weekend."

"I'm afraid I'll have to cancel my membership in the ladies sky-diving club and may not even get to continue playing in the bagpipe marching band."

Both enjoyed the banter, but the reality was starting to sink in that the regular date night they had enjoyed for years would have to be put on hold for a while. They would no longer be free to take the short travel excursions to places around the country they had included in their bucket list.

They wouldn't have it any other way, of course—Jack was their priority now and they were grateful to be able to show their love to him. They would continue to be together, which had always been their great desire and delight.

The conversation became more serious an hour or so after Jack went to bed. They were mostly comforting each other in the loss of their son and his wife, but also visiting the whole span of recent events when they were startled by Jack's scream.

"No! Dad! No! Swim! Swim, Dad!" The 'Hellish Darkness' had followed them to Kansas.

By the time they got to his room, Mikey was up on the bed, licking Jack's face, and the boy was shaking– half asleep, half awake.

"We're here, Jack. It's ok," Fred said as he wrapped his arms around his grandson. Susie was on his other side, rubbing his head and assuring him he was ok.

"It's ok, Jack. It's ok," she repeated softly.

He calmed down, still half-asleep, and said, "It's not ok. It never will be. They're gone."

She continued to rub his back as he lay down and soon went back to sleep, albeit with occasional whimpers. Mikey stayed next to him on the bed.

They left his room quietly. Susie took the wine glasses to the dishwasher and Fred went out the back door. She was concerned for his emotional state, but too fragile herself to have much to give him. The 'Hellish Darkness' attacks sapped their energy and left them feeling as if they'd been in a fight—which they had.

After several minutes he came back in without speaking. Not wanting to add to her troubles, he didn't want to tell her about the pain in his chest and his trouble breathing.

Neither spoke as they quietly got ready for bed. Once they were lying next to each other holding hands, Fred softly said, "Jesus, you're going to have to do this, we're just not able to do it ourselves."

He sensed Him saying: *I will. I'm always with you, all three of you. Trust Me.*

Knowing something was wrong with her husband, she continued praying in silence. Eventually they dozed off, each with damp pillows from their tears.

The "Really Is"

Fred and Susie let Jack sleep in on his first full morning at their house, which enabled them to enjoy their usual early time of reading, journaling, and listening to Papa (or Jesus or the Spirit, it didn't seem to make any difference Who was part of the conversation on any given day).

On this day they were both still wanting answers to the "why" question. Fred was refilling his coffee cup from the pot on the counter that divided their dining room and kitchen. He was about to speak when they heard Jack and Mikey coming down the hall.

"Pops, Nana... I'm sorry about last night."

"What do you mean, Jack?" Fred asked quizzically.

"About saying it would never be ok. I didn't mean that it won't be ok with me being here with you and everything... I just meant..."

"Oh, honey, I didn't even know you were awake when you said that!" Susie said. "Listen, you never have to apologize for things like that. It's not ok for us that your mom and dad are gone, either. Please don't worry about hurting our feelings. We're in this together and Jesus has helped us not let our feelings get hurt very easily."

As she hugged him, Fred interjected, "Nana's right. Never worry about hurting our feelings over things like this. However..."

Jack looked at him, fearing a rebuke.

"However, always make sure that you, and Mikey, have clean feet when you come in from playing outside. Nana turns into a bear when mud gets on her nice, new carpet!"

"Oh, Fred... you know I apologized after I blew up at you for making tracks in the living room when we got our new carpet last spring! I haven't raised my voice since then... much," She smiled.

As they enjoyed their breakfast, Fred talked about some of the things they'd need to do that day.

"After we help Nana with the dishes, we'll take a walk to your new school, then put the top down on the Really Is and head out. When we get back, we'll unload the trailer and then take it back to the local U-Haul place."

Unsure if he heard his grandfather correctly, Jack nodded in confusion, content with whatever was to happen.

The Trusting Axe

"I'm going to show you the way we'll walk to school every day in warm weather, then when we get back we'll go for a ride."

They made their way out the back door, through a wooded area adjacent to their back yard, and down a little hill where they came to a concrete path.

"I didn't know there was a sidewalk here, Pops!"

"It's a nature path. A few years ago, when the city was growing, they built a new school past the edge of town– Windsor Elementary, where you'll be going. The city leaders bought a wooded area between here and the school and converted it into a nature park. They paved this trail, which has entrances from several different adjoining neighborhoods. As you'll see, they created several unique little areas along the creek, at the top of the big hill, and in different settings."

Mikey had a wonderful time exploring the limits of where his leash would allow, and to Jack's delight, they encountered an abundance of wildlife. In the half hour walk to the school, they saw rabbits, squirrels, turtles, a myriad of birds, and evidence of beavers, deer, and voles.

Jack made mental notes for his sketches.

Mikey carried a dead vole in his mouth for about 15 minutes and Fred prayed it wouldn't become a habit for him to bring similar prey into the house. He knew Susie would not approve.

Several times Jack asked Fred to take a picture with his phone so that he could later make a sketch of what they saw.

When they arrived at the school, it was closed for the holiday, but Jack got a close up look at his new hangout.

As they left to go home, both were quiet.

A few minutes back into the woods on the nature path, Fred asked, "What you thinking about, Pardner?"

"Oh, uh, no offense, Pops... but I was remembering my mom and dad taking me to school when I was younger, and then walkin' with my friends the last couple of years... and just, uh, missin' all that."

Fred wisely didn't speak right away. After a few minutes, he asked, "Want to talk about it some?"

"I just get mad, sometimes, Pops. I want to fix it. I want to bring them back. I want to make things right. I want us to be together. But, there's nothing I can do."

"I know those feelings, Jack. You know I want them back, too. And... about wanting to fix things, most men are like that. We see a problem and we want to fix it. It's a good thing to realize when we're powerless, when we can't fix it. That's when we use the 'trusting axe', or the 'axe of trust.'"

"Huh?"

"I'll show you when we get home."

Soon they departed the trail at the edge of their property and entered the wooded area that led to the backyard. As they entered the yard, Fred walked over to a huge, old, walnut tree with an enormous, gnarled trunk. Some of the branches seemed to be dead, but it was mostly alive.

"Look closely at the trunk, Jack. What do you see?"

It took a few moments, but eventually he observed, "It kinda looks like someone tried to chop it down a long time ago, but they didn't get very far."

"That's exactly what happened! You and Mikey wait here, I'll be right back." He disappeared into the barn and soon reappeared, carrying an old, weathered axe. Handing it to Jack, he said, "Try it out."

"You mean... hit the tree?"

"Sure!"

The old tool was extremely heavy and very cumbersome since most of the weight was at the bottom. Having run his finger across the blade, Jack knew it was also pretty dull. But willing to give it a try, he awkwardly drew it back and was able to put a weak hit on the side of the tree. It didn't leave a noticeable mark.

"I don't think I'd make much of a lumberjack, even though that's part of my name," the boy grinned.

"Neither did I or your dad, Jack. But here's what we did. My dad actually taught me. Whenever I was really frustrated… when I was angry about something I wanted to fix or accomplish, but I just couldn't do it, I would get this axe, come out here and swing away at this tree for all I was worth.

"At first I thought I'd probably cut it down. Then I got to where I realized that wasn't gonna happen, but it sure felt good to take my frustrations out on something I couldn't really hurt. Then, after a while, I'd be exhausted, but I'd somehow feel better.

"My dad called it the 'trusting axe.'"

"What's that mean, Pops?"

"After trying as hard as I could, I could hardly make a dent in the tree. My dad taught me to use that as a reminder that I couldn't fix whatever situation I wanted to fix, but to trust Jesus. Give it to Him. To say, 'Jesus, I can't do it. So, I'm gonna let go and give this to You and trust You. Jesus, You know what I need and what to do. I know You love me and You are good, so I trust You.' Then I let it, whatever *it* was at the time, go.

"Whenever you need to, Jack. You can use the 'trusting axe'– unless I happen to be using it first! But only use it here, on this tree… nowhere else, and *never* use it on a person or animal, ok?"

"Ok."

Fred opened the back door and called to Susie, informing her that they would be taking the 'Really Is' for a spin. Then they headed to the barn-garage where Fred kept his prized, silver 2007 Pontiac G6. Jack was fascinated as he watched the hard top and accompanying parts go through a series of maneuvers and gyrations which soon transformed an ordinary looking vehicle into a sporty convertible.

After covering the back seat with a heavy, old blanket, Fred had Jack call Mikey to get in the car, and the threesome took off on the first of what would be innumerable special times together over the next several years.

The First Convertible Conversation

As Fred slowly drove down their lane and then proceeded on a street leading downtown, he asked, "What do you think?"

"This is a really cool car, Pops! I remember seeing it when I was here before, but I never got to see the top go down into the trunk. I didn't know cars could do that!"

Silently taking in his new surroundings, Jack didn't speak for a bit, but then said, "Oh, I forgot. Tell me about the 'silly, uh … riz… what was it?"

Fred smiled, "The Really Is? That's what I call this car."

"Uh, what does that mean, Pops?" Jack questioned.

"Well, you're gonna learn soon, if you haven't already, that things aren't always what they first seem to be.

"You can look at my car from a number of different angles, you can even ride in it, and it appears to be a hardtop. You can say, 'Pops' car is a hardtop.' But as you just saw, you'd be mistaken!

"I've found that something dramatic usually has to happen for us to change our mind, to come to see that something's not what we thought it was.

"As you saw this morning, this car is a hardtop convertible– it's capable of being changed. If you weren't familiar with my car, you wouldn't believe it's a convertible because what you *see* tells you differently.

"There's a guy who I like to read a lot. He lived about 2,000 years ago, and he was really sharp. His name was Paul. He wrote these words in a letter one time: '*We are not keeping any score of what seems so obvious to the senses on the surface; it is fleeting and irrelevant; it is the unseen eternal realm within us which has our full attention and captivates our gaze!*' 2 Corinthians 4:18 MB

"What this guy, Paul, was talking about, Jack, was *seeing what really is.*

"The word convertible means capable of being converted or changed from one thing to a different thing. The picture of the top opening up in my car is a great metaphor for our minds being convertible… being able to open up, open to seeing things that we have never seen before.

62

"When the hardtop is up, nothing from the outside can get in… it can feel safe. But while it may *feel* safe, it's very restricted, limiting, and closed off. It's exclusive. You're inside, all walled in and protected, and you're also excluded from what really is!

"You're secluded and insulated from the wind, the trees, the sky. Look over to your right, up high there– what do you see?"

"A bunch of big buildings. The tallest one has two flags on the top."

"That's Frazier Hall at KU. It's kind of a landmark for the University skyline. But, if we had the top up, you couldn't see it. All you could see would be the trees and houses on this street– you couldn't see what really is. Right?"

"Well, yeah. But Frazier Hall would still be there, I just couldn't see it."

"Exactly! That's a fitting example of the problem of small thinking– when you keep yourself from being able to see the big picture of what's really out there in life. The concept is true about all kinds of things, but maybe, most importantly, about God.

"You know that my definition of 'religion' is any attempt to gain or maintain a right relationship with God by our own efforts. Religion fosters judgment, condemnation, shame, exclusivity, and generally believes in a fictitious god of our own imaginations, not Jesus's Papa, the only true God!

"Your dad and I found that the most important thing in all of life is for people to be able to see the big picture about God, about who God *really is*, and not be stuck with some bad religiously incorrect picture about God.

"Convertible means much more than a type of car, it means 'able to change,' 'able to be converted'– as in converted from a closed in, restricted view, to a wide open, top-down view. Then we can see what really is!

"What really is, what is real, is wide open, free, glorious– not limited! I can see things I didn't realize were there. I can feel the wind. I can relate to those who are around me.

"I've had convertibles almost continuously since I was in college… a *long* time ago! I love the freedom, the openness, the ability to relate to my surroundings. And for the past seven years or so, I've become convertible in my beliefs. Your dad helped me a lot with that, Jack."

"He did? My dad taught *you*... his own father?"

"Yes sir! He taught me the real meaning of a Greek word that was used a lot 2,000 years ago, 'metanoia'. It means to change your mind, to think differently about something now than I used to think."

"He and I came to realize that what we thought about a lot of things weren't true! We needed to be convertible! We needed to change our minds!

"He helped me come to the realization that a lot of the things I had believed about God were not true. That was pretty shocking for a guy who'd been a pastor for over 20 years!"

"Was that hard for you to do? I mean, didn't you feel like you already knew everything about God and the Bible and stuff, about being a pastor and all?"

"That *was* the problem!" Fred laughed. "I thought I had God figured out even though there were a lot of things that just didn't add up. But we really weren't allowed to ask questions.

"Jack, I grew up going to church every time the doors were open, right here in this town. I continued that as an adult. Those were good churches with good people in them, and I'm grateful for the opportunities I had. It may seem like I think all churches are bad, but I don't.

After I got out of the army, I eventually became a pastor and had a lot of training about who God is, what He's like, and what we're supposed to do to try to get Him to be merciful with us rather than torture us forever.

"I heard things about God and about the Bible all my life, and I never questioned them... I just assumed they were true. Actually, in the church settings I was part of, it was taboo to question anything!

"I was virtually certain about what I believed, and I was pretty miserable. I could put on a good front, but those closest to me knew the truth. What I was doing just wasn't working for me... or really for anyone else in the church. But none of us wanted to admit it.

"Do you know the story about the Emperor's new clothes, Jack?"

"Sure, this guy was naked and everyone knew it, but no one would admit it!" he laughed.

"That's exactly what it was like for us in church... in religion! We talked about a lot of this stuff as if it worked, and all the time we knew a lot of it really didn't!

"So... what happened, Pops?"

"Well, your dad grew up, went to college, learned some things, moved to Houston, started his career... but in his spare time, he took online classes and started learning even more. About seven years ago, he started telling me about some things he was learning in Houston.

"I realized I had a hardtop spiritual mentality, that I needed to put the top down and be willing to change... to be convertible. So, I started on an amazing journey that literally gets better every day, because I now realize every day that God is not like I used to believe.

"Every day, I learn something new about Him that shows me He's even better than I thought He was yesterday! God is in the revelation business. He is continually revealing to you how much better He is than you previously thought!"

"Pops, you and my dad talked about this kind of stuff a lot?"

"Yep, especially the last seven years or so, ever since your dad started *seeing what really is* and helping me to see, we talked about it all the time when we were together and on the phone, emails, Skype... a lot!"

"Pops?"

"Yeah, Jack."

"Did you talk about this kind of stuff all the time with my dad when he was 10 years old?"

"Uh, you had enough for today?"

"I was thinking maybe you could take me by where the Jayhawks play basketball. Me and Dad watched a lot of their games on TV. It's a cool place! Allen Fieldhouse, right?"

"Right," the old man smiled. He could take a hint.

After seeing Allen Fieldhouse and driving through the rest of the beautiful, hilly campus, they took care of their errands and drove home for lunch. They spent the afternoon unloading the trailer and putting things away.

After they returned home from returning the trailer to the local U-Haul store, they parked Rachel's car in the garage next to the Really Is and Nana's sedan.

"Will we need to get rid of Mom's car?" Jack asked pensively.

"No, the convertible doesn't do all that well on snow and ice, and when you're fifteen you'll need something to drive, don't you think?"

"So this is *my* car?!"

"*Will* be… your bike will do just fine for now!"

"Oh, yeah."

Fred made sure that there was no more 'God talk' for the afternoon. It seemed to him that Jesus was saying: *Just wait… let Jack bring it up.* So, he did.

At dinner, the three talked about the Kansas City baseball team and kidded each other about who was the better team– the Royals or the Astros.

They decided on a trip to Dairy Queen in the Really Is. Susie wore a scarf and sat in the front seat while Jack enjoyed the wind in the back seat with Mikey. He wanted to hang his head over the side and stick out his tongue like his dog, but he thought better of it.

They got their treats and drove a short distance to South Park where the Lawrence City Band was playing the performance of the day at the Labor Day Fall Arts Festival. They were just the right distance where they could hear the music, but also hear each other as they talked.

"So, how do you like the Really Is, Jack?" Nana asked.

"Oh, I love it! So does Mikey!"

"Did Pops tell you how it got its name?" Fred tried to motion to her not to ask, but it was too late. He didn't want to violate his commitment to stay away from 'God talk' for the rest of the day.

"Yeah, he told me, and I've been thinking about that. He said that with the top down, we could see what really is… and that was good, because we can't see everything with the top up.

"But I've been thinking about this… what if what we see… what *really is*… is not good. What if it's bad… like *really bad*.

Praying earnestly for Jesus's help, Susie said, "Give me an example."

"Well, my mom and dad are dead. Gone. I'll never see them again. That's *what really is* and it's really bad. It's not good." His angry tone conveyed the deep hurt and loss that was now the prevailing reality to Jack.

As soon as he started talking, Fred started feeling anxious and the chest pains re-appeared.

"Jack," Susie said softly, but loud enough that he could hear over the Star Wars medley coming from the city band, "This is actually a perfect time for us to see what *really is*.

"Yes, your mom and dad are dead and gone. They aren't with us here. And that is really bad. There's nothing good about it. It hurts. It's not fair and it should never have happened. That's all true. It seems like God let us down. It seems like He could have kept that from happening, doesn't it?"

"Yes! He could have saved them!" Jack shouted.

"That's what we can see, Jack. It seems like we'll never see them again. But that's not seeing what really is. *What really is*, the big picture thing, is that while we won't see them for a while, they really are fine right now, and before we know it, we will see them again, and we'll all be together… forever.

"Remember, 'til we meet again'…what Pops said at the celebration?"

"Oh, yeah…I just forget sometimes."

"We all forget, Jack, that's why your Pops reminds us over and over about these things. That and he just likes to talk a lot and is getting forgetful."

"Hey… I resemble that remark!" Fred interjected, trying to keep them from seeing his physical pain.

Susie continued, "In the life-after, we'll be with God and there will never again be any pain, death, evil, nothing bad. I know that doesn't take away the pain and hurt right now… and I don't want you to think I'm saying to just be happy and everything will be fine. It's not. But we do know the truth. We have certain hope. Not like you hope the Astro's beat the Royals, but *certain* hope.

"God takes everything, even the bad– especially the bad things– and then works His divine plan into the bad to ultimately produce good. Good and bad are present all the time. Sometimes because we can't see *what really is*, we don't see how anything good could ever come from something as bad and your mom and dad being gone.

"But... God is working in that. I'm not saying that it's good that they are gone. It's not. It's bad... awful. But, God is with us in that, and right now, He's in the process of working good to come out of it. We can't see what that is right now, but one day we will. One day He will make everything right, for everyone.

"When Jesus was murdered on the cross, it was awful– the worst ever. But He knew His Father, our Father God, was with Him and was working everything out for the good, even then. So because He knew that, because He had that faith, He could endure it all.

"And in the same way, we know God, our Father, is with us now. He loves us. He's taking care of us. He will be with us and you will be with your mom and dad before you know it. And if it's important, He'll show us what good ultimately comes from all this. If it's not important for us to know, it will still be good... forever.

"Bad stuff happens here on earth, even to wonderful people... like you and your mom and your dad. But that's not all there is. We can see enough of *what really is* to get us through this. And even though it hurts now, we know we'll be ok."

That seemed to be enough for the moment. Jack was thinking. Susie and Fred were praying, and they were all listening to the band music.

America's Favorite Pastime and the Sin of Certainty

Labor Day weekend, Fred was concerned that his chest pains persisted. Susie knew something was wrong, but wrongly assumed it was "only" grief.

The fall youth baseball league started that weekend and one of Freddie's childhood friends, Duane Goldman, whom Fred had coached in little league baseball 20 years previously, was now coaching his own son, Wayne, who, like Jack, would was in 5th grade. As fate (or Providence) would have it, one of their players broke his arm and they had an opening, which Jack was excited to fill.

The Barnstormers consisted mainly of boys in their neighborhood who all attended the same elementary school. They usually practiced Saturday mornings and had a couple of evening games each week through October. Coach Goldman knew about the flood and Jack's situation. He called the players and told them about their new teammate and his recent loss.

Fred took Jack to the park early that morning to practice When they arrived for warmups, the boys all welcomed Jack to the team. Their awareness of the reason for Jack being with them eliminated what could have been innumerable uncomfortable questions.

Soon the Kansas sun became hotter than the 70-year-old could handle. He heard voices in his head condemning him for not being up to the challenge and responsibility of raising a 10-year-old.

The fact that Fred still loved being on the diamond with the feel of his old glove, and the smell of leather coated with Neatsfoot oil only added to his disappointment. Somehow he made it through the two hour session.

After practice they drove to Jack's new school so he could get a feel for it. Several cars were in the parking lot, so Fred decided to take his grandson in, hoping he might get to see some of his teachers. They were in luck as many educators were there on their day off preparing for the next week.

The air-conditioned building seemed to help Fred's physical condition. A friendly custodian escorted them to Jack's new classroom and he seemed to like his young, bubbly teacher, Miss Cass. This was her third year of teaching and she was full of enthusiasm. Because Fred had called the principal while they were still in Texas, she had been alerted as to Jack's circumstances and mentioned that she would do her best to alleviate any potential awkward moments.

He also met the physical education and band teachers and enjoyed touring the school, which was bright, colorful, had state-of-the-art media and computer equipment and the interactive library was cutting edge. His happiest moment was meeting the art teacher, Mr. Garcia, and there seemed to be an instant bond between them.

While the new building was all a marked improvement over the age, equipment, and space in Jack's old school in Houston, he still longed for the familiarity and for his friends.

Most of all he longed for his parents.

They went home for lunch and he told his grandmother about the school, especially Mr. Garcia.

Late afternoon they went to Jack's first ball game. Things went well for Jack and his new team until the father of one of Jack's teammates got increasingly louder and angrier at the home plate umpire who was calling balls and strikes. This fellow had a loud, booming voice and had apparently missed the class on good citizenship when he was growing up.

The ump, a young African American man, most likely a college student, was inexperienced, and *was* calling a lot of pitches wrong. However, that was no excuse for the unruly parent's continual barbs and accusations.

The volume and acidity of the taunts, coupled with thinly veiled racial slurs, reached the point in the third inning where the umpire took off his mask, walked to the screen separating the fans from the field, and ejected the parent from the game. He instructed him to leave the stands and not return that evening (which was proper protocol... although rarely employed.)

The man's wife was extremely embarrassed and tried to get her husband to calm down, which made him even angrier and then he lashed out and blamed her for his problems. Their son, who was with his friends on the field, was mortified... as was Jack.

Unfortunately, the event also triggered chest pains in Fred and this time he couldn't conceal them from his wife. She was relentless in getting him to reveal the nature of his discomfort and urged him to let her call 911.

"We can't do that, Sue. Jack can't handle another tragedy. I have to tough this out."

She couldn't help him see how illogical his reasoning was and didn't want to cause a scene that would further worry Jack, so she sat and prayed, "Jesus, please... do what it takes."

As fit the rules, the umpire notified each coach and the fans that the game would be halted until the man left. After a few loud parting remarks, the unruly dad yelled for his son to get off the field and forced he and his wife to come with him and they left. Play resumed and there were no more obvious problems.

Fred's pain subsided, leaving him weak, but thankful.

After the game, both coaches thanked the ump and made sure that he and the other umps got to their cars safely.

There was still plenty of daylight left when they got home. Fred and Susie both took naps before their dinner while Jack worked on a sketch. Later at dinner, Jack asked his Grandpa, "Pops, what was up with that guy who got sent out of the ball park? Why do you think he was acting like he did? I really felt bad for his son, Brandon."

"I'm not sure, Jack. I don't know the fellow, but I do know he has a story. Remember, everyone has a story. Who knows what might have happened to him today. Maybe he had a bad day at work and his boss got on him. Maybe things aren't going well in his marriage. Maybe he has an aging parent who he has to take care of and he's worried about them. It could be any number of things."

"Oh, so he's not just a hot-tempered drunk who likes to be loud and complain? Scooter, our third baseman, said he knew him and he was like that all the time. Scooter said the guy drinks too much and is always telling other people they're wrong and he's right. Scooter says he's scared for Brandon."

"What do you think about tonight, Jack? Was he right or wrong about the umpire? Was the ump missing a lot of calls?"

Jack laughed and said, "Did you see how far low and outside that pitch was that he called strike three on me? I would have to have run across the plate to be able to reach it with my bat! He wasn't a very good ump!"

"No, he wasn't tonight. Umpires have bad days too, but at least he was an equal opportunity ump. He missed a lot of balls and strikes for both teams! But that's not the point.

"You know, of course, Jack, that having good manners and being a good sport is more important than whether or not the ump or ref in basketball and football gets the call right. Everyone wants to win and we want the games to be fair, but people are human and they make mistakes. *And*, as much as we like to win, a few weeks from now no one will really remember who won which game in the season. At least most people won't! But there's something even more important here."

"What, Pops?"

"I call it the 'sin of certainty.' Some people call it 'the wrongness of having to be right.'"

"Huh?"

"Like with that man tonight, Jack, you will notice that some people just have to be right. They have to be right about sports. They have to be right about politics. They have to be right about religion. They just have to be right. They have to be right about how to stack the dishwasher or fold the clothes.

"Their way is the right way, according to them, and if someone is different than them– a different race, different political party, different religion– they think the other person is just wrong… about pretty much everything. They see everything as black and white, either/or, good or bad.

"They exclude and label people and for them, life becomes a perpetual contest between them, who are right, of course… and everyone else, who are wrong, of course.

"Not everyone is like that, and certainly people take it to different levels and even act out. I think that's part of what happened with the angry man tonight. It's possible that because he thinks he's right, he also thinks that it's ok to be mean and yell and criticize other people.

"That leads to judging– being judgmental, and lumping people into all good or all bad groups. When they do that, they're unable to see anything good in people who look, think, or act differently than those in their little group.

"And because they think being right is the most important thing, they're unable to see that there might be reasons why someone else is having a bad day.

"Because they are certain that they are right, and they believe that being right is the most important thing, they can't see that it's really not that important who wins a little league ball game."

"Is that kinda like not *seeing what really is*?" Jack asked.

"That's exactly right! Good thinking, Jack!"

Continuing with his explanation, his grandfather said, "Sometimes you'll see brothers and sisters and one just has to tell the other one that they are wrong all the time. That happens with married couples as well. People can be certain that they are always right… and the other person is always wrong… and thus, bad.

"For example, some white people are certain that all blacks are bad, and vice versa. They're sure they're right about that.

"Some Democrats are certain that all Republicans are bad, and vice versa. Being right is the most important thing to them. They're certain that they are right about that.

"Then when a person has a bad day… something doesn't go well at home or work, they may have a few too many drinks, which makes things escalate and become magnified.

"Drinking– having a beer or wine or whatever– isn't bad. But each person has a limit… a point at which they start to say and do things they wouldn't normally do if they weren't drinking. Many times, people can get angrier more easily and even belligerent… as this man was."

"Do you drink beer, Pops?"

Laughing, his grandfather said, "I don't, but not because it's wrong. I just don't like the taste of beer and when you get my age, it's pretty easy to get a beer belly, which I don't want. Nana and I drink wine, though, and other drinks, but we will only have a glass or two and we don't judge other people as right or wrong because they do or don't drink.

"Some religious people, though, are certain that it's wrong to drink. They think being right is the most important thing, and they're all certain that they are right. They can make it known in no uncertain terms that a person is bad if they have a drink. They are certain that they are right.

"When people judge and label others like that, they put up an invisible barrier, Jack, that keeps them from seeing the good in other people. It's hard for them to trust or like people who are different than they are. They are certain that they are better than those other people… and then it's easy for them to treat other people badly."

"Pops?"

"Yeah, Jack?"

"What's gonna happen to that man who got angry at the

game?"

"Hopefully he will come to realize that he has a problem, and will go to someone who can help him, and then he will change."

"Could you go tell him he needs help and then help him? I don't like to think about his son having to experience that all the time."

"Oh, Jack. You really have a good heart... just like your mom and dad!

"But, I don't know that man, and when you don't have a relationship with someone, I don't think you have the right to step in to a situation. Also, most people will reject help until they come to the realization that they really are in need and want to change."

"So, what can we do, Pops?"

"We can pray. Let's do that right now.

"Lord, we don't know this man, but you do. We know you love him just as much as you love us. You know what's going on in his life, what caused him to act like he did today, and exactly what he needs. I pray that real soon he realizes his need and I pray that you will put just the right person into his life who can help him. Lord, protect his wife and kids and show us if there's any way we can help."

"Now what?" Jack asked.

"Now we trust Jesus that He knows what's going on and He knows what to do... and we let it go. If you're still concerned about the boy, whenever you think about him, you can ask Jesus to protect him."

Since they'd finished their dinner, Nana asked, "How about some ice cream? We didn't have treats after the game and I have a sweet tooth."

They went out to the picnic table in the backyard and Mikey ran all over the place, darting here and there... occasionally coming up to them, as if to make sure they were going to stay and not leave him alone like they had in the afternoon.

The next day the threesome slept in, then after brunch they enjoyed a leisurely time at the Fall Art Festival in South Park on the southern edge of the downtown business district. Jack could have stayed hours longer surveying the various artist's work, but his Grandparents started tiring mid-afternoon.

On Labor Day Monday they slept in again, partially because the events of the past few weeks had taken not only an emotional, but also a physical toll on the three. They took a picnic lunch to Clinton Lake and let Mikey and Jack explore during the afternoon.

That evening they ate at the picnic table in their back yard then Fred and Susie chatted about old friends they'd seen the last two days at the art fair and game, and commented on various things they saw and heard from them. Jack was pretty quiet, periodically throwing a stick for Mikey to fetch.

"So, did you see any drawings as good as yours at the fair yesterday, Jack?" Pops grinned.

"There were some pretty good ones, but I'm gonna show some things next year. I think I can hold my own," he said confidently.

"That you can!" His grandfather replied. "I'm continually impressed with what you come up with. Do you have anything new to show us?"

"Yeah, just a minute," Jack said as he went in to get something from his room.

He opened his sketchbook to reveal a curious blend of two school buildings. After studying it for a while, Susie remarked, "The part on the left side looks like your new school and then right in the middle it looks like an earthquake or something happened and there's a split between the part on the right, which is a completely different school."

Fred joined in, "And out in front of the door, there's a boy looking at the school, scratching his head. Is that it?"

"Yep."

"Tell us about it, Jack," Susie invited.

"That's me. I have a lot of questions. I don't know if I'll like this new school like I do *my* school." Although he wasn't being dogmatic, he conveyed this obvious understanding that he viewed his former school as *his* school.

"I don't know what to expect. Will I fit in? Will I like the other kids? Will they like me? What if I don't know as much as them? They probably all have moms and dads, and I don't…"

Wanting to make sure Jack knew he was listening and not just quickly throwing out cheap platitudes to million-dollar questions, Fred prayed silently: *Jesus, this precious little boy needs You and Your wisdom and compassion right now. Would You please speak to him… as me?*

"I know those questions, Jack…I had similar ones… often. When I was an army bandmaster, every two or three years, people who I'd never met at some headquarters who-knows-where would reassign me to a different band at a different installation in a different city… sometimes a different country.

"The last 10 years, your dad was growing up and he changed schools four different times between kindergarten and when we moved back to Lawrence and he got to settle in here.

"Each time we moved, I would wonder how I would fit in with my new band and new headquarters. The people there had known each other for a while. I didn't know if I'd be as good as the person I replaced. I didn't know if they'd like me. I didn't know if my new bosses would like my style.

"And I remember your dad having almost the same questions you did, Jack. Four schools. Four new sets of teachers and students. Four different homes in different cities. It was unsettling, to say the least."

"So how did he do? How did you guys do?"

"Each place was different, Jack," Fred said. "We didn't have any bad experiences… just different, especially since two of those were in different countries, Germany and Korea. Korea was the worst, because I was there for a year before your dad and Nana came. There was a big cultural adjustment, but the people we worked with and the students at your dad's school were all Americans."

"Freddie made new friends each place we went," Susie said. "The hardest thing for him was leaving them each time. You know what that's like, don't you?"

Jack nodded, a little too emotional to speak.

His grandmother continued, "Jack, you're a very smart guy. You're talented. You make friends easily, as you found out from your new baseball team. Your teachers know your situation and they've assured us that they will do everything possible to make things go smoothly for you.

"Pops and I have great faith in you. But most importantly, Jesus has faith in you."

"Nana, I thought *we* were supposed to have faith in Jesus. What do you mean?"

"Jesus knows you better than you know yourself, Jack. He lives in you. He knew you before you were born. He was responsible for your creation to begin with. He loved you before you were born. He loves you right now more than you can possibly imagine!

"He has given you obvious gifts with music, art, and doing well in school. He's given you a wonderful personality and He's given you a very tender, compassionate heart. You really care for other people and don't like to see anyone get hurt or taken advantage of.

"Most importantly, Jesus has faith in you, because He is in you and He guides you!

"Your teachers and most of the kids will notice those nice things and want to be around you because they are actually seeing Jesus when they see you!" She smiled.

Fred continued, "That may not be the case with everyone, son. There will always be a few people that see things differently than you, and as you know, everyone has a story. There will be some kids who have a real rough time at home and some kids who have sick parents whom they're worried about.

"There will be kids in your class who's mom and dad don't get along and there's a lot of anger and shouting at home. That will certainly affect how they relate to the other kids. Everybody has a story."

"I sure have a story… I'm just not sure how it's gonna end. I don't even know what tomorrow will be like…"

"Jack, I believe it will go well," Nana said. "But you know what, the next day may not. Or the third day of December may not be the best. Or March 30th. Not every day will go the way we want it to. Situations and circumstances change.

"But Jesus never changes. He is always with you. He is always for you. He is always working things out for the best for you and everyone. As you remember to trust Jesus, ask Him to show you what's going on, and as you ask Him to live as you, you'll experience Him doing that more and more.

"Then, even when things don't go just as you hoped, you will be okay knowing that Jesus is with you and working out things for the best."

"Ok. Can I go in now?"

"Sure thing! See you in the morning."

Once in his room, Jack got his sketchbook out and began drawing while Fred and Susie enjoyed some time together in the back yard. Eventually Susie said, "Tell me more about the 'sin of certainty.' Are you certain you're doing the right thing by *not* doing anything about these chest pains?"

"Oh, Suze, I really don't know what to do. You know I used to have anxiety attacks and have pain like this. The doctors always said, 'Relax, don't take things so seriously, don't work so hard.' I think that's all it is."

"What if it's not? Have you thought about what it would be like for Jack and me if you died of a heart attack?"

He never liked this tone of voice coming from her, because it almost always meant he was wrong.

"So…" she continued, "What are you going to do?"

"I guess I should ask Jesus…"

"That would be a good start."

He hugged her, then left to go outside. As she was getting ready for bed, he came back to the bedroom.

As she looked questioningly at him, he said, "I'm going to see the doc as soon as I can get an appointment."

"Thank you, *Jesus,*" she exhaled as she hugged the love of her life for the past 48 years.

First Day of Fifth Grade

At six the next morning Fred texted his friend and family doctor, Phil Goode.

"Been having some chest pains. Can I get in to see you today?"

The doctor's answer came back immediately: "Are you having

pain right now?"

"No."

"I'm out of town, but will be back tonight. My office 8:15 tomorrow. No coffee."

"Dang! I'll be there. Thanks."

Soon Jack was up and thinking about his first day at his new school. He knew a few boys who would be in his room, had his supplies and a new backpack. Technically he was ready.

Mentally and emotionally... he wasn't.

He kept thinking about his childhood friends in Houston, many of whom he started with in kindergarten and had been friends with ever since. He looked at his yearbook from fourth grade, which seemed an eternity ago and like it was in an alternate universe.

There was his gang that produced their little school newspaper. He had a special, different feeling when he saw Clara's smiling picture. There were the guys on his old baseball team. There were the kids who lived on his block, the ones he walked or rode his bike to school with. There was the PE teacher whom he'd had for five years.

There was his art teacher, Mr. Silver, who encouraged him with his sketching and often stayed after school to teach him about drawing.

And he thought about having breakfast with his mom and dad and their hugs, encouragement, and little lectures about how to do the right thing that day. He remembered not wanting them to hug him out in the yard as he left for school because he would be teased by the other kids. How he longed for their hugs right now...

He wondered if he would be at the same level as his new classmates. Would they have learned things and progressed beyond where he was at his old school? Would he be embarrassed? Would he fit in? Would they make fun of his Texas accent (he didn't think he had an accent at all, but some of the guys on his new ball team sure thought so.)

Fred, Susie, and Jack had a good breakfast, cleaned the kitchen, took care of their toiletries, and the time finally came to head out.

Susie gave Jack an assuring smile, hug, and encouraging words, then playfully admonished Fred not to dawdle in the woods after he left Jack at school.

The two, accompanied by Mikey, went through the back yard, made their way down to the concrete path, and started their daily warm-weather routine of traversing the nature park on the way to school.

Jack didn't mind not walking with other kids, especially since he didn't know any who lived on the direct route to school, and he loved being in the woods. He always enjoyed having Mikey with him and knew that unless Pops was along to take the pooch home, he wouldn't have that time with him.

Best of all, he loved the opportunities for Fred to take pictures of things they saw so that he could sketch them later on. He enjoyed being with his grandfather, too, even though many times he wished it was his dad who was at his side.

On this September 5th morning, the sun had already been up for a couple of hours; he was a little warm even wearing a t-shirt and shorts, and was grateful for the occasional water fountains the city had thoughtfully placed on the trail.

After walking a few minutes, they came across a dead blue-jay lying on the path. Stopping to look at it, Jack commented, "I wonder what happened to it?"

"I don't know, Jack," his grandfather responded. "Sometimes birds, like other animals and like people, just get old. Their body wears out and their heart stops beating. That could have happened to this guy while he was flying over the path.

"Or maybe a predator like a falcon or something got him and lost control when he was flying and carrying him somewhere for breakfast and dropped him here. Or could have been something else. What do you think?"

"I don't know, either. I just know he can't fly anymore… would you take a picture of him for me?"

Fred didn't ask why. He pulled out his phone, got down close to the bird, took a picture, and showed it to Jack.

"That's good, Pops. I'll need it when I get home tonight."

Fred made sure to talk about other things and point out animals and birds they saw as they got closer to the school. Periodically, other parents with children would appear on the path, and eventually, after coming up a steep hill, the woods stopped and Jack's new school appeared across the street.

They encountered a pleasant middle-aged crossing guard who diligently watched the different streams of people coming to the round-about intersection. "You want me and Mikey to go across with you and go up to the school, or should we leave you here?"

Looking around at the other parents and their young charges, Jack said, "You can come with me."

Many parents of younger children accompanied them up to the school, but Fred noticed most of those appearing to be Jack's age were with friends, not parents.

As they neared the school, Jack rubbed Mikey's ears, thanked Fred for walking with him, awkwardly waved goodbye, and watched them backtrack to the roundabout. As they crossed the street Fred looked back and saw his grandson wave at them. As Fred and Mikey went back into the woods, Jack took a deep breath and looked for someone he knew just as one of the guys on his team said, "Hey Jack! Over here!"

Fred prayed on his way home, "Jesus, thank you for living in Jack and for taking care of him, especially today. I trust you. Thanks."

No worries, Fred. Relax!

Fred's step was then a little lighter and he enjoyed being with Mikey and greeting the latecomers hurrying along the trail.

Miss Cass did a wonderful job of including Jack in her classroom and making sure he was aware of how things worked at his new school. Of course, he wasn't the only new student in his class, but he thought he was probably the only one there because of tragic circumstances.

At first, he made mental notes of how things were different from his Houston school, but by lunch time he was caught in the flow of his new setting and adjusting comfortably.

As soon as Fred arrived home, Susie wanted to know how it went.

"Great! No problems, I'm sure by now he's fitting right in. I'm sure gonna get my exercise with a forty-five minute walk twice each day!"

"Remember not to overdo it– stop to rest when you need to and drink plenty of water!"

"Yes, Nurse Nana," he smiled wryly.

"I'm not worried about Jack. Miss Cass has both our cell numbers and emails, and she promised to let us know if there were any problems, so I'm sure he'll be fine. I'm just worried about you and your health. You don't have any concerns about Jack, do you?" she asked, wanting to be assured.

"Not really. Just one little thing... we saw a dead blue jay and he wanted to take its picture so he could have it tonight. I assume it's so he can sketch it. Not sure why he'd want to draw something that's dead, though."

"Hmmm..." she wondered.

Blue Jays and Groundhogs

That afternoon when school was out, Jack ran up and hugged his grandfather before he embraced Mikey.

"You were right, Pops! Everything went well and I have some new friends already. It was a good day!"

Thank you, Jesus! Fred said silently.

"All right, Pardner, let's get some gone."

Jack happily played with Mikey on the way home and talked a lot about his day, but never mentioned the blue jay.

Susie had fresh-baked oatmeal raisin cookies for them when they arrived, and she too was grateful for Jack's good first day. Finding out that he had no homework, she said, "Feel free to play outside with Mikey, or do whatever you'd like, Jack. You have about an hour before dinner."

Jack asked his grandfather if he could print out a picture of the dead blue jay, which he did without question. The boy grabbed it and thanked him, took Mikey out to the edge of the back yard, and sat down to draw with his sketchbook and pencils.

His grandparents were curious, but didn't talk about it. Susie started dinner and Fred worked on some things in his office.

After eating, Fred suggested they take the Really Is to get some frozen yogurt before they watched the Royals game that night.

On the way, Jack and Mikey enjoyed the wind from their backseat perch and Susie did her best to keep it from blowing her hair.

As they slowed down and then came to a stop sign, Fred hoped that Jack wouldn't notice the roadkill groundhog on the edge of the pavement. But he did.

"Pops!"

"Yeah, Jack?"

"Could you, uh, pull over and take a picture of that animal for me?"

As he pulled the convertible to the curb and put on his hazard lights, Jack asked, "What is it, Pops?"

"It's a groundhog. They come up from the woods sometimes and get in to town a ways, but they're not used to navigating cars and trucks. Someone probably didn't see it and hit it without even knowing that they did."

Flies covered its mangled head, congregating on caked blood and still open, but bugged-out, eyes. There was a gash on its stomach and some entrails had spilled out. It was truly grotesque. Susie looked away.

Mikey was still in the car, but desperately wanted to come and get at the carcass.

Fred took a couple of close up pictures, showed them to Jack, and after his agreement that they passed muster, they got back in the Really Is and continued on.

"What do you want the pictures for, honey?" Susie asked.

"Sketches."

"Anything special?"

"No…"

She dropped the subject for the time being.

They got their treats at the yogurt store and enjoyed them while driving on a historic river road by the Kansas river.

After they got home, Jack reminded Fred of the ground hog picture and asked him to print it out, which he did.

After a while, it was time for the Royals game. Fred and Susie both had their laptops with them and caught up on email and social media as they enjoyed the game and their time together.

Jack brought his sketchbook in and was absorbed with it, but occasionally commented on the game. Mikey was by his side.

After some time, he closed the book, leaned back, and seemed to be interested in how the Royals were doing, but he made it clear they weren't *his* team… the Astros were.

"Care to show us what you've been drawing?" Fred asked.

As Jack opened his sketchbook, Fred and Susie moved to the couch and made space for the boy to sit in between them so they could all three see the drawing.

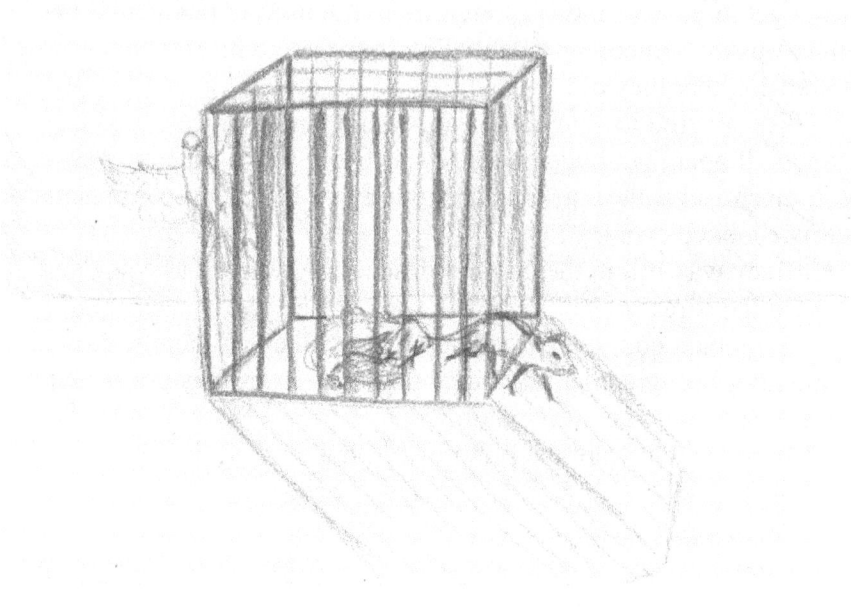

They saw what appeared to be a jail cell with bars all around and no door. On the floor inside were a dead bird and opossum. On the left of the cell was a ghostly figure of a bird flying away and on the other side was a ghostly opossum running the opposite direction.

They were all aware of the dead blue jay and groundhog.

"Tell us what you're thinking with that drawing, son," Fred asked gently.

"Well, they don't want to die. Death is like a prison where you can't play. You can't do anything. You can't be with your family and friends. You can't… live. And what they want to do is fly and run and play and be themselves, like you see the ghost figures doing, but it's just a dream. They can't… live."

Jack spoke softer than usual and the sadness in his tone of voice was palpable.

Pausing for a moment, Susie then said, "How do you know that's how they feel?

"Cause that's how I think my mom and dad feel. They want to be alive. They want to be with me. But they can't. I feel like that sometimes too. Even though I'm here and alive, sometimes I feel like I'm watching myself from behind bars. I want to be like I used to be… and I can sort of see that in my mind, but it's like it's out there somewhere and it's not really me."

Putting his arm around his grandson, Fred lovingly said, "Jack, I feel like that too sometimes. I see you and I think of my son, Freddie. I watched you play a ball game and I thought of how he and I used to do that. I dream sometimes that he and I are playing catch again… but I wake up and he's not there."

"So, what do you do, Pops?"

"Sometimes I just let myself have those feelings, because being able to feel means I'm alive. And I know that if I had never had good times with Freddie, then I wouldn't have anything to miss. There's an old saying by a guy named Tennyson: 'better to have loved and lost, than to never have loved at all.'

"Both loving and experiencing a loss are part of our whole experience of life. We don't like losses and we'd choose to never have any. But we'd never really live… never really know how good something is, if we never experienced the loss of something good.

"But there's way more to it than that… here's where I always remember to go with my mind Jack, and it always comforts me. We know the end of the story. We know what happens after life here on earth.

"As much as we like our life and love to run and play and be with friends and enjoy cool things, our life here is just a black and white picture of what real life is like with Jesus.

"It's hard for us to understand this, because we miss them and we know they must miss us, but I know that your mom and dad now see *what really is*. They now know, because Jesus has shown them that in the blink of an eye, you, and Nana, and me, and Mikey will be there with them where we'll be together forever!

"And you'll get to meet and enjoy my mom and dad, and Nana's mom and dad, and our grandparents. We'll have forever to meet and be with and enjoy all the people we ever want to meet.

"But more important than that, we will be in the very presence of Jesus. We'll see Him and look into His eyes. He'll hug us and laugh with us and joke with us and hang out with us. And we'll have new bodies that will never age, never get sick, never hurt. We'll never die again.

"There will be nothing bad there. Nothing bad will ever happen to anyone! No one will get mad, no one will hurt anyone else, no one will make fun of someone else. There's no sadness, no more tears. No more feelings of loneliness or sadness... ever!

"The food will be even better than Nana's cooking! We'll have really fun things to do! The music will be better than you've ever heard. And the artwork, some of your drawings will be there, and you'll continue to draw remarkable pictures that are more fantastic than you could ever imagine now!

"It's all good all the time because God is all good and He loves us and has taken care of everything for us.

"So, Jesus reminds me of that when I get sad and think of Freddie and Rachel. Then Jesus shows me that they're never sad, never lonely, never unhappy, never frustrated, never wishing they could be alive... because they're actually more alive now than they ever have been before!

"You know when you lived with your folks in Houston, Nana and I missed you and we wanted to be with you, but we always knew that we'd see you soon. Either you'd come and visit us or we would have a trip planned to go to Texas. So, we wouldn't dwell on missing you, we'd be excited about seeing you soon. We'd make plans of what we'd do and we'd tell each other how much fun it would be when we got to be with you.

"That's what your mom and dad are doing right now! Because they know how much Jesus loves them, how good God is, and that we'll soon be together, they are excitedly talking about that and thinking of the places they will show you and the people they will introduce you to and the good times that you'll have… forever!

He'd been talking fast and excitedly, and then paused, took a deep breath, and squeezed Jack's shoulder. "It's a little hard now, son. But your mom and dad are great and they are making plans for when we all get together!"

Jack said, "Do you really believe all that, Pops?"

"Oh, it's true, Pardner. It's really true. Jesus tells me that all the time and we can trust Him!"

The Second Day of School

Early the next morning, Fred was grateful that his grandson was still asleep when he left home. As he left, he prayed "Jesus, you know what this is and you know how to take care of it. I'll do whatever you want."

Good.

The receptionist was expecting Fred and took him to a patient room immediately. His charts were already in the plastic container by the doorway.

Within a minute Dr. Phil Goode, the Miller's family doctor for over three decades, appeared and was all business.

"Tell me what's going on Fred. Don't sugarcoat it, ok?"

Fred accurately told him about the chest pains and shortness of breath that had occurred five or six times since the tragedy.

After performing the usual listening, poking, and coughing tests, Dr. Goode asked a few more questions, then looked at Fred's charts.

"Well, you have a history of panic attacks… I thought I remembered that correctly. You don't appear to have anything physically wrong, but we need to do a full stress EKG to make sure. One of our Physician Assistants will take you back and monitor everything. We'll send a file electronically to the hospital and go from there. Relax, if you can, my friend."

All this time, Susie was having breakfast with Jack, simply telling him that Fred had an early appointment. And she was praying. She dropped Jack off at school, promising him that most days he and Mikey would get to walk with Pops. Then she went home to anxiously wait.

By mid-morning, an exhausted Fred had been taken back to the patient room and given a bottle of water. He was in good shape, so he thought, but the stress test took a lot out of him.

After a few minutes, Dr. Goode reappeared. "Good news and bad news, Fred. Which to you want first?"

"Give me the bad."

"You're not going to live forever."

"How long am I going to live?" he smiled.

"Unless you do something foolish, probably a long time, my friend. Your heart is fine. Consistent with your past history, I think the chest pains are from built-up stress and anxiety."

"So, what should I do, Doctor?"

"Listen carefully, Fred. Ok?"

"Sure."

"Trust God. Have you tried that?"

"Dang! You know it's easier to teach this stuff than to do it sometimes!" He smiled.

"I do know that. Seriously, though… you and your wife have been through a tremendously devastating experience. Don't try to be Super Godman and think it won't affect you like everyone else. Don't overdo it, and especially avoid the heat. Stay hydrated. Do some breathing things to relax. Find someone besides Susie to talk to about all this. My guess is that you want to appear strong to everyone and have kept all this in."

"Busted."

"Ok, I'm giving you a 'script for some anti-anxiety pills– they will help. But please consider the things I've just said."

"Thanks, Phil. Thanks for working me in so quickly."

After picking up his medicine, Fred felt much lighter as he drove home. As he went in the kitchen and hugged his anxious wife, both were relieved when Fred relayed his diagnosis to her.

In unison they said, "Thank you, Jesus!"

So, What Do You Teach?

Jack and Mikey soon became acclimated to their home and surroundings. His grandparents showered Jack with love and grace, and did everything they could to assure him that they would be ok as they moved ahead in this new era of their lives.

After a 20-year career as an Army Bandmaster, the two semi-retired for the first time at the ripe old age of 42 and moved with their young son back to Fred's home town of Lawrence. Susie continued her career as a nurse, and Fred taught music lessons, guest conducted bands, performed clinics, judged music contests, and played trumpet with some local groups.

But their real passion was the church. Along with some friends, they soon started a small church in their home which rapidly outgrew the space, triggering a series of several moves around the city. Fred continued with music endeavors and they raised their son enjoying a nice life with a variety of friends and interests.

In the last few years, just as Susie was ready to retire, many people in the church grew older, moved away, and/or left the church for different reasons, and the church could no longer afford a commercial meeting space. Fred and Susie adapted and the smaller version of the church group continued to meet on Sunday evenings at the Miller's home. They even had a wood-carved sign hanging over their front door that said: The Grace Gathering.

Relieved of having to manage a church building, staff, committees, and most meetings, they had been enjoying having the freedom to do whatever they wanted whenever they wanted, as many of their friends were doing. However, now they had new responsibilities that would limit their leisure freedom.

In no way were they bitter or resentful of this unexpected change. Jack was family, he needed them, and they thanked God every day for the wonderful opportunity given them to love and raise their grandson just as they had their only son.

They would soon start to understand and empathize with some of their friends who had adult children and grandchildren living with them, which they found was a pretty common occurrence due to a variety of reasons.

Jack was enjoying school and the twice weekly ball games. At one of the games Jack noticed that his grandfather was sitting with Brandon's father, the man who'd been ejected from the park for harassing the umpire. He hoped the dad wouldn't repeat his tirades with the umps this night.

During the game, with a runner on first base and two outs, Jack hit a nice line drive to the gap in left-center field and slid into second base ahead of the outfield relay throw for an obvious double, scoring the tying run who crossed the plate seconds later. Except it wasn't a double and the run didn't count!

"Yer out!" said the ump.

Jack remembered the coach's admonishment before each game, "Under no circumstances are you players to argue with the umps. If I think a call is wrong, I'll talk to the ump. That's my job, ok?" And per the coach's instruction, each player had to individually say, "Ok, Coach Goldman."

He knew he was safe and wanted to stay on base, but did the right thing by not saying anything. He expected his coach to go out and argue with the ump, but surprisingly, he didn't.

They played the next three innings with neither team scoring and lost by a run.

On the way to meet the rest of the team at Dairy Queen, Jack asked his grandfather, "Did you see the play where I was called out at second base, Pops?"

"Sure did. You were safe by a mile."

"Why didn't Coach Goldman go and talk to the ump? He told us not to argue, but he said if he saw a bad call, he would talk to the ump... but he didn't!"

"Son, Coach Goldman called me this afternoon. He works with that umpire at the car dealership. He told me that because sales were way down, the owner called a meeting at the end of work today and said they were gonna have to let several people go. That umpire was one of the mechanics there and has a wife and three kids... one is a newborn baby. He lost his job just hours before the game.

"Coach knew the ump missed the play. And he knew that the ump's mind was on how he was gonna provide for his family. He had to come straight to the ball park for the game before ours and he hasn't even been home to tell his wife yet.

"Coach decided that in the big picture of things, *seeing what really is*, that call at second base or even who won the game, wasn't the most important thing."

"So that ump lost his job… and he's home telling his wife right now?"

"I imagine so."

They arrived at the Dairy Queen and Jack didn't really feel like going in, but other teammates were arriving, so he did. The boys sat at a couple of adjoining tables and parents and grandparents were scattered throughout the place.

After a while, Jack noticed Pops and Nana sitting at a table with Brandon's mom and dad. He wondered what was going on.

After they got home, he said, "Pops, I thought you didn't know Brandon's dad?"

"I didn't, until tonight. I just happened to sit by him at the game," he smiled.

"What'd you talk about?"

"Well, after I introduced myself, I told him what a shame it was about the umpire losing his job, and how badly I felt for him and his family, especially with him not being able to tell his wife yet. He seemed to take that pretty hard. I was kinda surprised."

"Did you talk about other things?"

"Oh, sure. I told him I was your grandfather. We talked about baseball, kids, the Royals– stuff guys talk about."

"Did you talk about the umps?"

Jack smiled "Only once. After your play at second, when I didn't say anything, he just looked at me and said, 'Did you see that?' and I said I did. I said, 'That poor guy has so much on his mind, he must have not even seen the play. But you know what, it's no big deal to me.'"

"Wow. What about sitting with him and his wife at Dairy Queen? What did you talk about there?"

Susie spoke up for the first time. "Brandon's dad, Mr. Lundquist, saw us come in and waved at us to join them. After we sat down, he said, 'I don't know anything about you. I don't even know your name or what you do.'

"Then Pops, as he likes to do, told him his name and introduced me. We met his wife. She's Linda and he's Kent, and then Pops said, 'I'm a teacher.'"

"Huh?" Jack said.

Susie continued, "Then, as happens almost every time, Kent said, 'Oh, at KU? What do you teach?' And your grandfather said..." She motioned for Fred to continue.

"I told him that I'm not part of the faculty at KU. I freelance and I teach people how much God loves them," he smiled.

"It was classic, Jack!" Susie smiled. "Kent said the same thing a lot of people do. He said, 'After all I've done, I don't think that even my mother loves me sometimes.'

"He went on to tell us how he lost his job earlier this summer, then how he'd started drinking too much and getting angry, and how he doesn't know what he's going to do because he doesn't have the money for his house payment and he's afraid they will lose their house... and he said he really needs help."

"Pops! We prayed that he would realize he needed help!" Jack exclaimed. "And we prayed that Jesus would put him with someone who could help him!"

Susie and Fred both beamed. "That's the way Jesus works, Jack. Sometimes He wants us to help people. Other times He asks someone else. Our part is just to be available."

"Wow... so what happens next?" Jack wanted to know.

"We're having breakfast tomorrow. We'll see what Jesus does," Fred responded.

"Oh, Jack..." Susie cautioned. "We need to tell you what we told your dad when he was growing up. Because Pops is a pastor, we're involved in a lot of people's private lives. Sometimes we thought it was right for us to tell your dad some things, but most of the time we didn't.

"When we did tell him, though, we made sure he knew it was confidential and that he wasn't to share things with his friends.

"It's ok for you to know that Brandon's dad lost his job and they are struggling financially. They have told people that publicly. But it's not appropriate for you to talk about that to anyone else.

"Pops will probably learn a lot more about their lives as he tries to help them, but for the most part, he won't tell us. Do you understand?"

"Yes." Jack thought for a moment, and then said, "I hope I can remember not to say anything!"

Jack seemed satisfied to leave it with that and he went off to play with Mikey.

Answered Prayers

That weekend the Millers were shopping at the local grocery store, but Jack stayed in the convertible with Mikey. Soon a pick-up truck drove up to them and right away Jack noticed Kent Lundquist and his son Brandon from the baseball team. Brandon came over to talk and pet Mikey while Kent went in to get their groceries. Just as he was going in, Fred came out.

"Hey Fred, so glad to see you. I called your friend at the paper company, and just like you said, they're getting ready to open a new department. They're gonna hire two guys, and I think have a great shot at being one of them. Thanks again!"

"Great, Kent! Keep me posted!" Fred didn't let on that he'd been called by his friend at the paper company to get an off-the-record reference. Fred had developed a reputation for shooting straight while at the same time looking for the best qualities in people.

They each loaded their groceries while the boys visited some more, then Kent asked, "We still on for lunch Tuesday, Buddy?"

"Looking forward to it, Kent. See you at Fuzzy's Taco Place."

As they drove away, Jack asked, "Are you friends with Mr. Lundquist now, Pops? Remember how angry he was when he got kicked out of the ball game?"

"We are becoming friends, Jack. He's really excited to find out that God's not angry at him and that Jesus loves him and has already taken care of his relationship with God. I think he and his wife might come to our Sunday night group when we start up again in a few weeks. Brandon will probably come with them and you boys can hang out, if that's ok."

"Sure! Brandon's cool!"

Trumpet Lessons and Respect

When Sunday afternoon came, it was time for Jack's first trumpet lesson. Band was to start the next day. He'd had a meeting with the director, and after he explained the different instruments, Jack chose trumpet… the instrument his dad and grandfather both played. Delighted at his choice because that was what he played and because he didn't have to buy a different instrument, Fred offered to help him get started on his old trumpet.

They agreed on a formal lesson each week and Jack committed to practice 15 minutes a day.

This provided a great teaching moment to start learning about finances and respect. Fred wanted Jack to realize the value and importance of the private lessons, so he told his grandson that each lesson would cost him $10, which would come from his allowance. He was to put his trumpet and music in the case, go out the back door, come around to the front and ring the doorbell, call his teacher "Mr. Miller" during the lessons, pay him when they finished, and reverse the process leaving by the front door.

Susie joined the process in being the one to remind Jack to practice and in making sure he remembered when the lesson was and to be ready to go a little early. "One of the best lessons that your dad ever learned, Jack, was to always be prepared, show up a little early, be polite, and work hard."

"Did he take trumpet lessons from Pops, too, and did he have to come in the front door and call him Mr. Miller?"

"He did for a while, and then he started taking lessons from the KU trumpet teacher."

"I thought Pops was a good trumpet player…"

"He was, but not all good players are good teachers. Some just don't have the patience," she grinned.

"Oh…" Jack was concerned.

"Uh, I mean, I'm sure he will have patience with you, uh… sure he will!"

Wednesday afternoons, soon after getting home from school, Jack would warm up, pack up his horn and music, put a $10 bill in an envelope and write "Mr. Miller" on it, go out their back door, come around and ring the front door bell to greet Mr. Miller.

As it turned out, he was a natural, was eager to learn, and

enjoyed practicing. Fortunately for Fred, patience wasn't an issue!

The '10-10-10-70 Plan'

Although Jack enjoyed learning how to play the trumpet, he had trouble understanding why he had to pay for the lesson to his own grandfather with money his grandmother gave him.

So, one day he said, "Nana, I don't think it's really fair for me to have to take your money to pay Pops for trumpet lessons, doesn't he have enough money already?"

That provided an opportunity for another teachable moment.

"Yes, Pops has enough money. That's not the point. This is actually a really good time to start you on your allowance and the 10–10–10–70 plan."

"The what?"

"Let me explain. We're going to start giving you an allowance. You don't have to work *for* it, but you will soon start to have some chores to do to help out around here.

"Your mom and dad left us money for your allowance. Your trumpet lessons, meals at school, clothes, shoes, school supplies, and fees for the baseball team and things like that don't come from your allowance. Your mom and dad provided for all those things. The allowance is for other things. It's also going to be flexible, to a degree, depending on what your needs are.

"We'll give you money for trumpet lessons at the beginning of each month, then you manage it… which means you put it in an envelope and don't use it except for trumpet lessons.

"In addition, you will get $100 a month allowance."

"$100… really?"

"Yes. What I'd like you to get in the habit of doing is saying thank you to me each time I give you your allowance. Then I'd like you to thank God, because He's ultimately the one who's providing it. It's a grace gift. 2 Corinthians 9:15 says, 'Gratitude is the language of grace.'"

"Is that it?"

"No, there are financial principals that you'll get to start learning. Here are four plastic cups… red, yellow, green, and blue. When we give you your allowance in cash the first of each month, you'll put 10% of it, which is $10, in each of red, green, and blue cups. 10%, 10%, and 10%, that's $30 dollars total. How much does that leave?"

"$70."

"Exactly! I've taped a word on each of the cups. The red one is savings. Each month you'll be saving $10.00. Occasionally, we'll put that in the bank and it will be there for you when you want to do something special, like take a trip with the baseball team or the band or something like that.

"The blue one is giving. That money is for you to give to church or a charity or to someone who needs it. You only give this when there's someone or some organization that you *want* to give to. You don't have to give it to someone every month, but it stays in there until you give it to someone or some group. I want to make very clear that you are not giving this money to gain brownie points with God or to get Him to bless you. We give because we want to. We're made in God's image and He's a giver!

"Please don't feel like you're 'paying your tithe to God' as some mis-informed people believe. I'm just helping you develop a good habit to get started. You're always free to give more than 10%. Of course, when you're 18 and you leave home for college or the military or whatever, you don't have to give anything. It should always be because you want to.

"The yellow one is for business."

"What's that, Nana?"

"Well, you're getting to be old enough that you can start to do some things to make extra money for yourself. We don't know exactly what that will be, but let's say next summer you decide you want to mow lawns to make some money. There are probably some people in our neighborhood who would give you a chance to mow their yards, maybe for $20 a week, depending on the size of the lawn. If you did four a week… you'd make?"

"Eighty bucks!"

"And with four weeks in a month, you'd make?"

"Three hundred and twenty bucks!"

"Sound good?"

"Well, yeah!"

"Ok, what would you need to mow lawns?"

"Uh… I know, a lawnmower!"

"Do you have one?"

"No…"

"A good used one would probably cost $100. Do you have $100?"

"I don't think so."

"Well, after you save $10 a month in your business cup, when mowing season starts next spring, you'll have at least enough for a good down payment on a mower and some gas.

"Wow… so then I won't need to put any more money in that cup?"

"No, you'll keep on doing that because your lawnmower will need gas. You might have to buy a part to fix it. You'll need to pay for some flyers to be made to take around to the neighborhood advertising that you mow lawns. This money will make sure you can do things like that. And one day you'll need a bigger, better mower, which will cost money.

"That leaves the green cup. You'll have $70– 70% of $100– to put in it every month."

"What does that go for?"

"Anything you want! If you want to go to a movie with your buddies, you can pay for it with that money. If you want a special cap or something other than the clothes we buy you, you can use it for that. If you want to buy baseball cards or a new sketchbook and pencils, or candy… or buy a girl a coke…"

"Nana!"

"Just sayin'!"

After thinking for a moment, he said, "Nana… what I get to spend is really $70 a month, right?"

"Yes."

"Then why don't you just take the rest of the money and do all that stuff with the cups and all that instead of me doing it?"

"Why do you think?"

"Uh… cause you already know how to do it and I need to learn?"

"That's certainly part of it, Jack. But it goes deeper than that.

Jesus, who lives in you, absolutely refuses to be God apart from you."

"Uh, what in the world does that mean, Nana?"

"Well, when you look at Jesus' life, He could have done all His miracles by Himself. He could have turned water into wine, raised the dead, fed 5,000 people with a sack lunch, provided huge, miraculous catches of fish... all by Himself. But He didn't do that!

"Instead, He always involved people. For example, instead of just having 5,000 individual box lunches drop on everyone's lap that day, He asked a boy, probably a guy about your age, to give Him his lunch. Then Jesus took it and started giving food to the disciples to pass out to everyone, and it just kept multiplying and multiplying and multiplying! My point is that He involved people in what He was doing.

"Similarly, He could just drop money in our bank account, but He likes to do life with us. He provides and then He teaches. The concept I'm giving you comes from scripture but there's no rule that we have to do these concepts or have to do exactly the same percentage or anything like that.

"But we do know from our experience that learning some type of finance and work principals and then practicing them will put us in a better position to flourish in this life. It's not a guarantee, but it's an opportunity for us to let Christ in us show us how He wants to do life with us!

"So, how do I decide how to use the money in the cups?" he asked.

"As opportunities come up to give some money to a worthy cause or person with needs, or to start a little lawn mowing business or whatever, you can then talk to Jesus and let Him show you what is the best thing to do with your money. You do it with Him!"

Susie smiled as she continued, "Now, for the $70 that you have left after the cups and all that, you don't have to spend it all every month, but if you want to, you can. You need to plan ahead, though, because you might spend it all in three weeks and then get invited to go to a movie or ball game or something with your friends and not have any money left."

"Then what would I do?"

"You can borrow money from one of your other cups, but you have to put an IOU in when you take the money out, and you have to pay yourself interest… 10%. That means if you borrow $10 from your business investment cup to go to a movie, you put an IOU note in that cup saying that you owe $11. Then when you get your next allowance the first thing you do is take $11 from your green cup money and pay back the loan. Then you can tear up the note."

"Nana…"

"Yes, Jack."

"I don't know if I got all that straight…"

"I'll help you Jack. I'll give you your allowance the first day of every month and I'll help you remember how it works."

"Nana, what can I do with the money I make from mowing lawns next year?"

"You can use these same four cups with that, so 10% to savings, 10% to giving, 10% to business, and 70% to anything you want!"

"Did you do this with my dad?"

"Something pretty similar. I think it helped him a lot!"

"Nana…"

"Yes, Jack."

"Thank you."

They shared a nice hug, and then he went out to play.

Part 3
Close Up Horror

Jack was excited about band starting at school on this Monday, but before the day was over, his excitement turned to horror accompanied with stark fear.

Just before it was time for Fred to start his afternoon walk to pick up Jack from school, he was interrupted with a phone call on their land line. It was with a "long-talker," as Fred and Susie called certain irritating people. Long-talkers often repeated phrases, explained the background leading to every decision they made, but never said much of substance.

He was becoming more and more anxious, realizing that he was going to be late and Jack would wonder where he was and what he should do.

Eventually he was able to end the call and set out on his walk. His mind wanted to hurry, but his legs wouldn't comply, so he did the best he could. He was almost to the school when he heard sirens coming from some kind of first-response vehicle.

Cresting the hill where he could see Windsor Elementary school, he saw a police car, fire truck, and ambulance parked at the front entrance and several people crowded around. Fearing the worst, he picked up his pace and hurried to the edge of the crowd.

The familiar face of a parent who regularly walked her daughter home from school greeted him with, "It was awful! Just awful! I sure hope the kids will be alright!"

A man standing next to him said "I hope the poor man will be alright, but either way, there will be hell to pay for William Kelly. Coming here against a restraining order, hitting a defenseless man with a ball bat, and screaming, 'I'm gonna kill you!' Yes sir, there will be hell to pay for him. I'll be glad to testify against him… saw the whole thing."

The sound of a stern voice coming over a loudspeaker got everyone's attention.

"Moms, dads, students… any of you who witnessed the, uh,

unfortunate event, please come to the front doors. Detective Hicks would like to interview you. Parents who witnessed the event can bring their children to the gym door where they will be with their teachers, and you may then proceed to the front door to talk with Detective Hicks. The police have asked that everyone else leave the area as soon as possible."

Ignoring the command, most of the crowd stayed while some parents made their way to the gym.

Moving closer, Fred could see the paramedics attending to someone on a gurney in the ambulance, and closer to the front door were three police officers trying to restrain a very belligerent man in handcuffs.

Then he saw Jack.

Just a few feet from the gurney, the little boy stood still with an expression of sheer horror on his face.

Teachers and administrators were herding students off in all different directions. No one had taken charge and the scene was chaotic.

Rushing over to Jack while trying to restrain Mikey, Fred was exhausted by the time he got to his quivering grandson. He wrapped his free arm around the boy, drew him close to him, and hugged him for all he was worth.

"I'm here, Jack. I'm here. We'll be okay. Jesus is with us." Jack wrapped both his arms around his Pops, and hugged him tight as he started shaking and sobbing.

Fred was struggling with the dog, surrounded by chaos, and wanted to help his grandson more than anything.

He managed to sit on the ground, still hugging Jack and holding on to Mikey but was only there for a second when a police officer came over and said, "I'm so sorry to bother you, but I understand this boy was a witness to the event, and I have to take down his testimony as to what he saw.

Fred's mind was swirling. He summoned every ounce of energy to compose himself and started to pray silently when Mikey lurched, pulled his leash free from Fred, and took off across the school yard.

"No, Mikey!" Jack yelled, broke free from his grandfather, and took off running after his beloved companion.

Fred started off after him as the officer said, "You'll have to get control of him and bring him right back, sir."

Scowling at the policeman, Fred restrained himself from saying something he would later regret, and pursued Jack and Mikey amidst the chaos of wailing students, police sirens, teachers, parents, and administrators all trying to do something... but with no direction.

Moments later he spotted the boy and dog a football field's length away at the edge of a densely wooded area that was off limits to people because coyotes were known to live there. Mikey was after something and Jack was running after him, crying and calling for him to come back.

As Fred ran after them, he started to feel pains in his 70-year-old chest and his legs started cramping. "Not now. Jesus... please... help me."

Jack and Mikey disappeared into the woods and Fred, chest heaving and out of breath, eventually got there and went in after them, shouting, "Jack! Jack! Where are you? Jack!"

The woods and underbrush were very thick and contained lots of thorn trees and sticker bushes. Fred feared the worst.

Continuing to yell for his grandson, he pursued the easiest route through the brush, knowing he might be going in the wrong direction.

Eventually he collapsed in exhaustion on the ground, too weak to shout anymore. In addition to the physical challenge, Fred sensed the "Hellish Darkness' enveloping him again.

Just then, a couple of men appeared who had witnessed his plight and came to try to help. One stayed with him and the other went in search of Jack.

Feeling light headed, fear stricken and still having chest pains, Fred managed to ask the man to call for medical help but also to be sure Jack was safe.

His helper immediately dialed 911 then called another parent whom he knew was also on the scene. Quickly, a relief group formed and began to scour the woods.

Moments later a couple of dads found Jack sitting on the ground. He was leaning up against a tree, with Mikey guarding him and licking his motionless face. The "Hellish Darkness' was at work.

In addition to the ambulance already at the school, two more quickly appeared with one set of attendants helping Jack, and the other working with Fred.

Before he fainted, Fred gave someone Susie's name and phone number and pleaded with them to be sure Mikey was okay.

Prying the dog away from Jack only added to his traumatic episode and both ambulances left in tandem- one with a non-responsive 70-year-old, the other with a traumatized 10-year-old.

Mikey barked at Jack's ambulance and nearly yanked his restrainers arm out of his socket trying to chase after his boy.

Within minutes, Susie arrived on the scene, trying to make sense of the barrage of stories coming to her from a number of different people including a hysteric Mom's wailing, "How will the kids ever recover? Lord help us!"

Struggling to get the basics, she was greatly comforted when Jack's teacher, Miss Cass, arrived and hugged her.

"Mrs. Miller, Jack and your husband each left in ambulances. I'd like to take you to the hospital so you can be with them. One of the parents has Jack's dog and he'll make sure he's safe. Won't you come with me?"

Shocked with the suddenness and gravity of the situation, Susie replied, "Yes, thank you. Let's go."

The trip to the hospital took about 15 minutes, and on the way Miss Cass related the story to Susie as best she could piece it together.

The parents of one of the students were separated and there was a restraining order against the Dad. He was to have no contact with his son or wife.

"The mom had a live-in boyfriend who had come to pick the boy up from school. The Dad decided to do the same. He'd apparently been drinking and had a baseball bat. He snuck up on the boyfriend and hit him in the head from behind. When he collapsed to the ground, the dad continued to beat him with the bat. There was screaming and blood everywhere…"

"Mrs. Miller, it appears that Jack was waiting for your husband to come and pick him up, and he saw all this happen. I'm not sure what all happened after that, but more ambulances were called and they left with Jack and his grandfather right before you got there."

"Oh, dear Jesus…" Susie prayed. They rode in silence the rest of the way to the hospital.

Upon arrival, Miss Cass took Susie to the emergency room desk and explained who they were. Fred and Jack were in different rooms and Jack's teacher suggested that she go to Jack and Susie go to her husband.

Jack was relieved to see his loving and compassionate teacher, but was distraught about the assault he'd witnessed, and at the same time, extremely worried about his grandfather and his dog.

Miss Cass assured him that someone was taking care of Mikey, but Jack picked up on her lack of confidence that his grandfather was going to be all right.

"Where is Pops?" he asked.

"He's in another room here in the hospital, Jack. Your grandmother is with him and I know he's getting the very best care possible."

"Is he close to here?"

"I'm sure he is. This is the emergency room and he can't be very far away."

Before his teacher or the nurse could react, Jack jumped up and ran out of the room calling, "Pops! Pops! Pops!"

Susie, who was just a few rooms away, heard the familiar voice and stepped out to the hallway.

"Jack! Over here!"

The boy ran to his grandmother and she kneeled down, wrapped her arms around him, and said, "I'm so glad you're all right, Jack. I'm here now, we'll be ok."

He was relieved, but then looked up to see his beloved grandfather on a bed with tubes and monitors attached to him, his eyes closed and motionless.

"What's happening? What's going on?" the boy asked.

"Pops is resting. He either passed out from exhaustion or had a heart attack. We're hoping for the best. We just have to wait now."

Jack went to his grandfather and took his hand in both of his. "You have to be all right, Pops. I can't lose you too." He put his head on his grandfather's arm and sobbed.

Just then, Miss Cass and the nurse came in the room. The nurse said, "The boy can't stay here. He has to come back to his room."

Susie stood between them and said, "Over my dead body. Jack stays here with us. Understand?"

Retreating, the nurse said, "I'll need to get the doctor."

Quickly, the nurse reappeared with the E.R. doctor.

"Hi, Susie. You here to see someone in the church?"

"Oh, I'm so glad you're on duty, Dr. Hull! We've had quite an afternoon. Our grandson witnessed a brutal attack after school, Fred was late to get him, the dog ran away, and when Fred chased him, he collapsed. As you can see, they have him all hooked up to things."

"Actually, he was my next patient to see, but I didn't realize it was Pastor Fred. Is this your grandson... Freddie's boy?"

"Yes, he lives with us now."

"I'm aware of that... and I'm so sorry..."

Getting back to the business at hand, the physician said, Nurse, can you give the chart?"

"Shouldn't I take the boy back to his room, Doctor?"

"You can give me the chart and I'll take responsibility for Jack, Nurse Phillips." The tone of his voice wasn't mean, but there was no question about who was in charge. Susie, Jack, and Miss Cass were all relieved.

Taking a minute to look at the chart, Dr. Hull then checked the monitors and said, "We'll need to do some tests to see if he might have had a heart attack. From what you told me, it could just be a stress, dehydration, heat and exhaustion combination. They started a fluid iv, so that will help with the dehydration. I'll order the tests right away. You can all stay here while I do that. Nurse, I'll need your help with this." He motioned for her to follow him.

"But what about the boy?" she questioned again. He ignored her.

Soon, she brought back a couple of extra chairs and expressed her apology to Susie. "I'm very sorry, Mrs. Miller. I was just following protocol, doing my job."

"No apology necessary. I was a nurse for many years. I understand. It's an unfortunate situation all the way round. I hope

I didn't get you in any trouble…"

"No, we're fine."

"What's everyone doing here? Where are we?"

Everyone turned to see Fred raised up and wide awake in his bed. He had a little trouble gaining his bearings, then looking at his wife he said, "What happened?"

Hugging him and ecstatic that he was awake, she said, "Honey, we're in the E.R. What do you remember?"

"Uh… Oh, I was in the woods chasing Jack…then everything went dark." Looking at the boy, he said, "Oh, you're ok! I was so worried. Jack, if I'd just have been on time to get you… you wouldn't have experienced any of this. I'm so sorry…"

"It's ok, Pops." He half crawled on the bed and hugged his grandfather. "I was worried about you Pops! I was so afraid of losing you…"

They all laughed, cried, hugged, and shared their mutual relief.

Fred continued to lament his remorse over being late… then Susie interrupted him, "Pastor Miller, I'm going to preach one of your sermons to you… but I won't take 45 minutes like you sometimes do. This wasn't your fault. There's no way you could have known. The dark, evil voice you're hearing is not your own and it's certainly not Jesus. You don't have to listen to that voice. Listen to Jesus… what's He saying?"

They were all quiet for a moment.

"He's saying you're right, honey."

"Ok, then. No more blaming yourself. Jesus said so." She smiled.

There was a pause, then Jack said, "Mikey?"

Miss Cass quickly assured him, "Jeremy Palance's dad has him. He's taking great care of him. They live on a farm and have lots of animals. I know Mikey's fine and you can get him whenever you go home."

They were all relieved. Then Dr. Hull reappeared.

"Oh, hey, Pastor Fred! You gave us all quite a scare!"

"Sorry, Danny. I'm glad I'm in your good hands! What's the scoop?"

"Well, you certainly appear to be fine. We're hydrating you and going to do some tests, which will be much easier to do since you're awake and alert. We want to see if you may have had a heart attack or if it was a heat-stress-exhaustion situation. Either way, we're going to get you back on your feet and back home as soon as is best for you."

"You're in charge, Danny. Whatever you say."

"I've ordered the tests and the attendants are actually here to take you to another room. We'll bring you back here in an hour or two."

Two young men made sure that Fred was unhooked from the monitors and everything except the saline drip that was hydrating him.

After their goodbyes, Dr. Danny Hull said, "Let's visit a bit, shall we?"

Closing the door to the room, he addressed Susie, Jack, and Miss Cass. "I think Pastor Fred will be fine, these are just precautionary tests, but he's presenting very well for a man his age. Has anything like this happened recently?"

"Actually, with all that's happened with us this summer, just a few of days ago he did have a couple of anxiety attacks. He saw Dr. Goode, they did a stress EKG, but everything was ok."

"I'm so glad to know that." Turning to an attendant, he ordered him to get those results from Dr. Goode's clinic. "That will give us a great recent base-line to compare with today's tests. Now, young man, you've had a pretty rough afternoon. Would you mind telling me about it?"

Feeling comfortable with those in the room, Jack was able to recap what he saw happen, starting with the brutal beating of Pat Kelly's mom's boyfriend.

Dr. Hull was very compassionate and asked some probing questions, especially about how Jack was feeling. He didn't think it necessary to tell them that the victim of the beating was down the hall having emergency surgery.

"Well, son, bad things happen in this world… I know, I see the results of many of them here in the E.R. Unfortunately, you saw a very bad thing happen right in front of you. You have absolutely wonderful grandparents who will help you through this.

"You may have some nightmares, so I'm going to prescribe something to help you sleep and something else for anxiety. Your pharmacist will explain the particulars to you, Susie. But you call me if you have any problems, okay?"

"I sure will, Doctor."

"Now, you can wait here or out in the waiting area, but I'll personally find you and let you know what's going on with Pastor. Any questions?"

There were none and the Dr. left the trio alone.

Miss Cass offered to find someone to bring Susie's car to the hospital, and after giving Jack a hug, she took Susie's keys, assuring her that she'd be back soon.

Jack and Nana got some refreshments in the waiting room and within half an hour Miss Cass returned with Susie's keys and information about where she'd parked the car. Receiving their heartfelt thanks, she left them, making sure they would call her if they needed help.

Presently they met a smiling Dr. Hull who confirmed the diagnoses of heat/stress/exhaustion, and after being released, the three made their way to Susie's car.

"What about Mikey?"

"Let's call Jeremy's dad."

After stopping at the pharmacy to pick up some prescriptions, they were able to go to the Palance's farm and pick up Mikey who was as glad to see them as Jack was to see him. Even Nana, who swore no more pets years ago, was relieved. She'd grown quite attached to the Lab as well.

Some friends who'd heard about the events graciously brought dinner for them. Afterwards they gathered in the living room, and Fred said, "Want to talk about today, son?"

"I'm so glad you're ok, Pops. I was really, really worried."

"Me too! But that's past us now and I'll need to take it easy for a few days."

"Maybe a few months would be more like it!"

"Yes, nurse Nana!" he grinned. "What I really want to know is about what happened at school."

"Pat Kelly's dad is not like us, Pops. He's mean. Real mean."

"Oh?"

"Pat told us the first day I was at school that during the summer his dad beat his mom up and when Pat tried to stop him, he got beat up. He told us the police came and took his dad away and that he's not to see him anymore…which he's glad about. But his mom has a boyfriend who came to live with them and Pat says he's pretty weird. Some of the other kids have said that they sell drugs.

"Our social worker lady comes and gets Pat from our class the next day and we didn't see him for a few days. He doesn't want to talk about it."

I bet he doesn't, Fred thought.

"Jack, whatever is going on, it's not good. But we can't help things by speculating about situations that we don't know about. The best thing to do is for us to pray for them, and to ask Jesus to show us whatever He wants us to do to help.

"And we always need to remember that everybody…" Jack joined him in union, "has a story."

"I don't think this story has a happy ending, Pops. When you were late to get me, I knew you'd come, so I was just hanging out with Pat… then his mom's boyfriend… who Pat's afraid of… showed up to get him.

"All of a sudden, Pat's dad came out of nowhere and hit him with a bat. We were shocked. Then his dad wouldn't stop… the look in his eyes was like a wild animal… I never saw anything like it.

"Everybody was screaming for him to stop… but he kept hitting him. Finally Coach Swartz tackled him from behind and somebody got the bat and coach held him down until the police came. Pat was crying and I guess I was in shock.

"The next thing I remember was seeing you… then Mikey ran away."

They were startled when Fred's cell phone rang. "Is Jack there?" A young voice said. "It's for you, Jack."

Looking at his grandparents for permission, Susie said, "Go ahead and take it. You can go in your room if you want."

In a few minutes he returned.

"Pops… Nana… that was my friend Eddie from school. His mom works at the police station. He told me how Pat Kelly's dad is in a lot of trouble now. He got arrested today for… let's see, I wrote it down… parole violation, assault and battery of a police officer, resisting arrest, violation of a restraining order, and premeditated attempted murder with a lethal weapon. I don't think that's good."

"Oh, honey, it's not good at all." Nana said gently. "That poor man will have to face the consequences of his actions... and so will his family. It must be awful for Pat and his mom."

"Eddie said that Pat is in protective custody. He said that when the police went to his Mom's house to tell her what happened, they caught her in the middle of selling drugs to people the cops had been looking for. So she's in jail, too, and Pat may be put in a foster home. I feel so bad for him."

"Let's stop right now and pray for them." They formed a circle, held hands, and Fred continued, "Lord Jesus, you know all about this situation. You know their stories... each one has a story. I know you're working in their lives to draw them to you because You're the only one who can give them what they're searching for. Thank you for protecting them all, especially Pat. Lord, show him that You're there with him and use us to help any way we can. In your name, Amen."

"Pops?"

"Yes, Jack?"

"Eddie said that there's a special place in hell for guys like Pat's dad. He said God will pay him back many times over for what he's done. He kept talking about payback. I don't think that's true, but I didn't know what to say to him, so I didn't say anything."

"You did well, son... very well. We're both so proud of you." His grandfather continued, "Let's talk about the 'hell-to-pay' thing so you'll know for sure, and maybe know what to say when the time is right. Okay?"

"Yeah."

"Here's how it works, Jack. Let's say one group of religious people believes that getting drunk, selling drugs, and beating other people up is awful. Well, that's true... those things are awful.

"They don't do those things... and that's good. But, they also think that someone like Pat's mom and dad are as far from God as you can get. They are certain that God feels that way too. They judge them and they act like God... judging for Him.

"They come up with Bible verses that they are certain prove that drunks, drug dealers, and wife beaters are going to hell and they think God delights in sending them there.

"They believe it's impossible for a person like that to be a Christian. They think those people are separated from God because of their lifestyle and that God will burn them in hell forever with a sadistic smile on His face. They think God can't stand to be around them and that they don't deserve for anything good to happen to them.

"They think God is justified in paying those people back for all eternity for the bad things they do here on earth. They call it 'payback.'

"It seems to me that, in their minds, they are certain that it's ok to hate different groups of people, keep a distance from them, not be around them, not let them live in their neighborhood, not be friends with them. They think it's fine to be angry with people just because they're sinners... because they believe God is angry with them.

"They come to the conclusion that there's nothing good about such people, that they're totally bad, and it's ok to be mean to them, tell them they're wrong, be hateful to them, not let them come to their church or club or be on their sports team. It's ok to exclude them and punish them... because they are certain that God feels the same way about them.

"They tend to have more than one group they treat that way... like gays, people of other religions, people from other countries... even other political parties. They seem to be certain that those people are bad, that there's nothing good about them. They think those people deserve punishment from God... and from themselves.

"When you become certain about something...all you see is black and white. You can't see any good in the other person.

"You're not willing to be open to the possibility that you could be wrong. You're not willing to see anyone else's point of view. You're absolutely certain that you are right. Now obviously what Pat Kelly's dad did was wrong. You can never justify that. But, you can seek to understand what's behind it. After all, everyone..."

"Has a story." all three said.

"Right. And God knows everything about our story. And God loves us. He's for us. He's not into payback at all... He's into putback."

"What's putback?"

"I'll be glad to answer that question, Jack... but I'm getting pretty tired. I think this day has taken a lot out of me. How 'bout we all head to bed and maybe we can talk about it tomorrow."

Fred and Susie quickly fell asleep. Jack, however, had a hard time getting the picture of the beating out of his mind. Eventually, Mikey curled up next to him on the bed, and he dozed off.

Payback or Putback

They just started breakfast the next morning when Jack said, "I still want to know about payback and putback."

"Well, Jack, God is continually working things out so everything will one day be restored, put back, to God's original intention. His desire is that we would all know that we're in His family and that we'd all know Him and how good He is. He wants us to know that He has forgiven all our sins and made us all right with Him and He loves us all exactly the same way. That's grace.

"Once we truly get that, then we'll start to see everyone else like He does. We'll forgive them and love them and accept them and give them grace and include them... with no payback. We'll participate in putting everything back the way God originally intended!

"Pops, I don't understand why it's like this. I mean, couldn't God just have created a world where there was no evil and nothing bad ever happened? He's God... couldn't He have done that?"

"Yes, He could have– listen, let's get you ready for school and we'll talk about it as we walk."

Soon they were in the woods and on their path. Pops continued, "Jack, God is all powerful. He could have created a world with no evil where nothing bad ever happened. I don't fully understand it, no one does... but I think it has to do with the fact that He wanted us to love Him because we want to... not because we have to. If you *have* to love someone, it's not really love. And when you give people choices, they can choose poorly. They can choose to hurt other people and themselves. Then evil things happen.

"But He's always there with us, always working everything together for the ultimate good. We just can't see most of that here on earth.

"So where did sin, where did evil come from? Did God create evil?" Jack asked.

"No, only good comes from God. There was no evil on the earth until after God created people. Evil comes from us. But we don't like to admit that.

"People have always blamed their evil on someone else... Eve blamed it on the devil and Adam blamed both God and Eve.

"The first result of evil... is even more evil... lying and blaming.

"Their first son murdered his brother. And, in effect, blamed God, then blamed his brother for God being pleased with his brother's offering and not with his.

"That pattern continued to Jesus' day– religious people call evil 'good'... and good 'evil.' For example, Jesus cast out evil demons from people and the Pharisees, the religious leaders, labeled what was obviously good... as evil!

"They said Jesus– God, who is all good– was casting out evil spirits by the power of the devil– by evil's power! Then Jesus gave them a little talking to.

"They didn't know Jesus was God, because their minds were darkened and they were so into rules– like no work being done on the Sabbath– even if that work was compassionate and helped people by casting out evil spirits on the Sabbath– they believed Jesus must be evil.

"They valued their interpretation of the rules way more than they valued people and relationships. Jesus, however, valued people and relationships and restoration way more than He valued rules!

"That pattern continues to this day. Many religious people value rules– their interpretation of rules– way more than they value people and relationships. I'm not accusing your friend, Eddie's family, and their church of knowingly doing that… most likely they are just continuing what they were taught and what their people before them were taught. Your father and I used to think like that… we know all about it!

"Unfortunately our experience has been that most every time you talk to a religious person about Jesus being love and God including everyone… they go, 'But, what about…' and then they talk about their interpretation of someone or some group of people… breaking the rules!

"I'm doing all the talking and giving you some pretty deep stuff. You want me to stop or are you interested in some more?"

"Keep going, Pops… I want to know."

"Back to the beginning," he continued, "throughout all that time, God continued to love Adam and Eve, Cain– and everyone else. Jesus loved the Pharisees– and everyone else… most just didn't know that… just like today.

"Also, especially in the Old Testament…in the Jewish Bible, it appeared that from time to time, God punished people because of their sin and rebellion. However, we've learned through Jesus's life and the teaching of the New Testament which was written to Christians, that it was not God punishing people.

"Sin itself punishes people– the wages of sin is death. Pat Kelly's mom and dad are being punished right now… and may be even more after they have their day in court. But it's not God punishing them… it's their own poor decisions that are punishing them.

"Evil itself, which is sin, punishes people. There were times in the Old Testament when people thought they were hearing from God, but instead they were hearing from Evil spirits.

"Any time you read that the Lord told them to murder men, women and children, for example, that wasn't God they were hearing. We know that because Jesus is the exact representation of God and Jesus never did anything like that.

"They had no concept of the evil one. They thought God was both good and evil. They thought God was paying them back…

but He wasn't. God always wants to put things back like they originally were!"

"Then it was the same thing in Jesus's day with the Pharisees– they thought they were hearing from God– but they were obviously hearing from evil spirits to accuse Jesus of being an evil spirit!

"A big problem is that Christians have said for 2,000 years that God's love is unconditional, that it never fails, and that we can never be separated from it. But at the same time, many Christians have also said that while God's love is unconditional… there are conditions to it! The Pharisees said that, all religions say that, and unfortunately many Christians believe that."

"That sounds like lying, Pops."

"Well, I don't think they're lying. I used to say the same thing, and believed I was telling the truth. Now I'm amazed that I never questioned how unconditional love could have conditions. Seems silly now."

"Yeah!"

"I would guess that at Eddie's church, they talk about God's love being unconditional. But then they start adding conditions like we used to. I think the reason we said that was because we have conditions to *our* love for *others*– and we have believed the lie from the evil one that God must have conditions too.

"People believe that other people must be punished for certain things. They think God is bound to punish them by some sort of Divine decree… pay them back.

"This is based on a lie. The worst lie– the worst representation of God– in my opinion, has to do with God… and evil. To really grasp the ramifications of this lie, we first have to see what the truth is.

"Are you okay with this, Jack? Want me to go on, or pick it up again another time?"

"Maybe later… I'm kind of overloaded right now."

"No problem."

Jack was glad to get to school, and Fred was equally glad to get home and take a nap. Instead of walking to pick his grandson up from school in the mid-day heat, he drove up in the convertible.

After having snacks, since there were no evening activities,

Fred asked Jack to help him wash their three cars. He put the top up on the Really Is, filled two buckets with soapy water, and instructed Jack to watch him... then do the same thing on his Mom's car, then Susie's.

As they were soaping down the vehicles, Jack spoke up. "Pops, I've been thinking about Pat Kelly's dad and the awful things he did yesterday. Everybody at school today said that Eddie's right... surely God has to make him pay for that evil, doesn't He?"

"I sure used to think that way, Jack. I think most humans do. So to learn the truth, we look at what Jesus Himself did.

"The truth is in seeing how Jesus, God himself, responded to the worst evil ever conceived. It was bad enough for religious leaders to accuse him of being the devil... but they did far, far worse.

"Let's start with John 3:16. When you look at the original Greek language, I think the best translation into our language is For God so loved the world (everyone forever in the entire cosmos) that He gave His only Son (Jesus), so that all believe in Him and not perish, but have eternal life.

"So God has always loved His people, everyone. We humans got so far off that we didn't realize that. We even thought that God was both good and evil. We were lost and perishing... and God Himself came to show us the truth of what He is like.

"Jesus showed us what God is like. Jesus loved people. Jesus himself said He didn't come to judge or condemn.

"Jesus had enemies– the religious people and the government. They hated Jesus.

"One time Jesus said some things about enemies in regard to evil. People call that teaching the sermon on the mountain. Nobody had ever said this before. He said, 'Love your enemies! Bless those who curse you. Do good to people who hate you.' Now get this Jack– He said to do that, because that's what God does!

Later, the Apostle Paul wrote that we should speak nicely about people even if they want to take advantage of us. He said not to retaliate, not to get even, when people do us wrong.

"He wrote, 'If your enemy is hungry, feed him; if he is thirsty, give him a drink; these acts of kindness will certainly rid your enemy of the dross in his mind and win him as a friend. For in so doing you will heap coals of fire on his head. Do not let evil be an excuse for you to feel defeated, rather seize the opportunity to turn the situation into a victory for good. Do not be overcome by evil, but overcome evil with good.' That's my paraphrase of Romans 12.

"Jack, those are just some of the things Jesus wants us to do when our enemies come against us.

"Never repay evil with evil. Jesus said His father doesn't do that... and Jesus sure didn't do that. The Apostle Paul wrote that we shouldn't either.

"He said, 'Never seek vengeance. Love people, don't hate them. Give them grace. All this is perfect love which is How the Father loves us!' He said, 'Don't do payback... do putback... put the relationship back to being good by doing good.'

"Now, knowing all that– what did we, humanity, do to Jesus? We mocked Him, spit on Him, hated Him, lied about Him, cursed Him, unfairly tried Him, unfairly judged Him, condemned Him, called Him a liar and a fake and a blasphemer, we beat Him, whipped Him, crucified Him and killed Him.

"That's pure evil. That's the most evil thing ever done in the history of the world.

"And all the time we were doing that, He did not retaliate... and He could have. So now, we look at what Jesus did, and do the same. Instead of retaliating, instead of vengeance, instead of payback and punishment, Jesus kept loving everyone. He forgave everyone. He included everyone. He actually let us do the worst we could to Him... kill Him. He submitted to our evil... He let us do it."

Since all three vehicles were covered with soapy water, the 70-year-old showed his grandson how to hose them off without leaving spots.

Continuing their discussion, he said, "I know this is hard to understand– I don't know how He did it, but Jesus actually took us, who weren't even born yet, and everyone with Him on the cross!

"We died with Him, and He went to the depths of our sin and

darkness with us, and forgave it all!

"Then, when the Father raised Him from the dead, He raised us too! Our old self died and God created an entirely new us... a new spirit that is totally right with Him, that's pure, holy, and without fault as far as God is concerned.

"That's what Jesus, God the Father, and the Holy Spirit do. Instead of payback, They put us back to a right standing with Them and forgive us!

"On Easter Sunday, when Jesus raised from the dead, He was happy. He was full of Joy. He did not go to the people who just three days before did the worst evil ever to Him and take out vengeance on them. He did not pay them back. Just the contrary– He saved them, included them, loved them, and took up residence in each of them!

"So today, God's unconditional love is still given by God to us– even when we are rotten to the core and even when we do the worst things imaginable to God Himself. He still loves us– with no conditions.

"That's the way God relates to Pat Kelly's dad... and to every one of us!

"Ok, one more cleaning lesson. Do you know what this is?" He said, holding up a chamois.

"Uh, an old brown rag?"

Laughing, he said, "That's right, but it's an expensive one, and it's actually made of leather... pig or goat skin. It's called a shammy but it's not spelled like it sounds."

"What do we do with it?"

"We dry the cars off like this." After showing him, he produced a second chamois and they both went back to their task.

"Now, Jack– here comes the biggest lie of all time. Are you ready?" Without waiting for an answer, he continued, "That's when religion lies and says, 'Yes, God loves unconditionally and yes, Jesus did all that at the cross without taking vengeance on us... but He's gonna come back one day and that day will be payback day. There will be hell to pay... God will send you to hell and punish you there forever!'

"Religion, like at Eddie's church, says, 'You got it all wrong before, but out of His goodness, God made it possible for you to get saved. You got a second chance, but now… if you have never heard of Jesus, or if you just haven't believed what we told you about Jesus… or if you just don't want to have anything to do with Jesus, then there will come a day when everything that Jesus taught is out the window. Forget about loving your enemies, forget about not taking vengeance, forget about not paying back evil with evil, forget about unconditional love… God has a breaking point and He just broke,'… they say.

"Religion says that the day a person dies here on earth, that day is payback day and Jesus goes back on everything He said. He actually does just the opposite of what He told you to do.

"Religion says that Jesus totally changes character and goes from unconditional love to horrible hate and wrath and vengeance, and human blood is going flow as high as a horse's head all over the earth when Jesus slashes everyone with His sword."

"Oh, that's awful, Pops. I can't imagine Jesus doing that!"

"Their lie gets even worse, Jack."

Before he could contemplate what could be worse, his Pops continued, "Religion says that Jesus is not gonna just kill you… He's gonna supernaturally keep you alive in a special torture chamber called hell, where you will burn forever and weep and wail and gnash your teeth.

"Religion says all that, right after they say that, 'God is good all the time and He loves you unconditionally.'

"Pops… that just doesn't make any sense. How could people believe that?"

"They believe it because that's what they have been taught at church and by parents and pastors who believe it because that's what they were taught.

"Religion teaches that. I used to believe and even teach that. But then God revealed His truth to me!

"For the record: Jesus is not like that. God is not like that. There will never be any punishment from God for people who refuse to believe in a god like that!

"So today, Jesus wants us to look at all this in light of evil… like the evil we saw come out of Pat Kelly's dad… and like the evil that is done to us when people hurt us, lie to us, lie about us, leave us, condemn us, accuse us, abandon us… what do we do?

"In all situations when we witness evil, when evil is done to us, and when we do evil to someone else, Jesus wants us to remember what He said to His followers the night before He died. It's in John 13:34-35 MB. 'I give you a new commandment, keep on loving one another just as I have loved you. My love for you is the source of your love for one another. In this environment of your love for one another, everyone will come to know that I'm your teacher.'

"When we experience evil, when we encounter evil from someone, when we realize we have done evil, He wants us to love… just like He loved us when we rejected Him and killed Him.

"That's impossible to do, Jack, when we try to do it by our own strength and ability. We simply don't have the ability or capacity to do that as humans.

"Jesus knew that, that's part of the reason why He came to live in us. His love in us is the source of our love for others… especially our enemies.

"When we love others who do evil to us, people notice that!

"When we forgive someone instead of retaliating and repaying evil with evil, when we forgive, we go from victim to saint in our story. Our story becomes about us– not our offenders. Jesus gives us supernatural power to transform tragedy into good.

"We are touched by evil, but not defined by it. We overcome evil with good and our story ends up good, not bad because love always triumphs!

"That's what God does… He puts things back right, which is totally different from payback. That's totally different from the lie that Satan whispers to us. Satan influences religious people and he (evil) says, 'Get them, pay them back, make them pay, take it out on them.' He says that's what God would do. But that's a lie!

"Jack, Jesus forgives and He calls us to forgive. Forgiveness rewrites a storyline… it's no longer tragic– it's good. Forgiveness changes the final word from retaliation to restoration! The goal of forgiveness and the goal of God's justice is always reconciliation… never retribution!"

"I hear what you're saying Pops, but how does that even work? That man who was beaten by Pat's dad... how does that man ever forgive the guy who hit him. It's impossible, isn't it?

"Humanly speaking, it sure is impossible, Jack. We don't have it in us to forgive like that. Forgiveness is only possible when Jesus, living in us, does it as us."

"So, Pops, does that mean that Pat's dad should get out of jail free with no punishment and be allowed to go out and hurt people again? That wouldn't be right."

"Great observation, Jack. It sure wouldn't be right. Every society has civil laws that protect people. We have courts, juries, and laws that show what punishment should fit any given crime. And that's the way it should be. Actions have consequences.

"The law punishes people... and we are never to take the law into our own hands... let the system do its job.

"But that's all in regard to getting along in society. Laws protect. But spiritually, we're at a different level... in the unseen world... in our relationship with God, we can ask Jesus to forgive people as us, and He does. We can make the decision not to hold something against someone, to let it go. We can decide to release an offender from anything we think they owe us for what they did wrong. We can give that to God and let Him take it from there.

"That takes all the pressure off us and keeps us from getting bitter and hateful and all-consumed by something.

Rumors, Gossip, and Malicious Mischief

The next several days at Windsor Elementary school were filled with stories about Pat Kelly's dad, mom, and mom's boyfriend, who was still in intensive care at the hospital.

Since all the local news outlets in Lawrence, Topeka and Kansas City featured the initial incident and still followed the ongoing saga, there was plenty of fodder for those who seemed obsessed with passing judgment quickly on other people.

The school tightened up its security considerably. Even individuals like Fred, who had been well known there for three decades, now had to show their identification through a window before being allowed to enter.

Pat Kelly didn't return to school and no one knew exactly where he was, but that didn't stop outlandish rumors from being espoused.

Virtually every day the news featured reports on Pat's mom and dad, both of whom remained incarcerated. Reporters dug up the sordid past of their long criminal records and investigations by child services personnel. There were sporadic reports on the mom's boyfriend and his criminal record.

He remained in a coma with traumatic head injuries for several days before tragically passing away. Then the charge against Pat's dad was amended to pre-meditated murder and his bail was increased to five million dollars.

People wrote scathing letters to the editor bemoaning the rotten state of society. Some wrote sarcastic letters saying that we ought to ban all baseball bats from society, because, after all, "if there were no ball bats, this murder wouldn't have happened."

Others wrote that the government needed to invest heavily in having surveillance cameras covering school's public areas and that we should dramatically increase the number and training of monitors who could patrol schools en masse when students were being dismissed each day.

Preachers preached about a wide variety of sins from anger to hate to bitterness to drunkenness to lack of self-control to "thou shalt not murder"– and passionately, with quivering lips, red faces, and bulging veins, they railed against the alcohol industry and lamented the state of "worldliness."

All this was accompanied by ever-present warnings that "those of you sitting in the pews" are capable of the same actions and you need to fast more, pray more, study your bibles more, serve more, and especially give more to keep yourselves from the devil's wicked schemes. Parents were admonished to double-down on raising their children up "in the way of the Lord," especially concerning drinking, doing drugs, and marital infidelity.

Every day, Jack would report to his grandparents what the scuttlebutt was at school, and they watched the local news to see what the recent developments were.

Then, one morning, Fred's cell phone rang. The caller ID said

"Lawrence Police." Fred had their main number saved in his phone from years of "pastoral" calls ranging from "someone wants you to visit them in jail" to "a member of your congregation has been arrested and they'd like to speak with you."

"Hello, this is Fred Miller."

"Pastor Miller, this is Detective Ron Hicks with the Police Department. I think you're aware of the current situation regarding William Kelly."

"Yes, I am."

"He claims that he used to be a member of your church, and he asked if you would come and visit him."

"A member of my church? Really?" As was the case with many other people, over the last 25 years, some had come to church for a Sunday or two and never came back. However, when they'd run into Fred, they'd introduce him to their friends as "my Pastor."

The two arranged a time for that afternoon, and Fred started looking through the phone lists of church members for each year since they had started the church. There was no William Kelly.

Fred told Susie what was going on and she couldn't place the name either. So they prayed (not that they hadn't already).

Behind Bars and Broken

Fred knew the drill at the Douglas County Jail like the back of his hand. The building was sterile, stark and imposing... bars and double-lock gates were everywhere. The desk administrator greeted Fred sympathetically with, "This is a tough one. Isn't it, Pastor Miller?"

"Sure is, Mark. Good to see you... but not under these circumstances."

After signing in, Fred left his keys, cellphone, and identification with the administrator, went through the first set of large doors that were controlled by someone in a camera room in the bowels of the jail, then stopped to be patted down. After he was given his clergy visitor's badge, he waited for the next set of doors to open.

The double door procedure was repeated several times before Fred got to the top floor maximum security wing. He entered the small cubicle, picked up the phone, and said, "This is Pastor Miller here to see William Kelly."

In a couple of minutes, a deputy escorted in a thin, gaunt, 50ish man with unkempt hair and a scruffy beard and sat him down on the stainless steel stool on the other side of the wall. They could see each other through a thick glass and could communicate via the phone.

"Do you recognize me?" asked William Kelly.

"I'm sorry, Mr. Kelly, but I don't. When did you attend our church?"

"Uh, maybe 15 years ago. Me and the wife… actually I cain't remember if we ever got hitched… we thought it would be good to have our boy go to church, so he wouldn't grow up to be like us. We only went a couple of times… it was real hard for us to get up on Sunday morning, you know. Should have kept going. That boy's in jail now just like me…

"Anyway, you was real nice to us and we had a cup of coffee afterwards and you said if ever I needed help, to give you a call. I remembered your name…that's how I knew to have them call to see if you could come.

"You kept your word. I didn't think anyone would want to come and see me. The only visitors I've had have been lawyers and social workers and them kind of people. Guess I cain't blame nobody for not wantin' to be 'round a bad-ass like me."

William Kelly appeared to be a thoroughly beaten man. He mostly looked at the floor and rarely made eye contact with Fred. His body language conveyed shame, despair, condemnation, and hopelessness.

The numerous scars, missing and yellowed or blackened teeth, and deeply lined face reminded Fred of a saying his grandfather used when looking at horses to possibly purchase. "That one looks like he's been rode hard and put to bed wet." William Kelly had indeed endured a hard life.

"Well, I am here to help, and I'm so sorry you're in this situation. Would you care to tell me about it?"

"Oh, man… bad choices. Really bad choices. None of my

marriages worked out… that's just the ones we bothered to actually get hitched. I ain't no good with women. Then the booze and the drugs… meth, mostly."

Fred had guessed correctly about the cause of Mr. Kelly's dental appearance.

"Couldn't never keep a job, always in trouble. Little time in the slammer here and there, but this is the worst. I never really hurt nobody before, but something just snapped with me, Reverend, and then I took after that bastard with a ball bat. I couldn't stand the thought of my wife sleeping with him.

"I guess I done did more than enough to make the man upstairs fry me forever… that's if there's anything left after they fry me here. The lawyer-man said I could get the death sentence. It don't look good Rev. I probably won't ever see my boy again. He's a good kid, too. He don't deserve the life I've given him. What's gonna happen to my boy?" He sobbed.

Fred didn't know what to anticipate prior to this meeting, so he prayed that Jesus would listen to William Kelly and speak to him as Fred. He knew that on his own, he was incapable of helping the man.

Fred waited until the sobbing stopped, then he gently said, "Mr. Kelly… what do you like to be called? Bill?"

"I always wanted to be called Will." he lamented. "But everybody called me Billy."

"Will, I want you to know that I really am sorry that you and your family are in this situation. But more than that, I want you to know about the man upstairs. I can't help you much with your legal situation, but I can help you with God, if you're interested."

"I don't think there's no hope, Rev. I've been praying ever since I sobered up after hittin' that scumbag. I've been telling the good Lord that I'll change my ways. I'll quit drinkin' and quit druggin' and quit getting' in fights… that I'll get me a good job and keep it… that I'll straighten up and fly right if'n he'll just get me outta this fix."

"Will, do you think you could do all those things… turn over a new leaf?"

After a lengthy silence, Will Kelly softly said. "No, I'll go right back to drinkin' and druggin'– that's all I know. My old man run stolen whiskey and sold dope… taught me the ropes… when he wasn't beatin' me with his belt. I swore I'd never grow up and be like him… but I sure did. He died in jail too. 43 years old. I hadn't seen him in years."

Fred's heart ached for this man and he knew Jesus' heart did as well.

"Will, you've made mistakes. We all have. And you weren't dealt a very good hand to begin with. Now I'm gonna tell you about God, and you're gonna be really surprised."

Mr. Kelly looked up at Fred for just a brief moment, then sighed and stared at the floor again.

"Will, have you ever been dead certain sure of something for a long time, then found out that you were wrong all along?"

"Drugs…"

"What do you mean?"

"I was totally wrong about drugs. I thought they was good. I thought I could quit any time I wanted to. I thought they wouldn't hurt me. I thought I could make good money dealin' and not have to work some dumb factory job. But I was dead wrong. Now I'm gonna *be* dead…"

"Here's what I'm talking about, Will. You thought drugs were good… and you found out that was a lie, right?"

"Yeah."

"What do you think about God, Will?"

"I try not to think about Him cause he's got to be really upset with me. I 'spect He's got about the worst place of all waitin' for me. As bad as I've got it now, He's gonna really make me pay. I've just made a mess of everything…"

"You were wrong about drugs… dead wrong, weren't you?"

"Yeah."

"Will, you're dead wrong about God, too."

"Huh?"

"Will, God has always loved you. You. William Kelly. You're in His family. He likes you… He always has. When you hurt, He hurts right with you. When you cry, He feels your sadness. He's working all the time to take the messes you've made and turn them into something good for you.

"He's never hated you. He'd like for you to make better

decisions because then things would go better for you. But He never stops loving you.

"And, Will… you gotta know this– He doesn't have a special bad place prepared for you. He's not gonna punish you… the drugs and booze and your temper have already punished you. God's into putback… not payback."

"What's that mean?" Will looked up at Fred with a slight glimmer of hope in his eyes.

"What God is all about, Will, is putting you back together like He originally wanted William Kelly to be. He made you in His image. You're in His family and always will be. The moment you take your last breath here in this life, you will see Jesus Christ face to face."

"Get this, Will, it will be like the brightest white light you've ever seen, it will be warm– a good kind of warm. You'll see that Jesus is love– pure, total, unconditional love. You'll see that He's for you.

"His white hot, fiery love for you will burn away all the bad stuff and all that will be left is the real you… Will Kelly, and He will show you how much He loves the real you. And you will be with Him forever."

"But I thought… I thought He would punish me forever."

"That's a lie, Will… just like drugs are a lie. Most people have fallen for that lie… but it's not true. Jesus wants you to know right now that He loves you unconditionally… that means with no conditions. It doesn't matter what you've done. He loves you.

"Sure, you are suffering consequences with the law here on earth for what you've done, but Jesus has already forgiven all that. He took care of that at the cross. He loves you, He's forgiven you, He's accepted you, and He's included you in His family. It's a done deal."

"How come no one ever told me that?"

"Cause most people don't know that. Most people believe the lies they've heard. I believed those lies for a long time. Then Jesus showed me the truth."

"How'd He do that?" Will was sitting up straighter and was looking right at Fred through the glass window.

"Some of it through Bible verses that I'd seen before but

misunderstood. Some of it through other people coming and telling me. Some of it He told me Himself."

"What's that?"

"Will, Jesus's spirit is in you. He knows you better than you know yourself. He wants you to get to know Him. He will talk to you. You'll learn how to hear His voice. You ever hear that little voice inside you that warns you of something… or tells you to do something good? That's Jesus."

"Mostly I ignore them things cause I think I know better."

"How's that been working out for you, Will?"

"You can see, can't you? Look at me." He hung his head again.

"Will, Jesus doesn't ever condemn you or try to shame you or make you feel bad. Those thoughts come from evil, not from Jesus. Jesus wants you to know that even when you haven't listened to Him, He still loves you, He's still for you and He's still with you.

"Many times I've heard Him and decided to do my thing instead, and it's never worked out good. We're all like that. But Jesus loves us all and sticks with us."

"If that's true, what do I do now?"

"Listen, Will. You get by yourself and still your mind and talk to Him. Just say, 'Jesus, if you're there and you really do love me, I want to hear that from You.' Then be still and listen. You might get interrupted by someone else talking or the TV or whatever, but you keep on doing that and keep on listening. He will talk to you."

"Gettin' by myself ain't no problem. I'm in solitaire 'cept when somebody like you shows up. Will you come back and see me again?"

"I sure will. I'd like that."

"Rev?"

"You can call me Fred."

"Rev Fred… thank you." Big tears welled up in both their eyes. Fred really wished they weren't separated by the wall and glass window so he could give Will a hug, but he trusted Jesus to do that.

God's Will

Later that day, Fred and Mikey set out on foot on their familiar route to Jack's elementary school. As usual, the group of parents, grandparents, nanny's, or other child care-givers who came to pick up their children were all abuzz with gossip and speculation about William Kelly.

Fred's heart ached as he overheard accusations, innuendoes, and slander about his new friend. Wisely, he didn't enter any conversations.

Jack came bounding out the front doors, rubbed noses with Mikey and hugged him, and the three set off on their trek home. Each was grateful to be outside together in their routine.

"Pops, Miss Cass told us today that Pat Kelly is in a foster home in Topeka and that he probably won't be coming back to our school. I don't know him, but I feel bad that he won't get to come back to his school. I know what that feels like."

"You sure do, Jack. It's really hard... and sad, isn't it?"

"Yeah... I think of my old friends sometimes and with your phone I get to call and text and send them pictures... but it's not the same, you know."

"I do know. Remember, your dad had to change schools several times because the army moved us different places. Have you thought about what it might be like for Pat to come back to your school?"

"No... I just thought he'd like to see his old friends and stuff."

"I bet he would, but there have been an awful lot of bad stories going around and people have come up with terrible thoughts about his family."

"Yeah... I hear stuff all the time. Maybe it would be embarrassing for him."

"Could be. I think when kids need to be in a foster home for a while when something bad like this has happened and everyone knows about it, they try to put them in a different city for their own good."

"Pops..."

"Yeah, Jack?"

"Are his mom and dad as horrible as everyone says?"

"I don't know his mom, so I don't know what she's like, but remember Jack, everyone…"

"Has a story. I know, Pops. But I bet their stories are different than most peoples."

"Jack, what I'm gonna tell you now is confidential– you, me, and Nana will be able to talk about it to each other, but not to anyone else. Ok?"

"Sure… what is it?"

"I spent over an hour with Pat Kelly's dad this afternoon at the jail."

"You did?! Did he try to hurt you?"

"No. Not at all. I'm on one side of a thick wall and he's on the other. We can see each other through a thick, bullet-proof window and we have to talk over telephones. They have cameras on us and we're watched all the time.

"Now, I'm not gonna tell you everything, but here goes."

Fred told his grandson how the visit came about, how broken and full of shame Mr. Kelly felt, how he knew he'd let his son down, and how his own father affected the way he turned out. "Jack, there's no question that what Mr. Kelly did was wrong. It was evil and there's no excuse for it. He's not gonna try to convince anyone otherwise. But Mr. Kelly has a story."

"Pops, does God love him?"

"What do you think, son?"

"Well, you've told me that God loves everyone and everyone is in His family, and you've said His love is unconditional… so I guess so."

"How do you feel about that, Jack?"

"I dunno. Something inside me feels like it's really good that God loves everyone unconditionally. I mean, I sure want Him to love me even when I mess up. But… I hear everybody talking at school about how bad he is and how awful he was in killing that guy, and I have these thoughts that maybe he should get what he deserves…"

"Be honest with yourself, and with me, Jack. Do you want God to love him unconditionally?"

"I know I do. My stomach feels bad when I hear other people talking about how God's gonna really get him. I think about when I took that new baseball glove that wasn't mine... I sure wanted my dad, and God... to still love me and still want me. I do want God to love him unconditionally. So... why do I have these other thoughts sometimes, Pops?"

"Those are not your thoughts. Your heart is good, Jack. The evil one sends those thoughts into your mind to confuse you, to steal the peace and joy you have, to try to destroy what Jesus is doing in you, to try to kill your friendship with Jesus. He lies to you and he whispers lies into your mind.

"He's so good at that, we end up thinking they are our own thoughts. But they aren't. Our brains just process what we hear. We hear from Jesus, and we hear from evil. Many times evil comes to us through other people.

"The people aren't evil, they aren't bad people, they are not our enemies. They are just many times misguided and ill-informed, don't yet know how to discern what is true and what is false, and they don't know how to hear God's voice.

"We're always going to hear evil things and if we dwell on them, they can take us down into the "Hellish Darkness." But the good news is that we don't have to take thought thoughts...we can let them go, we can give them up and listen to God instead!

"Anything you hear that sounds different from what you know about Jesus, isn't true. He does love Mr. Kelly, Mrs. Kelly, Pat and everyone else... just the way and just as much as He loves you and me and Nana."

"I know, but... but we haven't killed anybody with a baseball bat..."

"No, by God's grace, we haven't. But we could. If our story was like Mr. Kelly's, if we got in with the wrong group of people, if we started drinking too much and doing drugs, if we didn't know Jesus... we could do really bad things too."

Jack didn't speak for a long time and his grandfather wisely left him to his own thoughts.

An Unpleasant Incident

Even after witnessing the horrible event and with the continual stories about the Kelly's, Jack started adjusting well to his new routine, school and friends, and his sketching seemed to have a renewed positive and optimistic tenor. Life seemed to be on an even keel as he, Fred, and Susie collectively settled into their new family dynamic.

Then one afternoon just after lunch, the grandparents each received the same text simultaneously, "Could you bring a clean shirt and clean pair of shorts to school for Jack? He will be in the office. There's been an incident." It was from his teacher.

Realizing he must be physically okay or the message would have asked them to pick him up, they quickly got the clothes, jumped in Susie's car, and drove to the school.

Going into the office, they saw their grandson sitting in one of the molded, stackable chairs that permeated the building. He was drawing something in his notebook.

The front of his shirt and shorts had noticeable dark red stains that appeared to be still moist. Knowing it couldn't be blood, or he wouldn't be sitting upright in the main waiting area, they kept calm and said, "Hey, Jack… what's up?"

Mrs. Belt, the pleasant school secretary who had held the post since Freddie went to the same school interrupted, "Hi Fred, Susie. Good to see you both. Why don't the three of you come with me back to the infirmary?" Nodding to her assistant, she said, "Hold my calls, if you would, please, Jennie."

Motioning for them to go in the unoccupied nurse's clinic/infirmary, she closed the door after they were in the room alone.

"I want you to know that Jack is not in trouble. He's been a real trouper through this. It seems that at lunch, another fifth grader in a different classroom obtained several packets of ketchup, squirted their contents in both his hands, then caught Jack by surprise and smeared his clothes and ran away." She looked at Jack and said, "Is that what happened?"

Jack nodded his head silently. He was obviously troubled by the situation.

"The incident caused some of the other students to laugh and caused a little commotion. The lunch room monitor, Mrs. Hills, actually saw the whole thing. She then brought Jack into the office and we called his teacher, who came right away. Mrs. Hills explained to Miss Cass what happened. You want to tell the rest, Jack?"

"Well, Miss Cass said she was really sorry that happened and asked me if I knew the boy and I told her I didn't. She asked if I had said anything to him or had any idea why he would have done that. I told her no. Pops, am I in trouble?" He asked, anxiously.

"No, Jack, you're not in trouble at all. Your clothes are messy and you've probably got lots of things going through your mind, but you don't have to worry about being in trouble at all. What happened next with your teacher?"

"She said that if she could get ahold of you all, you could come and take me home, or bring me some clean clothes and I could stay. She also said if she couldn't get ahold of us, there were some lost and found clothes I could probably wear. This afternoon we have art and I don't want to miss that, so I told her I'd stay."

"That's a good decision, Jack," Susie affirmed. Do you want to talk about anything else?"

"Uh, no. Can I change now?"

"Sure. Can he use this bathroom here, Mrs. Hills?"

"He certainly may. We'll meet you back at the front of the office, Jack."

While he was changing, Fred asked if there was anything else they should know.

"We called the parents of the boy who did it and they came right away. He's a real sweet little guy. He's in the Special Education resource room. He's on the autism spectrum and isn't always aware of what is acceptable social behavior and what's not. He got a two-day suspension and they took him home. He said another kid dared him to do it and he was just supposed to go surprise some random kid and mess him up. I don't think he even knew Jack."

"Do you mind telling me who his parents are?" Fred asked.

"Pastor Miller, if it was anyone else but you, I would not. But I know you always seem to come up with surprising ways to help everyone in these situations, and I trust you. They just moved here this summer. The dad is head of the Army ROTC program at

KU and teaches military science classes." She wrote down the parents' and boy's name, address, and phone number.

"If anyone asks me, I'll deny I gave this to you!" She smiled.

"Thanks, Ellie. We've been through some things together, haven't we?" They both smiled knowingly.

Just then Jack came out, awkwardly handed the soiled clothes to his grandmother and asked if he could go back to class.

Mrs. Belt gave him a hall pass and he waved goodbye as he went down the hall. She produced a plastic bag for Susie to carry the clothes in. They all thanked each other, then the Millers left to go home.

Once they got in the car, Susie said, "Bullying and peer pressure don't seem to go out of style. Do they, Fred? So, how you gonna handle this one?"

"Me?! I thought you could have the first one… ladies first, you know," he smiled. "Actually, what I'm gonna do is pray." Which he did, out loud with his eyes open. "Jesus, most of the things I'm tempted to do here are not good, wouldn't honor You, and probably wouldn't help Jack. I'm clueless, so I give this to You and ask You, in Your infinite wisdom, to show me and Susie what You want us to do to help this special little boy of ours."

That was enough. They were both silent as they drove home and went inside.

Susie took the clothes immediately to the laundry room and treated them before she started the washer. Fred went to his office, stilled his mind, and waited to hear from Jesus.

Nothing

Hearing nothing, after a while he fell asleep (as sometimes happened when he was waiting to hear from the Lord.) Now in his more mature years, he was able to tell his church friends and share a laugh with them. During his previous religious time, he would have been horrified to have church members find out their pastor fell asleep while praying!

He was startled from his catnap by the ring of his cell phone. He didn't recognize the number on his screen, but answered anyway. "Fred Miller."

"Mr. Miller, this is Major Boyd Frye. I'm Robby's dad. He's the boy who smeared ketchup on your son… uh, grandson today at school. I'm calling to apologize. My wife and I'd like to bring Robby over after dinner tonight to apologize to your grandson… and you all. Would that be possible?"

"I think so, Major. Frye… but let me check with my wife to make sure we don't have anything planned." After talking with Susie, he returned.

"That would be fine. Do you have our address?"

After exchanging information and agreeing on a time, Fred said, "It's very nice of you to call. I'll look forward to meeting you and your wife tonight."

Curious about why Fred asked her if they had anything planned for the evening, Susie had followed him back to his office and listened to the end of the conversation… not knowing why these people would be coming over.

"Do I get to know who our after-dinner guests are and why they're coming? Will this be another multi-level marketing presentation that you and I will both politely endure and then gag over when they're gone?" She grinned. Over the years, they'd had numerous newcomers to their church ask to meet, only to realize there was a motive to the meeting.

"Suze, I was praying, asking Jesus to show me what to do about this incident with Jack, and I heard nothing…"

"You fell asleep again, didn't you?" She joked.

"Actually… I did!" He smiled.

"I was wondering what Jesus was gonna do, and then I woke up to my phone ringing. It was the father of the boy who, uh… 'messed' with Jack… pun intended. He apologized and then asked if he and his wife could bring their boy over to apologize after supper. Wasn't that nice?"

"You mean nice of Jesus to answer your prayer that way… or nice of the man to call?" she smiled.

"Both… I think. I wonder what he's like, him and his wife. I wonder how they are handling this with their son?"

They both sighed as memories came to mind of former pastoral 'family counseling' sessions. Sadly, many of them revealed that the parent's overbearing, legalistic 'discipline-by-the-word-agawd' appeared to have exasperated their poor children, and all the parents wanted was confirmation by church authorities that their heavy-handed disciplinary tactics were 'justified by God.'

Throughout their military career, they also had their share of times when Fred, as a Commanding Officer, intervened in family's children discipline situations. Many of them were exacerbated by a heavy-handed, often absent, career army dad and an always-present mom who shouldered most of the parenting responsibilities, yet had to submit to an angry spouse during what few times he was around.

Painful memories of having to involve child protective services came to them both.

The term "autism spectrum" was new to them. They hadn't experienced that when Freddie was in school or during their army career. They would both Google it before their guests came.

"Let's pray it won't be like we fear, and that Jesus will use this for the good… for everyone." Fred said, in hopes that would indeed be the case.

"Ok, Fred. Before long it will be time for you and Mikey to start walking to school to meet Jack. How do you think that will go?"

"I don't know, Suze… but Jesus does. I'm gonna ask Him what He wants me to know and say and do. Would you do the same?"

"Of course."

This time he stayed awake because he distinctly heard the Spirit of Jesus speaking to him, as he often did in times like this.

Fred, you keep your ears open and listen to Jack on the way home from school. He will tell you how he's feeling and I'll show you what to say and do. I'll do it as you.

"Thanks. And about the Fryes?"

They are my children, as you know, but they don't know that. Mr. Frye's own father was very stern with him, and while he vowed not to be like that with his own son… he sometimes is, which frightens the boy and his wife. I have prepared you specifically to help them.

"What do You want me to say and do, Jesus?"

Do you have to know everything in advance? In his mind, Fred could see Jesus smiling playfully.

"Let me guess, You want me to listen to You as we go and You will do it all as me, right?"

You got it!

Fred let out a deep breath. He trusted Jesus. Jesus never let him down. But Fred would rather have things cut and dried. One time previously, Jesus told him: *This is what faith is all about, Fred... actually trusting Me and letting go of your need to control.*

Ouch!

Grace in Real Time

Jack came bounding out of the school doors, rubbed noses with Mikey, greeted Fred and they made their way across the street and into the woods.

"How'd the afternoon go, Jack? Did you enjoy art class?"

"Yeah! I really like Mr. Garcia. He showed me some more sketching techniques and told me I'm good at getting across the meaning of how I feel about something with my pictures. He made me feel real good!"

"You are good at that, son! How did everything else go?"

"Well, at first I was really embarrassed by the kid and the ketchup. Some of the other kids laughed and I just wanted to disappear. Then they took me to the office right away and while I was waiting on you, I thought about asking you to take a picture of me in my awful clothes."

"But you didn't…"

"No, Pops. I was thinking about that and wondering what you might think… and it came to me to ask Jesus what to do. So I did."

"And what did He say?"

"Pops… I heard Him. I know I did. It wasn't like an out loud voice, but in my mind, I heard, 'Don't take a picture. Just wait.'

"I still wanted you to take it, because I wanted to draw a picture of it… and, uh, I had in mind how to show what a bad guy the other kid was and how, uh…I could, uh…maybe get back at him." He confessed.

"But… Pops! I decided to do what Jesus said. After you left, when I got back to my room, all the kids clapped! I didn't know what was going on. I guess Miss Cass had told everyone what happened and that she said I could go home if I wanted… and that would be good. But if I came back, that meant I had a lot of courage!"

"Wow… that must have been pretty special!"

"Yeah."

"Then what?"

"Well, I don't feel so good about that. Some of the guys on the baseball team talked to me at recess and they said they were gonna get together when that kid comes back from suspension and de-pants him during recess and leave him naked on the playground. They thought that would be good payback and really funny. I just laughed with them, but I don't want them to do that. I wouldn't want that to happen to me."

"Anything else?"

"Yeah… I kept thinking what you've said before: 'everyone has a story.' I don't even know that kid, but I bet there's a reason why he did that. I don't want anything bad to happen to him. He's probably in trouble with his folks anyway."

Silently, Fred was overcome with emotion as He thanked Jesus for the tender heart his grandson had, and for the opportunity to minister love and grace to him. He didn't reply right away.

"Jack, I think we're gonna find out tonight part of what his story is. His name is Robby. His dad called me to apologize this afternoon and asked if he and Robby's mother could come over tonight so he can apologize. What do you think about that?"

"I bet Robby is scared to death. I remember when my dad made me take that ball glove I took back to the coach and confess what I did. I bet he's worried about it."

"He may very well be worried, Jack. What could we do to help him? What would you like to have happen if you were the one who had to go apologize to him?"

Jack thought for a moment, and then said, "You remember how you told me mercy was not getting what you deserve? Well, us not getting mad and telling him how bad he is and everything, that would be good… right?"

"Yep. Anything else?"

"Yeah. You tell me that grace is getting something good when we don't deserve it. Maybe we could do something like that…"

"You're exactly right about grace, Jack. There are a lot of good ways to describe grace. I just saw a new one from a friend on Facebook today. He said, 'Grace is when somebody hurts you and you try to understand their situation instead of trying to hurt them back.' Is that kind of what you're doing with Robby?"

Jack thought for a moment. "Well, yeah. I sure don't want to hurt him."

Thank you, Jesus, Fred prayed silently. "That's great, Jack. Your heart is really good."

Squirrely

They walked a ways in silence when all of a sudden they heard a piercing screech, then the sound of big wings flapping and branches moving as a falcon flew out of the woods and up to the sky. As they watched, something fell out of his talons several yards away from them.

Mikey barked and tugged for all he was worth on his leash. He pulled Jack off the trail a few feet into woods.

"What is it, boy?"

The lab made his way underneath a tree where a squirrel lay on its side, making squeaking sounds that indicated he was in pain. He was trembling and as they got near, Jack noticed a wet, bloody spot on its back, right behind its head. Telling his grandpa, he dug in his heels and kept Mikey from getting to him.

Fred pulled a plastic bag out of his short's pocket, and carefully picked up the squirrel by its tail. He assumed it was in shock, but also didn't want to get bitten. Carefully, he placed him into the bag, making sure he had air to breathe. He held him gently, but made sure he wouldn't fall or jump out of the bag.

As they hurried home, Jack asked, "What will we do, Pops? Is he okay? Will he die? Can we help him?"

"I don't know, Jack. But Jesus will show us." He'd just started to pray silently when he heard: *Listen– use your ears. Call your friend, Gary.*

"I've got a friend who's a vet. I'll call him when we get home."

"You should call him now, it might be too late when we get

home."

"Uh… yeah, I guess I could. Do you think you can hold the squirrel and Mikey's leash so I can use my phone?"

"Sure." Thankfully, Mikey was oblivious to the squirrel in the bag and was meandering along, sniffing as he went.

Fred found the number and dialed it. "Veterinary Clinic. This is Sheila, may I help you?"

"Hi Sheila, this is Fred Miller. Is Gary by any chance able to take my call?"

"I'll see. Just one moment."

After a moment, Fred heard his friend's cheerful voice. "Fred, I've been meaning to call you since I heard about Freddie… sorry I haven't called, and so sorry about, uh … what happened. Oh, and I got the records on Freddie's boy's dog that you dropped off a few weeks ago, so we're set there."

"Thanks, Gary. You guys were really close growing up. I remember good times when you used to come over with the other guys and hang out at the man-cave in our barn."

"Yeah… it always seemed silly to Freddie and me to call it a cave when it was actually in the attic, but we sure enjoyed it. Anyway, how can I help you?"

Fred told him the story about the squirrel and how Freddie's son, Jack, was with him, and asked if they could bring it over.

"Of course. But, you know I don't specialize in squirrels, so no promises, but I'll do what I can."

Fred told his grandson about Dr. Oldham and how he and Jack's dad used to hang out with their friends in the man-cave.

They rushed home, as much as the 70-year-old could rush, told Susie where they were going, left Mikey, and fired up the Really Is when Jack said, "Wait a minute," and ran back in the house.

"Nana?"

"You forget something Jack?"

"I just wanted to ask you, when the boy, Robby, comes over tonight, do you think you could have some kinda special treat that he and I could have and maybe take outside to eat?"

"Hmmm. I'll see what I can come up with."

He hurried off and Susie's imagination went into overdrive.

Fred didn't inquire about the momentary wait and as soon as

Jack was buckled in, they took off for the clinic. Jack was grateful that there didn't seem to be any change in the squirrel's condition yet.

They didn't have to wait long before Dr. Gary Oldham came out to meet them. He was a stocky, gregarious thirty-something guy with out-of-style, long hair that completely covered his ears and a nicely trimmed, thick, dark beard. He was wearing a white smock with some blood stains.

Holding up both hands to reveal rubber gloves, he said, "Hi guys, I'll visit with you after I see this little fellow and shake hands then, but right now let me take him back to my surgery table."

Fred handed him over and said, "Thanks so much Ear... uh, Dr. Oldham. We'll just be waiting out here."

Smiling wryly, the doctor turned and disappeared through swinging stainless steel doors.

As they were waiting, Jack whispered, "Did you start to call him something else, Pops?"

"Ah, I hoped you didn't pick up on that. You don't miss anything, do you? Dr. Oldham had a nickname when he was in school and friends with your Dad."

"What was it, Pops?"

"Ears."

"Ears?"

"He has really big ears that sort of stick out sideways. When they started playing baseball and he wore a cap, it was really obvious. You know how ball players like to have nicknames, well, your dad and his friends called him Ears. It stuck. All the kids started calling him that... even some of the teachers, if I recall correctly. He married a girl that was in their class, and she even called him Ears. I don't know if she still does," Pops grinned.

"I didn't even notice!"

"Do you remember anything about Dr. Oldham's hair?"

"It was really long! It covered his... ears!" Jack smiled.

As they waited, Fred chuckled as he remembered earlier asking Jesus what to do and He told him: *use your ears.* What a sense of humor, Fred thought.

Before long, a smiling Dr. Oldham came out holding a little wire cage containing the squirrel, which was lying still. "Don't worry, he's gonna be fine, I think! Has kind of a nasty cut where the Falcon dug his talons in. Sometimes birds of prey are like me at a buffet. Their eyes are bigger than their body can handle. I think the falcon couldn't fly well and carry the squirrel who was trying to get away, so he dropped him.

"I don't think the fall did any internal damage, but the whole thing had to be very traumatic for this guy. One minute he's going about his business in a tree, the next minute he's in excruciating pain and flying… then he falls fifty or sixty feet and hits the ground. All that probably happened in less than a minute!

"I had to sedate him to keep him still while I examined him, cleaned the wound, and stitched him up. You'll want to keep him in this cage until he wakes up, eats and drinks a little, then when he looks stable, you can release him in the woods. Might be a day or two… or could be tonight.

"You'll want to put some newspaper under the cage. He'll be pretty messy if you know what I mean. You can drop the cage back here next time you're in the area and we'll use it for the next squirrel. He'll be fine."

"Wonderful! Thanks so much! Now, Dr. Oldham, this is Freddie's son, Jack."

Jack smiled and stuck out his hand, which Dr. Oldham took now that he'd removed his rubber gloves.

"You look a lot like your dad, Jack! He and I were together all the time… played ball, played in the band, and hung out in the man-cave. How old are you?"

"10, soon to be 11."

"My son, Skipper, is gonna be 11. Maybe I can bring him over and show him the man-cave sometime and let him see where his old man used to hang out as a kid."

Jack nodded and Fred replied, "Anytime, Gary, anytime. Now, what do we owe you for seeing Mr. Squirrel here?"

"Oh, you get the limited-term pastor's discount."

"Which is?"

"No charge until you go over the limit."

"What's the limit?"

"Calling me by my nickname," he smiled. "Once you do that I charge you double!"

"You're very generous, Gary, and it's very good to see you again."

"No problem. Good to meet you, Jack, and you guys tell Freddie, uh, Susie… hi for me."

Fred gave him a big hug and Ears turned and quickly went back through the double doors hoping no one saw the tears streaming down his bearded cheeks.

"Let's get Mr. Squirrel home before dinner, shall we, Jack?" Fred said, choking back his own tears.

Fred didn't think Jack noticed their emotion. He was wrong.

They got home, put some water and trail mix in the sleeping squirrel's cage, left it on the back porch, cleaned up, and were there just in time for dinner.

When I Destroy My Enemy, I Make Him My Friend.

After they prayed, Susie started passing the fried chicken, mashed potatoes and gravy, corn, and coleslaw. She asked, "So, did Ears take care of you guys ok?"

"Nana, I don't think we should call him that. It will cost a lot of money and he might cry."

They both looked questionably at him and Susie asked, "What in the world do you mean?"

"Well, he told Pops that if he called him that, he'd charge him double the next time we brought in a squirrel, and then they both started crying."

"What?" She asked.

"Uh, I'll fill you in on the details later" Fred said. "Right now let's enjoy our dinner and talk about the folks coming over at 7."

"Ok, then." Susie knew not to ask any more. "I made apple cobbler and we have plenty of ice cream to offer them. I've already made a pitcher of regular tea. And I'm gonna make some sweet tea. Does that sound ok?"

"Nana?"

"Yes, Jack?"

"My folks never had sweet tea, but you always do. I like it. Do you just put sugar in it?"

"Fred, honey, would you do the dishes and put things away while I show Jack the *magic* of sweet tea?"

As her husband started to work, she started showing Jack her magic trick. "Jack, if you just make regular tea, then put sugar in it, it doesn't really taste good… to me at least. Watch what happens."

She poured a glass of regular tea, put a few teaspoons of sugar in it and stirred. "You can't see anything right now, but in a few minutes, you're gonna see a lot of sugar on the bottom of the glass. It doesn't dissolve, it stays separate. It's in the tea, but neither the tea nor the sugar has changed.

"Now, we're gonna fill this pan up about two-thirds of the way and put tea leaves in it." Showing him, she said, "To make a pitcher, I put in about this much tea. Now, we're gonna turn the stove burner to high and boil the water."

As it started to heat up, she continued to explain, "When it starts boiling, I'm gonna put the sugar in and stir it while it boils."

The two helped Fred by drying some dishes as they waited on the mixture to boil, then she added the sugar and stirred it. Having accomplished that part of the procedure, she said, "Now, I'm gonna use this strainer and pour the contents of the pan through it and into this pitcher. Watch and see that the tea leaves all get caught in the strainer."

As she finished, she emptied the boiled tea leaves into the trash, added cold water to the mixture, stirred the sweet tea again, then poured a glass and set it on the counter. "Ok, what do you see in that glass that I put sugar in?"

"Wow! Just like you said, there's a pile of sugar in the bottom."

"Right! Now you can come back any time today, tomorrow, next week, and look at this other glass, and there will be no sugar in the bottom. The boiling process actually changed the molecular composition from water, sugar, and tea into a totally new identity that didn't exist before. There is no more water, tea leaves, or sugar. There's only sweet tea.

"And get this, Jack. It's impossible to separate them and go back to what they were individually before. What do you think?"

"That's cool! So, it really does taste differently than just putting sugar in some tea?"

"Try some of each and see what you think."

After tasting both, he said, "Wow! I like the sweet tea a lot better!"

"We do, too… but there's something even more important that I want you to see. You've heard us talk about the Trinity– Father, Son, and Holy Spirit, and how they are One– three different identities, yet inseparable?"

"Yeah… a lot!"

"We do that… especially Pops! But we talk about them a lot because they're very important to us. They are like sweet tea, inseparable. You can't take Them apart and have Them each be separate… but there's something even more important. Do you know what it is?"

"No."

"Jack, They live in you… and in me and in everyone. You and I are one with Them! They included us in Their actual being. It's like when Jesus raised from the dead, They included us in Jesus and Jesus is in us. Like sweet tea after it's been boiled, you can't ever go back to just being Jack– you are one with Them. That's what is really cool!" she exclaimed.

Seeing that he was trying to process what she'd said, she asked, "Jack, I wonder if you'd do me a favor?"

"Sure. What is it?"

"You have a way of sketching things so that your pictures really show the meaning of what you've been thinking about. Over the next few days, whenever it's good for you, could you do a sketch that shows the Trinity– Papa, Jesus, Sarayu– being One, and us being one with Them? I'd love to see what you come up with!"

"Well, I don't know what that would look like, but I'll try."

"Great. Ok, let's get ready for our company. Do you have any thoughts about tonight?"

"Yeah, I think the boy, Robby, is gonna be scared and won't want to be here. He might even be worried that I'm gonna try to get my friends to beat him up or something. I don't want that to happen.

"I remember when we studied Abraham Lincoln in school last year, Dad helped me do some research and write a report. It was really cool. President Lincoln said something like, 'When I destroy my enemy, I make him my friend.'

"Dad told me that was like God. He doesn't really destroy us, like killing us and wiping us out, otherwise we couldn't be friends if we're no longer here. So, what he meant was when we become friends with them, we sort of destroy the bad feelings that made us be enemies."

Jack and Susie both exchanged looks that conveyed, "Woah... where did *that* come from?!"

"I'm not mad at Robby. Actually, a lot of kids seem to like me after what happened. Maybe we can be friends... Pops told me on the way home from school that grace is when somebody hurts you and you try to understand their situation instead of trying to hurt them back."

Touched by Jack's comment, and by his heart, Susie replied, "We'll probably get the opportunity to try to understand Robby's situation in about fifteen minutes, so we'd better get crackin' and get everything ready!"

Playing the "General" Card

At exactly seven p.m. the doorbell rang and Fred Miller opened it to meet the Frye's. A stocky, stern, 5'11" man in Class A uniform, with a military haircut and no-nonsense manner, stuck out his hand and introduced himself.

"Mr. Miller, I'm Major Boyd Frye. This is my wife, Annaliese, and this is our son, Robby."

Annaliese, a pretty, unassuming woman who seemed both embarrassed and obviously kowtowed to her husband, shyly offered her hand and said, "Pleased to meet you, Mr. Miller."

Robby, a shy, shorter-than-normal 5th grader, semi-hid behind his mom's dress.

"Come out here like a man and shake Mr. Miller's hand, boy." Major Frye's tone of voice and choice of words caused his wife to look down and a look of even more fear gripped his son's face.

Robby offered a limp hand to Fred, who kneeled down where

he was eye-to-eye with the boy, shook his hand warmly, and said, "I'm glad to meet you, Robby. I hope we can become friends."

Fred's warm words and genuine greeting were a cause of relief for Annaliese and Robby. Boyd seemed taken aback.

After introducing Mr. and Mrs. Frye to Susie and Jack, Fred asked them all to sit down in their spacious living room.

"Oh, we won't be staying, Mr. Miller. We have some business to take care of and then we'll be taking our leave," stated the Major.

"Please..." Susie gently grabbed Annaliese's arm and guided her to a seat on the couch next to Susie's chair. "I don't want to be denied the privilege of getting to know you nice folks. We're military too, you know, and it's always a pleasure to meet other service families. Won't you please sit?"

Susie seemed to take over the situation in such a kind, gentle, and welcoming way that before they knew it, they were all sitting comfortably... one a little less comfortable than others.

To help with any awkwardness, before Major Frye could begin, Fred said, "Thank you very much for calling me today. Being a parent who had a similar circumstance when my son was a boy gives me some understanding of the difficulty of your situation. I hope you can all be as comfortable as possible, considering the nature of your visit."

"I don't want this to be comfortable, Mr. Miller. My son needs to learn that being uncomfortable is part of the punishment for his bad behavior. Now, Robby, what do you have to say to this boy?"

Looking like a deer facing oncoming headlights, the little boy softly said, "Sorry."

"Stand up like a man. Look this boy in the eyes and say it like you mean it!" Major Miller's voice was intense and so was his body language.

"Sorry," Robby said a little louder.

"That's ok," Jack immediately responded.

His dad rolled his eyes, let out an exasperated grunt, stood, and said, "That will have to do. We'll be going now."

Fred immediately said, "If you wouldn't mind, *Major,* could you sit for just a minute?"

He attempted to brush his host off, but the next words out of

Fred's mouth got his attention.

"General White, your commanding general and I go way back. As a Captain, he was the aide to my Commanding General, Lt. General 'Bronco' McAllister when we were stationed at the Presidio. I reported directly to the General.

"I was a CW4 at the time, Commander of the 5th Army Band, which General McAllister considered his pride and joy. He was a Captain then. I called him Jimmy and he called me Chief," Fred laughed. "He still calls me Chief, and most of the time I call him General… especially in public. But when it's just the four of us…" he smiled.

"We share lots of memories, especially during both Gulf Wars, and Susie and I enjoy having dinner with the Whites often. They'll be having dinner with us here at home after the KU-Texas football game in a few weeks. He never lets me forget what the Horns' overall football record against KU is!

"He just called me yesterday to see about getting some tickets to a KU basketball game when his son will be back for Christmas. I never let him forget our record against Texas in basketball," he laughed.

"Usually generals have a lot of pull, but when it comes to KU basketball tickets, even *they* need a little help!

Major Frye's countenance changed from being stern, gruff, and commanding the situation to complete submission in about ten seconds. He was clearly concerned. His wife now had the deer in the headlights look. Robby and Jack were oblivious. Susie was amused, but didn't show it.

The Major was totally aware that, barring something unethical, he was at the mercy of this man whom he'd never met.

Stepping right in, Susie said, "I hope you all get to spend some time with General and Jennifer White. They are such wonderful people and have been close friends of ours for a long time now!

"I made some apple cobbler and have Braum's ice cream. Annaliese, would you help me serve those to everyone? And Robby, why don't you and Jack come with us to the kitchen?"

Having made his point, set his posture, and taken command of the rest of the evening, Fred then relaxed, asked the Major if he minded calling him Boyd, and started asking him questions about his military career. The Major was stunned. Less than 30 seconds ago, he was in charge and attempting to leave. Now he was obligated to stay and be submissive.

Fred was so gentle, affirming, and unobtrusive that Boyd found himself relaxing and not feeling like he was on the hot seat. However, he was very careful about what he said, not wanting anything negative to get back to the man who, at this period of time, controlled the fate of his yearly evaluation, future promotion,) and next assignment.

In the kitchen, Susie asked Annaliese if it was okay for Robby to have cobbler and ice cream. Receiving assurance, she said to the boys, "I'm gonna put this on paper plates for you two and why don't you go out to the picnic table in the back yard so you can be boys and not have to listen to all this boring grown up talk?"

Jack responded with, "Great. Come on Robby, I'm gonna introduce you to Mr. Squirrel!"

Robby wasn't sure and looked to his Mom for approval.

"You go right ahead, Robby. Don't worry about anything, and if you need us, you can just come on back in, ok?"

Reluctantly, the little boy moved away from his mom and tentatively followed Jack to the picnic table.

The Spectrum

As the boys left to go outside, Annaliese said, "Do you think they'll be ok? I know Robby did an awful thing to your grandson today, and he would certainly be justified to, uh, not be... welcoming. And, Robby is on the autism spectrum, and among other things, change and new situations sometimes are very difficult for him. He, uh... doesn't really know how to play..."

Touched by the compassion and concern of a fellow mother, Susie assured her, "I believe they'll be fine. Jack was more concerned with Robby getting in trouble and facing the consequences than he was having a messy shirt. When he found out that you all were coming, he asked if I could make a special dessert that he could share with Robby."

"Here, look out the window," Susie suggested.

The boys were standing, not seated, at the picnic table and excitedly talking about Mr. Squirrel in his cage on the table.

Relieved, Annaliese simply said, "Thank you, Mrs. Miller. This is not what I expected at all."

"It's Susie. Please, no 'Mrs. Miller.' I know from our army days how rank and protocol can be so important to some people, but it never has been to us. I was actually surprised at my husband tonight for saying Major and General and all that. Once he got to know the people in the bands he commanded, many of them called him by his first name… when no other officers were around," she smiled.

That was hard for Annaliese to comprehend, but she had never been around army bands, other than to watch them perform at a distance. She, along with most other people, incorrectly assumed they were just like all other military units.

The ladies brought cobbler and cookies to their husbands and listened a bit before they joined the conversation. The foursome shared military life stories for a few more minutes, and when there was a pause, Fred changed the subject.

"I'd like to visit with you all for a moment about what happened with Jack and Robby today."

Immediately, Boyd and Annaliese tensed up, fearing the worst.

"First of all, none of us are upset with Robby, and Jack especially, is concerned that Robby will have to face the consequences."

"Actions *have* consequences," Major Frye quickly said, and just as quickly wished he hadn't.

"Of course they do, Boyd, and parents have the responsibility to do what they think is best in raising their kids. I don't think it's ever appropriate for outsiders to tell parents how to discipline their kids."

Major Frye let out a sigh of relief. His wife hoped he wouldn't be emboldened to continue with what was, in her opinion, over-the-top discipline.

Continuing, Fred said, "I just want to make sure you know there's no ill will, no animosity, no hard feelings on our side.

"I also understand from my contacts at school that Robby is a very nice little boy, and that some other kids dared him to take ketchup and smear it on some random kid. My understanding is also that one of the possible effects of being on the autism spectrum is that children aren't always able to discern what's socially appropriate, and as a result of trying to please a peer group, they can attempt to do what they think is the right thing, then get in trouble for it, and not understand why."

"Oh, that's so true, Mr. Miller," Annaliese said. "That's been such a struggle for us in raising Robby. Just when we think we've found a good school and autism specialist who's helping him, it seems like we get transferred and have to start all over somewhere… and change is *so* hard for Robby…" her voice trailed off.

"I can only imagine, Annaliese," Fred said gently. "And please do call me Fred. Both of you, please.

"While we haven't had a lot of experience in that arena, we do understand how unsettling it can be for kids to move around a lot, as we did with the army. And our situation now with Jack is yet another new situation for us."

Puzzled, Annaliese asked, "How is that?"

"Jack's parents, our son and his wife…" Fred pointed to a family picture on the wall, "were killed in Houston while rescuing people in the flood earlier this summer, where they had lived all of Jack's life. After their deaths, Jack came to Lawrence to live with us. We sort of became instant parents again…"

Susie interjected, "As you can imagine, Jack has had his life turned upside down. Talk about change! And for the most part, he's doing as well as can be expected. He wasn't sure if he would make new friends here, so I know he's enjoying having Robby with him right now."

As if on cue, Jack ran in through the kitchen door and excitedly said, "Hey everybody, come out quick! We're gonna release Mr. Squirrel!"

The Frye's had no idea what was going on, but followed the Miller's to the back yard.

"Look, Momma. That's Mr. Squirrel. He has an ouchie, but he's better. He gets to go be with his friends now." Robby said, excitedly.

"Pops, Dr. Oldham said we could let him go when he seemed to be back to normal. Robby and I have been watching him eat and drink and he sure looks like he wants out of the cage. Can we let him go?"

"Let's take a look." Seeing that Mr. Squirrel was indeed ready to leave the confines of the cage and six pairs of human eyes scrutinizing him, Fred said, "First, put Mikey in the house so he doesn't go after him, then you can let him go."

After securing his dog in the house, Jack came back and said, "Pops, could you take some pictures of him leaving the cage and going back to freedom?"

"Sure!" Fred positioned himself, got his phone camera lined up, and said, "Free Mr. Squirrel!"

As soon as the cage door was opened there was a streak of brown flying across the picnic table, through the yard, and disappearing into the woods. The boys were yelling and high fiving each other and even Major Frye seemed to enjoy the moment.

As things quieted down, he said, "I always wanted to be a vet. I love small animals. But my dad insisted I be an infantry officer…"

The very rare and vulnerable statement embarrassed Boyd, while at the same time gave Fred and Susie tremendous insight into their new friend.

"I never knew that, honey," Annaliese said, seeing a side of her husband that she didn't know existed.

"Yeah, well…" Boyd's voice trailed off and he turned quickly to conceal tears welling up in his eyes.

"Hey Boyd, let me show you something before it gets too late and we need to get these boys to bed. Excuse us, ladies."

As Susie and Annaliese started cleaning up the dessert plates, they let Robby and Jack hang out a little longer. Annaliese gained a much better understanding for the Millers as Susie explained the details of their summer.

An Invitation

Going into the barn, Fred took Boyd upstairs to the cave. "I wanted to show you this so you'd have an idea where the boys might be playing in case Robby and Jack become friends and he ever comes over. This was where my son, Freddie, and his buddies hung out when he was a kid."

"I'm sorry about your son and his wife, but with all due respect, I don't think you invited me up here just to see this place." As soon as he said that, he remembered Fred's friendship with his boss and immediately said, "I don't mean to be rude, Chief Miller. Uh, just forget I said that if you could." He was clearly worried.

"You're very perceptive, Boyd. And don't worry about my friendship with Jimmy White. I can be such a name-dropper. Old Army habits die slowly! Susie will probably give me a little lecture on that after you all leave," he smiled.

"I did ask you up here for a reason. My dad wanted me to be a baseball player, or at least a coach. I was an ok player, and I loved the game, but not like I loved music. At first, I spent time equally playing ball and playing trumpet. But after a while, I gave up my pursuit to be a major-league baseball player and concentrated on music.

"My dad was a great guy. But he had a different paradigm. He grew up in a farm family during the depression. No one in his family had ever been to college. There were no musicians. He thought music was sissy stuff and made fun of it. He told me all the time that I could never make a living at *that music thing* and I ought to do something manly, like play ball and coach.

"I didn't hear him ever say he was proud of me until about a year before he died. I was leading the Army Field Band at a concert in Washington D.C. for a celebration at the end of the Gulf War. My folks were there. So was our Kansas senator, whom I'd gotten to know pretty well.

"After our concert, the Senator came up to visit, and I introduced him to my mom and dad. He made some nice comments about me and my career, and said to my dad, 'You must be awfully proud of your son, Mr. Miller.'

"My dad said he was. I hoped he meant it. But he never said it again.

"Fortunately, I eventually ran into a wise fellow quite a bit older than me who had grown up in a similar relationship with his dad, and my friend was able to help me process that, eventually forgive my dad, and feel better about things. Unfortunately, that didn't happen 'til several years after dad died.

"I spent all my life trying to get him to approve of me. So, Boyd, when you said you wanted to be a vet, but did what your dad wanted instead, I detected some, uh… sadness there. I invited you up here, not knowing if I'd ever see you again, so I wanted to let you know that I have a sense for how you feel, and that if you ever want to talk about it, I'd be honored to listen."

Fighting back emotion, Boyd haltingly said, "I'd like that. I know I need help. I get so angry sometimes. I hurt Annaliese and Jack. I mean, I don't hit them or anything, but I hurt their feelings… and they're the ones I love the most. I don't understand this autism stuff. All I know is how my dad treated me…

"Even though I did exactly what my dad wanted, it was never enough. It still isn't. I used to call him and tell him when I was getting an award or getting promoted. Every time he said something like, 'It's about time. Your brother did it five months quicker than you did.'

"I don't go and see him any more than I have to. And with him and Robby… he thinks I ought to kick Robby's ass into shape and be like a drill sergeant with him. I don't want to be like that, Fred, but I sometimes find myself treating Robby just like my dad treated me. I hate that. I hate that I hurt Robby. Sometimes I hate *myself*."

All the time that Boyd Frye was bearing his soul to a virtual stranger, Fred was silently praying for Jesus to listen for him, show him what was going on, and to say what He wanted to say. Jesus didn't disappoint.

"Boyd, I know those feelings. They are real… and they are frustrating. You want to fix it but you don't know how. It's not a good way to live, is it?"

Hanging his head, he said, "No…"

"To top that off, there's such a big paradigm shift between our army responsibilities and our home life. I bet you can relate to how I used to feel. I was the Commanding Officer. Everyone had to salute me, call me Sir or Chief. I was in charge. I made the decisions. Then I'd come home and it was hard for me not to act the same way with my wife and son."

"Oh, man, you're telling my story… and it's not a pretty one, at home at least it isn't…"

"Look, I have a pretty flexible schedule at this stage in my life, why don't we get together for lunch next week to visit and see if maybe an old man's experience can be of help?"

"I'd like that. Are you fully retired now?"

"No, I'm a teacher."

"Oh, do you teach music?"

"No."

"So, what do you teach?"

"I'll tell you at lunch next week. We'd better get you off and get these boys to bed."

A New Friend

The Millers waved as the Frye's drove down the lane to go home, and right away Jack started talking about Robby.

"I'm sure glad they came over! Robby's a nice guy, but he's afraid, and I'm not sure he knows how to play. He needs a friend. Can I ask him to come over again?"

"Of course you may," Nana replied. "I enjoyed meeting his mom, too. I know what it's like being a military wife and just moving here. I hope I can be her friend, too. What about you, Chief Warrant Officer, Army Band Director, Commanding officer, friend-of-the-general Miller?"

"Friend of the Senator, too," Fred said sheepishly.

Rolling her eyes, she said impishly, "Did Jesus tell you to say all those things?"

"He said He'd provide an opportunity," Fred smiled.

"I've heard of pulling rank before, but I've never seen such a blatant display of it!"

The two continued to kid each other playfully and Jack went off to his room. Soon he came back and asked, "Pops, could you print out the pictures of Mr. Squirrel being set free?"

"Sure, Jack. This has been quite a day, hasn't it?"

"Yeah!" Thinking a minute as he rehearsed his day, he said,

"Mr. Garcia showing me more good stuff about drawing, helping the squirrel and meeting Ears, uh… Dr. Oldham, and playing with Robby. It was all good!"

Both Fred and Susie were touched and pleased that their grandson had seemingly forgotten the ketchup incident. They thanked Jesus, because they knew that without His guidance, that incident could have been the defining moment of the day in a negative way for Jack. Instead it was a non-event.

Part 4
Grace Community

After their summer hiatus, Fred and Susie resumed their Sunday night group the first Sunday in October. Normally they took a few weeks off in August each summer, but this year their entire schedule had taken on a different look. For almost two decades the two had considerable freedom with their time.

Jack now had a full month under his belt at his new school and was enjoying several new friends. He wasn't sure what to expect with his grandparent's Sunday evening group, but was learning to 'go with the flow.'

The group consisted of several couples and a few singles. Most were in their 60s, 50s, and 40s. The core had been part of the church the Millers started and occasionally some new people would come.

While they thought of this as their "church," they didn't like to use that word, primarily because so many people have a negative concept of church, and because many have been hurt by well-meaning but misinformed religious people. They called their group a Grace Community.

They usually had a pot luck dinner and socialized for a while before Fred would make announcements and they'd take an offering, which was always used to help those in need. The group agreed to send it to aid flood victims in the Houston area.

The majority of the group had "been through the fires" together. They all came from various forms of "bad religion." Some had been hurt from legalistic, judgmental, controlling churches.

Others came from "faith" churches that told people if they just had enough faith, their Down Syndrome child would be healed instantly. Another side of those groups condemned their members when prayers weren't answered by stating, "Someone here is living in secret sin and God's not gonna answer our prayers until you repent, confess, and change."

A few came from "feel-good" churches that had a social-justice agenda, but little regard for scripture, seemed to believe in Jesus only for appearance sake, and had little concept of God's love, grace, forgiveness, and community, especially when it came to tolerance for those who had a different understanding of religion.

And some came from good churches where they had wonderful friends, good teaching, and no manipulative guilt trips.

As potential new group members came, the old timers tried to remind themselves of where they'd individually come from and not give the newbies a "drink with a fire hose." It wasn't always easy, but it was always worth it.

Fred and Susie prepared Jack for the first meeting of the fall, and he was excited to know that Robby Frye and Brandon Lundquist would be coming with their parents to check it out.

Fred had been meeting with Kent Lundquist, whose bursts of anger and heavy drinking were becoming fewer and farther apart. His new job with the paper company helped, but Fred's mentoring and showing him how much God loved him was the biggest reason. His wife, Linda, as well as Brandon, were grateful for the "new Kent."

Boyd and Annaliese Frye were like dry sponges as they soaked up Christ's unconditional love as demonstrated and taught by Fred and Susie. They were also very grateful for Robby's friendship with Jack.

On this night, the adults stayed outside after the meal and the three boys, along with Mikey, went to the man-cave.

Just before it was time to start his facilitating part, Fred got a call. "Unlisted" showed up on the caller ID, and Fred assumed it was a marketing person, but for some reason he chose to answer, "Fred Miller speaking."

"Mr. Miller?" Fred couldn't place the voice, but it had a vague familiarity to it.

"Yes?"

There was a few-second pause, then the person hung up.

Odd, Fred thought. He silenced his phone and got ready for the meeting.

The Frye's and Lindquist's joined 14 regulars as they all enjoyed their meal and visiting. After cleaning up and checking on the boys, Fred passed out a paper handout to each of them.

"Since we have some new folks tonight… and because it's always good to have a refresher when we start up after time off, I want to go through some basics with you all that come from our definition of Grace." Then they discussed the following line by line:

<u>*Grace is:*</u>

God's unconditional love and pure goodness perpetually in action working all things for the good to help everyone by:

* *Energizing and empowering us to be all God created us to be.*
* *Energizing and empowering us to do all God created us to do.*
* *Continually showing us that God is pure goodness.*
* *Continually showing us that God is totally for us.*
* *Continually showing us that God has forgiven, accepted, and included us in relationship with Jesus, His Father, and the Holy Spirit.*
* *Revealing to us what God wants us to say and do in every situation.*
* *Communicating with us how God sees us and everyone.*

Because we have an enemy who does not want us to know and remember this, and because we tend to forget, we continually remind ourselves and each other of these truths.

Therefore, we regularly meet and gather with others to remind each other, to encourage each other, to comfort each other, and share things God is revealing to us.

There were lots of questions, especially from the new folks. Fred and the rest of the group disarmed everyone by not being forceful or dogmatic, and assured them that, while this is the understanding of God that had been revealed to them, they were together to discuss things and encourage one another, not criticize or demand that anyone is right or wrong.

Everyone enjoyed the evening and left looking forward to the next Sunday evening.

New Insight on An Old Story

In a week's time the group, plus the boys in the man-cave, resumed their time together.

"I'd like to give you all some new insight I've received recently about an old story," Fred began, "Jesus' parable that we call the Prodigal Son. It's in Luke 15. As always, feel free to ask anything, interrupt me when you have questions, and we won't worry if we don't finish everything on your handout. There are no wrong or out of place questions, so don't be afraid.

"During the time Jesus was on the earth in a human body about 2,000 years ago, His country, Israel, was super religious. Religion was their whole way of life– their legal system was part of it, their commerce system, everything. Being Jewish wasn't just a race or nationality, it was a way of life.

"One of the two major parties was the Pharisees. They were stern, joyless, bound up by rules, condemned and judged everyone around them, were holier than thou, had the highest premium on keeping their rules and little regard for relationships, unless you believed exactly like they did.

"Does that remind you of anyone today?" Fred asked.

At almost the same time Scott and Becky Moore said, "The liberal Democrats," Wayne and Gwen Bysom said, "The conservative Republicans!" Everybody had a good laugh. The two couples were fast friends and agreed to disagree on their political leanings. In the past, each couple had erroneously felt that one couldn't be a "good Christian" and have an opposite political view.

Some others talked about the Westboro Baptist Church from nearby Topeka, while others mentioned some cult groups.

Then, Bernie Stapleton, a large, sixty-something man with a full head of hair and even fuller pot-belly said, "It reminds me of my dad… and sometimes, myself…"

Before he could even think, Boyd Frye found himself saying, "Me too. I thought I was the only one." Annaliese couldn't believe that her play-it-close-to-the-vest husband would be so transparent, but she was pleased.

Assured that everyone had the opportunity to speak who

wanted to, Fred resumed, "Well, let's take a look at what Jesus has to say. I don't mean just from the story He told 2,000 years ago, but especially what Jesus, the Living Word of God, has to say to each of us here this evening.

He put Luke 15 into his own words, "The worst sinners in the country– cheaters, hookers, gang members– flocked to hear Jesus, but the religious do-gooders complained that he was even talking to them."

"That was what church was like when I grew up," Bernie interjected. "My dad, our pastor, and the elders were on us all the time about staying away from those bad kids, which was everyone in town that didn't go to our church."

Logan McLane, a wiry little man who appeared to be anywhere from 50 to 70 years old, chimed in, "I was one of those kids who you should have stayed away from!"

Everybody laughed. His wife, Carole, Susie's best friend, chimed in playfully, "You haven't changed a bit, dear!"

Fred then summarized the story for them. "There was this rich farmer who had two boys and the youngest one asked for his inheritance before the old man died. The religious group had a law that said that if a boy was disrespectful to his father like that, the dad was to take the boy to the gates of the city where the religious leaders hung out, and they were to stone him to death!"

"That might keep kids today from being disrespectful," laughed Boyd Frye. His wife didn't smile.

Fred continued, "So everyone hearing this knew what the setting was. The 'sinners' were hoping there would be mercy and grace. The religious guys started keeping score and their first entry was a sin demanding immediate death. Jesus had their attention!

"Amazingly, the old man gave both boys their share, the youngest went to another country– whose people were considered deplorable by the religious group, and wasted the money with hookers and wild parties.

"The religious guys were filling up their tally sheets with this boy's list of wrongs. And get this, his boss sent him into his fields to feed pigs. Pigs were the most unclean of all animals to Jews. They weren't to eat pork, never to even touch a pig, and to be in a place where you would be covered in mud and pig poop and trying to feed them… hearing that made the religious listeners want to throw up. They had no way to process how bad that was!

"They were keeping mental lists of this boy's discretions, and by now the list was humongous!"

"Well, the kid finally came to his senses and thought, 'This ain't workin' out. I'm going home and see if my old man will at least hire me with the field workers so I won't starve to death.'

"Let me tell you my take on this," their facilitator said. "I used to believe that this boy 'repented'– saw the error of his ways, believed that what his father had taught him was right after all, and he wanted to go back and ask for forgiveness. But I now see it much differently!

"I think he would still be in that far country living a playboy-style life… if he just had the money. He's not asking for forgiveness… he's begging for food. There's a big difference. He also thinks that his father no longer loves or accepts him and the only thing he might be able to do would be to beg for mercy and ask to be hired as a servant. Anyway, he's rehearsing his speech… any of you ever do that?"

Almost everyone raised their hands and nodded assent. Linda spoke up, "I sure do. I find myself even thinking of what I'm gonna say next when someone else is talking to me. Then I sometimes get really embarrassed when I ask a question and find out they just covered that while I was thinking of what I was gonna say!"

The general consensus of the group was that they'd all done it, too.

"Now listen to this, my friends" Fred said excitedly.

"The kid's on his way home, like at the end of the lane coming into our place, and the old man was sittin' on the front porch waitin' for him! His dad went runnin' to him and hugged him and kissed him– even though he was covered with pig poop!

"The kid wasn't expecting that! Neither were the religious leaders. They were expectin' the father to throw the book at his son and then take him to be stoned to death.

"The religious guys freaked out. They didn't have any way to process that, except to judge the father as being equally as bad as his son! Now they had two people's lists that disqualified either from any kind of redemption.

"The kid tries to apologize and ask for a job, but the old man would have none of that... it's as if he wasn't even listening! He cut him off, didn't let him finish his prepared speech, didn't have a hint of condemnation, chastisement, shame, guilt, or judging, and instead, he told the servants, 'Dress him up give him full access to everything!"

"All that conveyed that he was completely and unconditionally forgiven and restored to his full position in the family. Unbelievable! The sinners who were listening had to be cheering, and the religious folks were sneering, jeering... and judging.

"And to top that off, the father threw a huge party and invited friends, family, and employees. He ordered the best food, had a cool jazz group playing, and they were soon all partying down!"

"Uh, Fred, I checked the original Greek, and it was a country band, not western!" Logan grinned.

"Nah, couldn't be... Jesus always wanted only the best!" Fred smiled, "Now comes the part that I really didn't understand until Papa started showing me a few years ago. Look at what happened with the older brother. He was out working in the field but he heard music and dancing. He asked a servant what was going on and the guy told him.

"Tell me, if you were the older brother, what you think your reaction would be?"

Boyd Frye spoke up immediately. "I'd be ticked. The kid got off scot-free. I'd be upset with my old man and be mad at my brother for getting away with it. Doesn't seem fair to me." His wife Annaliese looked at the ground in front of her, emotionless.

"A lot of us would feel that way, Boyd. Anybody else?"

Scott, who was the beneficiary of being in the group for a few years, and whose heart had been softened by Papa's love, quietly but confidently said, "I would like to think I'd be happy for my brother and grateful that my dad was so merciful and grace giving. I know I'd want him to be that way if it was me that had messed up. The golden rule, you know. But sometimes I find myself still hoping people get punished."

Major Frye rolled his eyes.

Jack, Robby, and Brandon had decided they'd like some more ice cream, so they quietly came up to the edge of the group, and respectfully not wanting to interrupt, they waited for the appropriate time to ask.

Before they could make their request, Bernie opened up... and they were all ears.

Religious Pain

"I actually had that happen to me, in a manner of speaking. When I was 14, before I got my driver's license, some buddies of mine and I borrowed a truck from my dad's business. He called it stealing.

"I was driving and didn't know what I was doing. I went around a curve on a gravel road going too fast and lost control. The truck crashed into a tree and totaled it. Some of us were hurt pretty badly.

"While I was in the ER at the hospital, my dad wasn't there, but the police were. He reported that I had stolen the truck and asked them to file charges. They did. Several days later when I left the hospital, I was taken to the juvenile detention center, where I finished the rest of my freshman year in high school.

"Pastor Davidson from our church came to visit me one day. He angrily told me that I had dishonored my family and the entire church. He condemned me and shamed me and told me that God caused me to have a wreck so that He could punish me and teach me a lesson and get me to repent. He was the only one from the church to visit me. My mom only came once... the first day I was there. I found out later my dad beat her up and told her he'd do it again if she visited me again."

Three 10-year-old sets of eyes and ears were riveted to the story. Jack noticed that Robby seemed especially bothered.

Bernie continued, "My dad never came to visit me. He wouldn't pay for a lawyer. The system gave me a public defender, who actually did a good job, and got a diversion for me. Mom took me home from court and explained that I should avoid my dad as much as possible.

"My sister, who was my dad's pet, was a year older than me. She would hardly speak to me, and ignored me at school. She thought I had ruined the family name and embarrassed her.

"I kept my nose clean and after three years, the charge disappeared from my record… but not from my dad's record, or my sister's. She and my dad continued to go to our church. Mom and I tried going, but we saw the whispers and the looks and heard the pastor's thinly veiled references to me as one of those rebellious kids."

Tears came to Bernie's eyes as his voice faltered and he haltingly said, "She and my dad never forgave me."

Knowing what was coming next, but unaware that the three boys were listening, Fred urged his friend to continue.

"My dad had always been an angry guy, but this whole thing seemed to push him over the limit. My mom, who had stood up for me and showed me her unconditional love throughout all of this, received the brunt of his anger and endured frequent beatings and continual verbal abuse. He blamed her for my mistakes.

"The first time I heard her pleading with him to stop hitting her, I went in their room to help her. He beat me so bad I passed out. Then he doubled down on her…

"I avoided him at all costs after that. When I was a junior, she left him. She was no longer able to cover the physical effects of the beatings up with heavy make-up or endure the constant shame from him and his church friends. My sister sided with dad and stayed with him.

"Mom told me what she was gonna do and gave me the option of staying with him. She made it clear that, financially, it would be much better for me not to go with her. I didn't care if we were dirt poor. I wanted love. I was scared of my dad. So, we left. I never saw him again.

"My dad made it real ugly. He accused her of stuff she didn't do, hired a big-time lawyer so he could save his ass… uh assets, and left her and me with nothing. We didn't have money to hire a lawyer. The church sided with him and told him his wife was responsible for my rebellion.

"It was really tough. We went to live with her folks in another state, and my mom worked two jobs. What made it even harder was, we found out that he stayed at our former church and was held out to be a 'strong man of God' for not giving in to 'sinners' like me and my mom.

"Within six months, my dad married the church single's ministry leader, who was 12 years younger than him. A year later, he died of a massive heart attack. They had a big church funeral, so I'm told. My sister made it clear that we wouldn't be welcome at the funeral, so we didn't go. His new wife and my sister inherited everything. He didn't even mention or include me in his will.

"I desperately wanted grace and forgiveness and acceptance. But I never got it. All I got was judgment, condemnation, and rejection… from my dad and sister, and from the church. I thought God was rejecting me too."

All that could be heard were the evening sounds of nature. None of the people could speak.

Eventually Fred looked at Bernie and simply said, "And…"

"And I wanted nothing to do with God, because I thought God was like my dad. My mom never wavered in her love and support for me. My grandparents helped us as best they could. We didn't go to church anymore.

"I didn't have money to go to college. But I was a pretty good trombone player. My high school band director really encouraged me and gave me free lessons. A few weeks before I graduated high school, I went to the army recruiting office, and as it turned out, recruiters were getting bonuses for enlisting band members on certain instruments. The army had a big shortage of trombone players. They needed me. It was wonderful to be needed, so I joined.

"I went to basic training at Ft. Leonard Wood and A.I.T. at Ft. Leavenworth. Then I got my first assignment. I was a Private First Class trombone player in the Big Red One band at Ft. Riley Kansas.

"Fred Miller, Chief Warrant Officer Miller, was my C.O.… but really, he became my dad."

At that, Bernie stood up, went to Fred, embraced him, and the two alternated between tears and celebratory laughter.

Logan spoke up and said, "Now we know why Fred sometimes calls you Sergeant Bernie. I always thought it was just because you looked like Sgt. Shultz from Hogan's Heroes!"

Everyone laughed because there was a real resemblance. Sgt. Bernie's normally jovial flushed face, neatly trimmed moustache, darting eyes, and mischievous grin brought about instant thoughts of, "I see nothing!"

The adults were so focused on each other and giving attention to Sgt. Bernie's vulnerable admission, that none of them knew three fifth grade boys had quietly sat on the grass a little ways from the group, patiently waiting to ask if they could have seconds on the ice cream. The boys heard the whole story.

Angry as Hell

Jack took the opportunity of the group's laughter to go to his grandfather and ask for the desired ice cream. That provided a bathroom break for everyone and some of the adults got seconds on their desserts and drinks as well.

As the group settled in for the second half of their study, Fred opened with, "I want to respect everyone's time, especially those of us who need to get boys to bed before school tomorrow, so we'll officially finish in about 45 minutes, but, as always, Susie and I will be available afterwards to visit with anyone who'd like to."

He passed out another handout that had the NKJV version of the rest of the story from Luke 15.

"Ok, the older brother, who would have been just like the religious leaders of that day, and unfortunately like many of us can be today, was really ticked with his father, who, of course, is the Father, God, in Jesus' story."

"Luke 15:28 says the older brother 'was angry and would not go in.

"Anger, as you know, is in our minds and our emotions. This son was physically on the outside of the party and mentally, he felt like he was on the outside of relationship with his father.

"So the dad came out and pleaded with him to come in and join the party. The son wasn't having any of it. He said, 'Look! I stayed home and kept the rules and served you all this time. Why no parties for me and my friends?"

Sgt. Bernie interrupted, "That's the way I grew up... thinking I had to serve my dad... and God. They were always watching me."

Many of the group acknowledged that this had been true with them as well.

Annaliese said, "Didn't he also get his inheritance... I mean, he could have killed whatever livestock he wanted and had a party whenever he wanted, couldn't he?"

"I never thought of that!" Linda stated.

"That's exactly right!" Fred exclaimed. "He didn't realize, for some reason, who he really was, especially in relationship with his Father. Many of us are in the same boat with the understanding we have of ourselves in relationship to our Heavenly Father.

"The older boy wouldn't even call his brother by name, he referred to him as 'your son,' and kept on putting him down.

Bernie interjected, "My dad and my sister wouldn't call me by my name either... but they had lots of other names for me..." his voice trailed off.

Fred resumed, "It seems to me that his problem was that he did not want his brother to be blessed, to be accepted, to be included, to be forgiven, to be celebrated, to be back 'in' the family. In his mind, his attitude, he wanted his own brother, his closest relative, to be cast out, punished, stoned to death, to be paid back 'evil for evil'... and so did the religious leaders."

Bernie interrupted, "That's how my sister felt about me..."

Everyone in the group looked at Bernie with compassion, and a few kept their similar experiences to themselves.

Fred asked the group, "Who do you think this son was angry with, and why?"

Boyd spoke up, "He was angry with his brother because he got away with his wild living. I think I would be too," he said honestly.

Gwen said, "He was also mad at his Father. He thought it wasn't fair and that his old man was letting the boy get away with murder."

Susie usually kept her comments to a minimum so that others could talk, but when she did speak, everyone always saw her wisdom, compassion for others, and deep insight come through. She said, "You know I never signed up to be a pastor's wife. I married a musician who was the life of the party and in the beginning, there were a lot of fun parties!

"When Fred started changing and being interested in God and spiritual things, I thought it was just another stage he was going through, and it would pass. But the change in his life was good, and so I went along.

"However, when he became a pastor, it was hard for me. I had to be really careful what I said and did. We'd be out to eat at a restaurant and I wouldn't have my usual glass of wine because I was afraid of what people would think.

"We'd be at a party and people would be laughing and telling jokes… and I felt like it would be inappropriate to laugh at most of them, even when they were really funny… if you know what I mean!"

They all laughed.

"So, for a while, I became kind of bitter. I thought everyone else got to enjoy life, but I couldn't because I had an image as a 'godly' woman and pastor's wife that I had to keep up. So, I found myself getting angry… that I couldn't have fun like everyone else.

"At different times, church people would complain to the elders that I shouldn't be doing this or that. I think maybe the older brother in this story may have been like those elders."

"How did you get through that, Susie?" Linda wanted to know.

"That's a story for another day. The short answer is Jesus… keeping my eyes on Jesus. But we'll get together and I'll tell you how He helped me. For now, though, I know we need to finish this parable so I can get Jack to bed!"

Fred resumed, "Ok, the Father said to the older boy, 'Son, you are always with me, and all that I have is yours.' He reassured him of his identity… and he showed what the heart of the Father is really like when he said, 'It was right that we should make merry and be glad, for your brother was dead and is alive again, and was lost and is found.'

"Jesus is making the point here that the Father is most concerned with those who are spiritually dead, who don't know the Father's love and grace and goodness, and His priority is that everyone knows what He's really like... and who they really are, as His children!

"Now, the story ends here, with the older son on the outside, but still in the presence of his loving Father. We don't know if he will ever change his mind. But here's the question I have to ask myself, and I want to encourage each of us to honestly ask ourselves: Do you hope he will change his mind?

"I have had to really look at this. For most of my life I believed that God was in to payback– retribution and revenge– because that's what I had heard in church and I never asked any questions, and I never researched or studied it.

"But once I started really experiencing God's perfect, unconditional love, and realizing it was for everyone and included everyone, then the Holy Spirit started showing me that retribution, payback, and revenge are incapable of producing reconciliation, God's ultimate restoration of all things.

"For God to be into payback, eternal punishment and separation of His creation would be the admission of Christ's failure at the cross and God's impotence to save, include, and restore everyone, which He says is His will!

"To believe what Jesus says about grace is to believe that God is, in fact, able to achieve what He wills... to happen!

"The key to grasping this, in my opinion, is whether or not it's what we want. I'm confident it's what God wants, but I won't really believe that about God... until it's what I want, too.

"I was embarrassed to see that I was into retribution, documenting every hurt and injury that I, and mankind, had received at the hands of 'those bad people.'

Some of the newer members of the group were starting to realize that's where they were.

"But God revealed to me that He keeps no records of wrongs! His love never fails. We can never be separated from His love... not even by our own actions!

"He is good. All good. We call that 'omnibenevolent.' God started revealing the obvious to me. He can't be all good, and at the same time, pay back evil for evil!

"Understanding this really affects how we live– how we relate to others, and to God!

"Only when we quit keeping a list of how we've been hurt and wronged, only when we quit keeping a list of the bad things other people have done to society… only then can we start to experience the freedom that grace, unconditional forgiveness, and acceptance provide for us!"

"Uh, Fred," Boyd said, "I like you, and you've been helping me a lot with things. But what you're saying is really different from what I've been taught growing up in the limited time I did go to church. With all due respect, Sir, how do I know if you're right… or they're right?"

"That is the question of the night, isn't it, Boyd?" Fred said gently.

"First of all, you… and everyone here, are free to believe what you think is true. I don't have the monopoly on truth! And, at least on my part, we'll be friends and there will be no animosity on my part if we disagree. I mean that."

Major Frye believed him and was relieved.

"What I've been learning is not something new. It's what most of the first church believed 2,000 years ago, and what pockets of people have continued to believe since then. It's not popular to believe it, because religious people get worried when you talk about God's love and grace being like Jesus said in the story we studied tonight. Without that fear, religious people know they can't control 'church' people.

"I'll be glad to give you more references and examples, and there are lots of good books that explain this a lot better than I can. The bottom line is, you have the Holy Spirit of Christ, the real Teacher, living in you. The Holy Spirit will confirm with you what is true. You'll feel your spirit resonate when you hear truth… and conversely, you'll be uptight and irritated when you think something is off. Eventually you'll learn to discern that what is off is anything that indicates God is different than what Jesus is like.

"Hang with us and give it a shot. Anytime you feel like you're being led astray, you're free to say so. I may be wrong about some things and I'm open to be corrected. And when we can't agree, we can agree to disagree. If you feel sometime you just can't go where I am, that's ok… but we'll still be friends."

That seemed to be good enough for Boyd. They started packing things up and agreed to meet again the following Sunday evening.

Fearing The Worst

The next morning at breakfast Fred and Susie were excitedly talking about the group from the evening before and commenting on how different people were coming to experience and enjoy God's unconditional love, grace, and forgiveness to greater degrees. However, Jack seemed a bit subdued.

"Did you and your friends have a good time in the man-cave last night?" Susie asked, trying to draw him out.

"Yeah. They're cool."

"What kinda things did you guys do?" His grandmother continued, oblivious to her husband's body language that was saying not to push it.

"Guy stuff."

"Good. Boys need to be boys, don't they?" Fred interjected, and finally Susie got the hint.

"Let's clear these dishes and head out for school, Jack. I think Mikey's been waiting long enough to get out of the house."

In a few minutes, Jack hugged his Nana, then the two Miller men and Mikey started on their familiar path. They made small talk for a while, then Jack gave the familiar indication that something was on his mind.

"Hey, Pops…"

"What are you thinking about, Jack?"

"Uh, last night when we came to ask for more ice cream, we didn't want to interrupt your conversation, so we waited 'til we thought was the right time. We, uh, heard Mr. Bernie's story… about his dad and everything."

"Oh…"

"Pops? When he talked about his dad being real mean to him… and hitting his mother…"

"Yes, son?"

"Pops, both Brandon and Robby started crying… and Robby got a strange look in his eyes, and he folded his arms like this and started rocking back and forth."

"I was really sad for Mr. Bernie… and his mom… but I didn't cry or anything. Is something wrong with me, or are they kinda sissy's… or what?"

"Neither, Jack. There's nothing wrong with you at all. And your friends aren't sissy's. Everyone reacts to stories differently, and it seems that Bernie's story had quite an impact on them."

"Why, Pops?"

His grandfather was hoping Jack wouldn't go there, but knew it was a teachable moment, so, as usual, he asked Jesus to speak as him.

"I don't know for sure, Jack. Why do you think?"

"I think maybe they've seen something like that… at home." He was afraid to say what he feared was true at his friend's homes.

"Oh, Jack…" Fred let out a deep sigh and trusted Jesus even more. "If things like that have happened in their families, we'd be really sad, wouldn't we?"

Acknowledging Jack's nod, he continued, "You know, son, there's no playbook or instruction manual that people get when they get married or when they have kids. Most of the time people just do what they saw their parents and grandparents do. I never saw my parents hit each other …and they never hit me… so that's a big part of the reason why I never did that to Nana or your dad."

"My dad never hit me or Mom. Never!"

"I never had any reason to suspect that he would, Jack," Fred said gently. "Your dad was one of the finest– no, *the* finest man I ever knew.

"Jack, even if Brandon and Robby's dads may have gotten angry at times, I'm confident that they are changing and it will be less and less… if at all. And they are good men, not bad men at all. They are most likely acting like their own fathers did. Remember, everybody…"

"Has a story," Jack said with his grandfather.

"Sometimes when guys have been hurt by their own dad, it takes someone who knows Jesus and has Jesus living as them to be able to show a man what God's love is really like, and then let Jesus do the changing in them."

"Are you helping Brandon and Robby's dads, Pops?"

"Jesus is helping them… through me and as me, Jack, and they are really coming along. But I want you to remember that I'm telling you confidential stuff, and it wouldn't be right for you to talk about my involvement with their dads to your friends, right?"

"I won't. But I want them to know things will be better."

"Then just be a good friend to them. Be yourself. Keep hanging around them. And if they mention anything about their dads, you can tell me confidentially, if you think I need to know."

"Ok, Pops"

Jack seemed content… for the moment.

Where Do Lies and Evil Come From?

A couple of days later after dinner Jack asked, "Pops, you told me that your church used to be a lot bigger. What happened?"

"Some people moved to other towns, some got old and died… we had a lot of funerals over the years, but actually the Great Exodus came when many left because we changed what we taught."

"What do you mean?"

"Up 'til that time we were a pretty standard church. We taught that God was really bummed with all mankind, that we'd all messed up, and He was continually watching us and taking notes.

"We taught Jesus loves you unconditionally… *but*. But you have to do this or that and if you don't God will really get you.

"We said it was great that Jesus made a way for us to keep from going to hell and that people needed to believe in Him, or they'd still burn forever. We taught it was up to us to get right and stay right with God. We preached against all kinds of sin and told people what they needed to do.

"But then we saw things differently and started telling everyone about God's grace– unconditional love in action. We told them that God loved everyone and wasn't mad at them. We told them

God was for them and Jesus already did everything to make us right with God forever.

"I thought everyone would be glad to hear that really good news, but they weren't. People started leaving.

"I realized that they were only friends with me because I believed what they believed. Some left nicely, some without saying a word, and some openly criticized us and tried to get other people to leave with them. Some people still criticize us today." Fred stated.

"What do they say, Pops?"

Fred laughed and said, "You won't believe this, Jack, but the biggest criticism we get is that people say, 'You're making God out to be better than He is… He's not that loving… He's also angry, harsh, and displeased with us and has to punish us.'"

"That's stupid!"

"It sure seems that way to us," Susie said. "But Pops and I have to remember that we believed the same things at one time. We had never heard the truth about God and what He's really like, we believed a bunch of lies, and we just didn't know any better. We loved God and wanted to do what was right. We were just ignorant of the truth and misguided.

Most of those who left also believed the lie that we have to do something to get right with God… they don't think Jesus did enough. That's a lie, but they don't know it.

Thinking for a moment, Jack then asked, "Where do those lies come from?"

"Ah, that is the question, my boy! You shucked right down to the cobb, boy. We have an enemy. Jesus calls him the evil one because he is totally evil and totally against God… and us. I call him Ophis, which is Greek for serpent or snake."

Jack laughed, "My dad used to say someone was a doofus. Is it kind of like that?"

"Doofus… close enough! Jesus told us that he's a liar– the father of lies and that he never tells the truth. His whole goal is to steal, kill, and destroy the truth about how good God is, how much God loves us, and how Jesus has already taken care of everything by His finished work at the cross.

"Ophis wants us to follow him and live like he does… lying,

deceiving, hurting other people, doing bad things, and above all, he doesn't want us to know the truth about how good God is.

"He's the one who pulls us into his 'Hellish Darkness,' that awful, sinking feeling of despair we have when we think we're being overcome by the bad circumstances and situations we're experiencing."

"I know that feeling, Pops, but I never knew what to call it. How does Ophis do it?"

"He lies to us. He's invisible, so we can't see him, but he's always around. Actually, he himself isn't, but he has lots of helpers... evil spirits. The Bible calls them demons... like an army of evil minions. They can't read our minds, but they observe us and see what's going on, and they whisper lies to us and tempt us to hurt people and do bad things.

"But worst of all, son... and this really is bad... evil beings tell us that God is evil. They tell us that God is judgmental, keeps a record of all our bad deeds, has to punish them, and will punish us in hell forever... unless we get certain things exactly right.

"Then they tell different people different things about what a person has to do to get right with God... so that we'll argue with each other over who's right. They tell us God has all these conditions for His love and grace.

"And Jack, when people have heard these lies all their lives... especially when preachers, like me, who are supposed to know... when preachers tell them these lies, people believe them. At least religious people tend to believe them."

"What's amazing, though," He explained, "is that people who never went to church, who never heard these lies... they don't believe them! They see the foolishness... you might call it stupidity.

"They see that it just doesn't make sense to one moment say, 'God is good and He loves you unconditionally' and the next moment to say, 'But if you don't do what we say, He's no longer good and He will punish you.' Non- religious people wonder how there can be all these conditions to His love and acceptance if it's supposed to be un-conditional!"

"Jack," Fred continued, "non-religious people especially see the absurdity of the false claim that a good, loving God, would intentionally create an eternal torture chamber where he would supernaturally keep 90% or so of all His children, people, for all eternity… forever… and continually burn them horribly, just because they never heard of Him, or didn't believe in Him. I no longer believe in that God either.

"Actually, son, non-churched, non-believers are more receptive to believing the truth about our good God who loves and accepts us all… than most religious people are who have been stuck with lies all their life.

"Sadly, I've found that most religious people just don't want to give up their concept of hell because they want some people to be there."

"Whew…" Jack exclaimed.

"Well, you've probably had enough 'God talk' for the morning, anyway!"

Jack was relieved. He was interested in these things, but, like most people, he could only process so much at any given time.

The Poison We Drink Hoping the Other Person Will Die

At the following Sunday night group meeting, the three 5th graders headed up to the man-cave, each with a couple of Nana's oatmeal raisin cookies and some lemonade.

"Ok, let's pick up where we left off last week– Luke 15," Fred said as he called the group together, "Jesus' story of the father who represents our Father God, and the two sons. You'll remember that the dad gave a big party for everyone and celebrated his son coming home!

"But, the older brother, the religious boy who kept all the rules, he didn't want his brother back. He wanted payback. He wanted vengeance. He wanted humiliation and retaliation. He hated his brother and he hated his father for loving, forgiving and accepting his brother. He didn't want to forgive and he would not go in to the party. He judged his father, who represented God the Father, and judged Him guilty!

"Where do you think he was?"

Major Boyd Frye was the first to speak. "I've been thinking about that ever since last Sunday night. At first, I didn't think the old man was being fair. I wanted that kid to get punished... get what he deserved. I could really relate to the older brother getting angry and not going in to the party.

"As some of you know, I've struggled with anger myself. 'Struggled' is not a very good word for it– I have been defeated. I never even put up much of a struggle."

His wife, Annaliese, kept her eyes on the ground. She didn't want people to see her pain from being the brunt of much of that anger.

He continued, "Well, Fred has been helping me see where my anger comes from and how Jesus can help me. Even though we went to church some, I never was much of a prayer guy, but Fred told me just to talk to Jesus and tell Him I don't want to be angry anymore and ask Him to help me. So, I've, uh, been doing that. I'm not lying, it's kind of weird to me!"

Several in the group light-heartedly, but genuinely, assured him that he wasn't the lone ranger.

"Anyway, I remembered that Fred told me that anger and bitterness are the poison that we drink, hoping it will kill the other person. But we're the ones who get sick. So I've got my own anger that I'm dealing with, then I see this older brother that's angry, and it hit me that maybe there's a connection.

"I got this thought in my mind to picture what it was like for that older boy in the story and see if I can relate. Boy, can I. That guy is on the outside looking in. Everyone else is relaxed and enjoying the party and having fun, and he's uptight and bitter and his stomach is in knots. He's on the outside.

"That's where I am when I get angry. Usually, everyone else is fine. They're having a good time and all... and I'm angry. Then I vent my anger and all of a sudden, I'm all by myself. I'm realizing that I'm by myself because no one wants to be around someone who's angry all the time.

"I don't know what all this means, but I do know I don't like being angry. I don't like being on the outside. I don't feel good when I'm like that, and I wish I could not let things bother me and instead, be at the party. Does that make any sense?"

"Makes a lot of sense to me now," Kent said. "But it wasn't all that long ago that I was the same way. Not that I'm perfect or anything now," he grinned.

Fred took the opportunity to share his insight with the group. "I call that awful feeling we have when we're angry or emotionally overwhelmed or seem to be losing it The 'Hellish Darkness.' It's no respecter of persons, it attacks us all."

He and Susie vulnerably shared about the attacks they had struggled with, especially since the loss of their son and his wife.

Several in the group confirmed that they struggled with anger and The 'Hellish Darkness' at different times, then Logan spoke up, "I've been thinking about that story all week as well. I think that older son who was on the outside… was in hell– the hell of his own creation. The father made it clear that he was included and that he loved him, but for the time being, at least, the older brother rejected that. He was in hell."

Then Fred asked, "And you know who was there with him? The Father!"

"I agree!" Logan exclaimed. "Hell is not some place separate from God. It is not an eternal torture chamber specifically designed by an angry god so that he can pour out his wrath on people who offend him. Nope, hell is a place we create in our minds when we reject the Father's unconditional love, grace, and forgiveness for us... and everyone else!

"And here's the kicker, when we do that… now, or in the next life, the Father is right there with us… just like He was with that boy in the story– loving him, accepting him, including him, assuring him that all He had was his, encouraging him to love and accept and forgive his brother.

"I think that's what hell is."

"I agree," Fred stated. "Maybe the biggest lie of all religion is the lie of separation. That's the lie that says people are separate from God until they ask Him to be with them… and that if they never ask, they are separate from Him for all eternity. But the truth is, there has never been and there never will be any chance of separation from God. He is everywhere present… all the time!

"When you don't want the good things God wants, you're in a

hell of your own creation. I've learned that when you are in the presence of God's fiery, consuming, white hot, unconditional love, and you see Him pouring it out and lavishing His love, forgiveness, and grace on people whom you want to suffer, burn, be tortured, and experience 'God's vengeance and wrath' because you think they deserve it… but you see God loving them instead, then His love feels like hell."

A Helluva Number

Nodding ascent, Carole asked metaphorically, "Oh, what kind of number has been done to us that we have to be convinced that God is more loving than we are?"

Susie responded, "A helluva number! You know, we used to focus on sin and how bad hell was, but now let's focus on what I think God wants us to focus on… the opposite of hell. Shall we?"

Hearing the chorus of, "Yes!" she continued, "When I was a practicing nurse… Fred still sometimes calls me 'Nurse Susie,'" she grinned, we had to know a little bit about everything, which was a real stretch for me! Especially when it came to science, which is really important in the medical field! But I do remember what an atom looks like, or at least the diagram they use. Can anyone describe it?"

Linda jumped in, "Oh, I love that stuff! You can't see atoms, but scientists use these three circles that seem to be intertwined and constantly moving. There's a proton, neutron, and electron. And there's massive energy in each little atom, which we know from the Atomic Bomb."

"That's exactly right," Susie affirmed. "I picture God– the Father, Jesus, and the Holy Spirit– in this circle dance that's a continual party. Actually, Jack drew a sketch of how I see it and I made a copy for each of you."

As she passed them out, she explained, "Jack drew this simple picture of God the Father, and Jesus being in Him, all of us being in Jesus, the Holy Spirit being in each of us, and everything being in constant, joyful motion!"

"It's a wonderful dance," she continued. "The power that flows out of Them and into everyone and just keeps flowing around and in and out and up and down… everywhere… is Their unconditional love!

"And Their love continually pours out an unstoppable stream of everything that's good: joy, peace, patience, kindness, goodness, gentleness, faith, compassion, mercy, and grace. And it's wonderful! Grace is actually the expression of God's love… that flows all the time.

"It's amazing grace! It reminds me of 1 John 4:8 and 16. God is love. Grace is unconditional love in action!"

"That's exactly right, Suze!" Fred exclaimed. "And I also think of Galatians 5:6 where Paul writes that, 'The only thing that counts (what is important) is faith expressed as love. Love expressed is grace! Continual unconditional love, forgiveness, acceptance, and inclusion for everyone!"

Boyd re-entered the conversation, "I love hearing about this, and it's all feel-good stuff and everything, but I keep having this thought that if we emphasize grace too much, there won't be any rules… and in my profession, in the army, if we didn't have rules and regulations, people would just screw up all over the place, wouldn't they?"

Fred answered, "Of course, we have to have rules and regulations in civil society, in business, in the military. No question about that. But when it comes to God, He's totally different. It doesn't seem that way to most people, because most people have never heard the truth about God and they don't know Him.

"Over the years, people have said to me, 'If you emphasize grace too much, you give people a license to sin. They'll just do whatever they want.' Well, personally, I've been able to sin pretty well myself without any license!"

When the group finished laughing and agreeing, Fred continued, "I've found that those who think we'll give people a license to sin, do not yet understand grace and they haven't yet really experienced the ever-flowing love and grace of God. If they had, they would no longer want to sin!"

Susie explained, "That's right! Did you know that it's actually grace that teaches us how to live right, not the law? All the law can do is point out what's wrong! But look at this– Titus 2:11-12 NKJV, 'For the grace of God has appeared, bringing salvation to all people, instructing us to deny ungodliness and worldly desires and to live sensibly, righteously, and godly in the present age.'

"The Mirror Bible says it like this: 'The grace of God shines as bright as day making the salvation of humankind undeniably visible! (God's undeserved kindness has burst in upon us, bringing a new lease on life for all mankind!)'

"And Titus 3:4-5 says, 'But when the kindness of God our Savior and His love for mankind appeared, He saved us, not on the basis of deeds which we have done in righteousness, but according to His mercy, by the washing of regeneration and renewing by the Holy Spirit…'

"Did you notice that both grace and kindness 'appeared?' Jesus, grace in person, appeared as a human, then His Holy Spirit was poured out in everyone 50 days after Jesus died and rose again!

"Here's what the Old Testament prophet foretold in Joel 2:28 NKJV– 'And it shall come to pass afterward that I will pour out My Spirit on all flesh.'

"That actually happened on what we call Pentecost."

Fred resumed his explanation; "Let me try to tie all this together: God is love. Love is expressed as grace. The most important thing to God is the expression of love. Love is continually expressed by the Trinity, manifested in, through, and as us by the Holy Spirit of Christ.

"We can reject that love like the older brother in the Prodigal story. We learned there that we get to choose whether we're in heaven or hell right now. Not just for some time in the next life… but right now. It has to do with embracing… or rejecting… grace: unconditional love in action. And some of us know what that hell is like, and we don't like it!"

Carole added her thoughts, "Not all of you have experienced this, but some of us who have been evangelical Christians have totally focused on the wrong point, I think. We incorrectly believed that everything revolves around whether or not someone is going to heaven… or hell. We believed that 'saved' means going to heaven and everyone who's not saved will be tortured for all eternity in hell.

"But now we've learned that God's goal is not to save us. Jesus *already* saved us all. He is the savior of the world! God's goal is ultimate restoration for all people and all things. Heaven and hell are not the issues! The issue is experiencing abundant life right now!

"God created us with His will in advance being for us all to experience abundant life, in Christ, in Their Divine Triune circle dance of love, joy, peace, patience, goodness, kindness, gentleness, faith, compassion, mercy, and grace... empowered by the Holy Spirit.

"I've been thinking about that and I made up a little thing I want to share with everyone, if it's all right?"

"Of course," Fred affirmed.

"You can look at it as I read. This is the lens that I now use to read the Bible... I have the lens and filter that: God is love; God is all good– there is no evil or bad in God; God is all about love in relationship; everyone is in God's family, the Holy Spirit of Christ is in everyone; God's will is the restoration of all things, for everyone to be saved and no one to perish; Jesus finished everything for us in our relationship with God at the cross; God's grace has taken care of everything and continually teaches and empowers us; God has accepted, included, and adopted everyone; God's way of treating those who think they are His enemies is: love, forgive, bless, serve, and pray for (not hate, payback, curse, take vengeance); God says that ultimately, everyone will worship Him and recognize that Jesus is Lord.

"Using that lens, then the concept of heaven and hell cannot mean what we used to think! They must mean something else... Jesus' story about the Prodigal shows us what hell is!

"God's goal is justice, which is making all things right for everyone. Then there will be no more pain, no tears, no sin, no evil, no hate, no vengeance... nothing bad! It's all good... a continual party!"

"But," Boyd asked, "what about God's wrath? I've had that drilled into me all my life."

Fred answered, "Boyd, that's a really good question and it needs to be answered. As we spend time together, I'll explain it in detail with the original Greek words and the history of how things got perverted, but for now, here's what's important for us all to know– in the original language of the New Testament, God's 'wrath' is the violent emotion of His white hot, fiery love that consumes everything bad– all evil– and only leaves what is pure. God's wrath brings about God's justice in stopping oppression, injustice, and all sin and evil.

"That's how He 'saves' everyone from human sin– greed, lust, pride, oppression, hypocrisy, dishonesty, violence, racism, chauvinism, abuse of power, and all injustice. He 'saves' us from those who are 'unjust'… from ourselves and from each other!"

"I'm not sure I believe all that yet, but I do know I need saving from myself," Boyd stated.

He didn't hear Annaliese whisper, "Thank you, Jesus."

Fred continued, "Boyd, we all need to be saved from ourselves. I'm learning that I need to ask: 'Am I on the side of justice or on the side of human oppression and greed?'

"To me, hell is experiencing human sin (greed, lust, pride, oppression, hypocrisy, dishonesty, violence, racism, chauvinism, abuse of power, judging, and all injustice)… and people are experiencing it all over the world right now. The army, as you know, can go into a country and free people from unjust dictators and governments, but only Jesus can help each of us see these things in our own selves."

Not wanting to overly dominate the discussion, Fred said, "Carole, thanks for your excellent handout on the lens we can use to read the Bible! Would you like to give us your take-away from this story?"

"Sure! Now, when someone asks me about hell, all I can do is say, 'I believe in hell… but I may have a different understanding of it than you do. Some people will experience hell, but I'm hopeful that no one will continue to choose to stay there.'"

"Great, Carole! Excellent summary. Ok, for next week, you guys email me things you'd like to talk about and we'll see how much we can cover. Let's get the boys from the barn and call it an evening."

Part 5
Autumn in Kansas

The rolling hills of eastern Kansas were drenched in red, orange, yellow, and gold as the maples, birch, ash, walnut, and box elder trees presented their annual fall majesty, appearing as a heavenly quilt covering the earth. This year's "Maple Leaf" season stretched past its usual third week of October into November.

Jack was enjoying the 360-degree panorama available with the top down on his grandpa's convertible. They rode silently for several minutes, taking in the stunning beauty of God's creation. Soon they passed by a little town that had a huge church on its outskirts. It was easily the most prominent thing on the landscape.

Noticing the church, Jack said, "Pops, you talk about God a lot. How do you know you're right and all those other people are wrong?"

"Ah, that is the question of the ages, isn't it, young man?

"The simple answer is: that's what Papa tells me. That's what I hear Him say. That resonates with my spirit inside me. It has the ring of truth to it.

"Of course, anyone can say that, and many people will laugh at you, make fun of you, and call you names when you tell them you actually hear from God. Other people hear things the evil one says to them and they think he's God… and he tells them to do bad things.

"Many religious people don't believe that God talks to people directly any more. They think the only way God communicates is through the Bible… as *they interpret* it, of course!

"Do you know what a decoder is, Jack?"

"Yeah, we learned at school about some special Native Americans back in a war who could decode the enemy's messages. We each got a little paper with words on it that didn't make any sense, then we got another sheet with holes all over it.

When we put the holey sheet over the other sheet, the words all made sense. That's a decoder."

"Exactly! Well, for a long time I never had a decoder for the Bible. I never had a filter, or a lens, to read the Bible to determine if what I was reading or hearing from other people about God was right or not... and it was terribly confusing since everyone had all these different ideas about what God was like, who He is, how to please Him, what made Him mad... there are all kinds of churches and denominations that have different ideas, and they can't all be right.

"If a new kid moves into your old neighborhood in Texas, and he hears what a neat kid this guy Jack Miller was, the only way he could really find out what Jack was like would be to ask his friends, those kids who know you well. They could tell him, right?"

"I hope so."

"So I started really focusing on what the three people who knew Jesus best said– John, Paul, and Peter. John and Peter were His two closest friends on earth, and then after Jesus went back to Heaven, He appeared to Paul and taught him personally in the desert for several years and even took Paul up to heaven with Him for a while then brought him back down!

"John wrote five books in the Christian Bible– the New Testament, and he stresses over and over that God is love and there is nothing bad about Him. He also writes about how Jesus told us that we are in Him and He and the Father are in us. He stated several times that Jesus is the savior of everyone and that He took away all the sin of the world and forgave it all.

"Paul wrote two thirds of the New Testament and never once mentioned hell. Over and over he wrote that Jesus died for everyone, forgave everyone, included everyone, accepted everyone, made everyone right with God, and that His grace covers everyone. He also stressed that Jesus is exactly like God... so God can't be anything different than what Jesus is like.

"And Jesus was all good! He never rejected anyone, never condemned anyone, never punished anyone. He hung out with people we would think would be rejected by God: prostitutes, cheaters, liars, drunks... and He didn't hang out with religious people!

"The book of Acts in the Bible is about some of Jesus's best friends– those who knew Him the best. They never ever talked about Jesus being mean or punishing people or about hell or anything like that!

"Paul also told a bunch of idol worshippers who had never heard of Jesus that they were already in Christ and in God's family and that Jesus had already judged them, and everyone, righteous... already right with God because of what Jesus did at the cross.

"Paul explained to us what grace is and told us that we were actually given grace, saved, and included in Christ before creation. That really should take all the confusion out of things!

"Peter said similar things and said that when the Father raised Jesus from the dead, He raised us all, too, and gave us new life... that's when we were born spiritually– when the Holy Spirit came to live in each of us.

"Jack, I had read the Bible clear through scores of times. I'd memorized whole chapters. I became a pastor, studied, took classes, and was taught personally every week by one of the most respected religious teachers in our area for years... and I didn't get it for a long time, because I didn't have a decoder.

"Even though I read in the Bible that Jesus was the savior of everyone, that we are all included, that God is love and Jesus is exactly like God... I had lots of questions, because in the Hebrew Bible– what we call the Old Testament– God appears to be completely different than Jesus. But we weren't allowed to ask questions. Or, at least, we had to accept the answers we were given or we were excluded. And many of those answers just didn't make sense.

"I don't know exactly how this works, but it seemed like when I was really ready to give up religion, because it wasn't working for me... when I couldn't accept that God was both good and bad, and when I was really ready and open to hear the truth, that's when God just started opening the floodgates of His unconditional love, forgiveness, grace, acceptance, and inclusion to me!

"Fortunately, God sent me a book that started to explain that God was only good... there was nothing bad about Him and He wasn't like religious people had told me. So, then I got more and more books and then found other people who believed what I was learning... people all over the world, and I started researching and found out that the people in the first church– right after Jesus died... believed these things... and it all started falling in place.

"Those books showed me that God's grace: unconditional love in action... was my filter for reading the Bible."

Jack let out a deep breath and Fred wasn't sure if it was because he'd just overloaded him with spiritual stuff, but he thought it best to be still for a while.

Out Home

Finally, Jack broke the silence. "I've never seen anything like this! Our trees in Texas never looked like this and I was never in Lawrence this time of year, but I guess I'll get used to it now..."

As Jack's voice trailed off, tinged with the ever-present sadness that his life as he once knew it was gone forever, Fred paused a moment before saying, "You'll spend several more fall seasons with us, Jack... but you'll never get used to the magnificence of this beauty. We seem to forget about it for 11 months and then, suddenly, it surprises us again. It's like having a cherished old friend show up unannounced."

Eventually they turned off the two-lane blacktop onto a dusty gravel road that led ever deeper into the woods. Jack was thinking there was surely no place like this in south Texas.

They came out of the woods as the gravel road turned to cinder and seemed to cut through farm fields. On the right, the corn was high, maybe two feet higher than the top of the car. In a few weeks, giant green John Deere corn pickers would level the growth, the stalks would be used to feed cattle, and the husked corn shelled and sold at the local co-op.

On their left was short, golden stubble where wheat had been cut a few months ago. It would soon be plowed and next year's crop would be planted.

After a mile, they came to a nice, rustic lodge. Fred stopped the Really Is to tell his grandson what this spot represented.

"Jack, when I was your age 60 years ago, my grandparents

lived in an old, white farmhouse on this very spot. I spent a lot of time here, especially in the summers. There were barns and out-buildings over here to the right. They always looked to me like they were about to collapse but they never did. This windmill sets atop their well where we got our water.

"My grandfather had an old, green John Deere tractor that he kept by a shed over there, and he had a big gas tank that a delivery man would come by and fill up every few weeks.

"My grandmother was born in the old house and when she got married, her parents, my great-grandparents, gave her this house and farm. They moved to another farm they owned which was a few miles from here.

"Over to the left were chicken houses. She never had less than 600 chickens and they ran everywhere. I would go with her to gather eggs. Every Saturday we'd go into town and take dozens of eggs, fresh fruit, and vegetables from her huge garden, berries and nuts from the orchard, and sometimes fresh meat, and they'd sell all that from the trunk of their car. Then we'd go to the stores and buy what we needed… which was not very much, since they grew or raised about everything we ate!

"My Mom grew up here and moved into town when she and my dad got married. Whenever she'd talk about coming here, she'd say, 'We're going out home.' After her parents died, my folks sold the farm to some sportsmen who built this lodge and they still use it when they go hunting and fishing. I know them and they give me permission to come out and hunt and fish whenever I want."

He started the car again, drove a little further west where the gravel road ended, and turned to a well-worn dirt road with high ruts. After turning into a grass lane that led to a padlocked gate, Fred opened the combination lock, drove through, and fastened the lock again. They drove through a rough field for about a mile and stopped a short distance from a picturesque lake lined on one side by an abandoned railroad track and otherwise surrounded by beautiful trees. This could be a picture in one of his U.S. Geography books at school, Jack thought.

"Shhhh…" Pops whispered, motioning for him to walk towards the lake. As they climbed up the side of the elevated, former railroad grade, he pointed to a small island in the lake that was surrounded by a large flock of geese.

The white-haired, 70-year-old man sat down and motioned for the 10-year-old to do the same. Without talking, they watched the geese paddle rapidly, dive underwater, then come up eating something. Jack guessed they were small fish. Occasionally, their piercing squawks would jar Fred and Jack from the peaceful tranquility of the moment.

Jack broke the silence with, "I miss Dad…"

After a deep breath and long exhale, Fred replied, "I do too, son."

In some ways it seemed like an eternity, but was actually now just short of two months since Fred Jr. and his wife, Rachel, had tragically died while rescuing people from housetops during Hurricane Harvey's flood of Houston.

"Pops, did God take my parent's lives to punish them… or me?"

There was no pause this time as Fred emphatically said, "No! Never! What made you think that, Jack?"

"Well, you know I went to that church youth group deal with my friend Wayne last Wednesday night and when the leader found out why I'd moved here, he said that's probably what happened."

"I thought you seemed worried when you got home that night. Did he say anything more, Jack?"

"He said there must have been a lot of sin in somebody's life that God had to punish and that God was probably trying to teach me something. He told me that if I didn't want to go to hell and be tortured forever, that I needed to ask Jesus to forgive me all my sins, then join their youth group and stop my evil ways and learn how to please God. What should I do, Pops?"

"I think you should stay away from that place! Jack, you know that's not what Nana and I believe… and I'm glad you're learning what your dad and I talked about and started learning right here on this very farm, when we used to fish right where we're sitting now.

"You know that even though I was a pastor, I still believed lies like you were told in that group. I didn't know any better. Your dad went to church with me and Nana, and we started to question things, but we didn't know where to turn to get our questions answered. Questioning is often not allowed in religious settings.

"We believed in God, although we didn't really know what God was like then. We also liked the people at church and we liked doing things like serving meals to homeless people, but our whole deal was based on trying to keep people, including ourselves, from being brutally punished by this angry god who had to get revenge when people disobeyed him.

"But as I thought more and more about grace and looked at Jesus' life and looked at verses that said God is love and He is for us, I started thinking… that just doesn't fit with the concept of an angry god who didn't really like being around us and whom people should be afraid of. It didn't seem to make sense any more.

"About that same time, your dad was especially concerned when he saw how badly some of his friends, like Coach Goldman, were hurt by the lies of religion… like you heard at that youth group last Sunday evening. He wanted to know the truth. So, he and I would talk about it a lot, many times right here at this lake, like we are now.

"We learned some things, and then after he graduated from high school, he decided to study and do research to find out where these lies started. He wanted to know if Christianity had always believed these things, or if it started out right and then got off track.

"As you know, he went to college to become a music teacher, and he was a really good one! He was so looking forward to starting you on trumpet this year. But, more than music, his passion was finding out what God was really like… he just couldn't believe that God was both good and bad."

"What does that mean?"

"Son, remember how I've told you before that you'll hear well-meaning, but misguided and misinformed religious people say, 'God is good… all the time! He loves you.' Then in the next sentence they'll continue, 'But, if you don't do your part to please Him, get right with Him, and stay right with Him, He will burn you forever in hell for all eternity.'"

"That's mean! That can't be good!"

"Your parents made sure to always tell you the truth about how good God is… and to protect you from hearing lies about God. That's why they kept you away from religion and taught you themselves. But they knew that, one day, you too would hear the lies. Your dad left me a letter stating that he and your mom didn't want anyone talking to you about lies like that."

"But… they're not here now…"

"No, Jack, they aren't. But Nana and I are. And, your dad left something for you. He had been working on a book for you that was to be one of your presents for your birthday tomorrow. I've been waiting 'til your birthday to give it to you."

"What's the book about, Pops?"

"He called it, 'Don't Believe the Fake News!' He wanted you to be able to see the truth about what God is really like. He wanted you to know how good God is, how much God loves you… and how much He loves all people. He wanted you to know that everyone is part of God's family, but most people don't know that yet."

"Oh, he said that to me all the time, especially at night before I went to bed."

"Jack, your dad did the research that proved what I always suspected was true, but never took the time to study and find out. He learned what the people and leaders of the very first group of churches believed… the church that started right after Jesus went to the cross for us all.

"He learned that for the first 400 years or so of the church, the people really knew what God was like… that He was all good and there was nothing bad about Him. They knew Him and talked to Him even after He went back to heaven. Their lives changed so dramatically and they were so different from religious people that people wanted what they had and their groups grew and grew and grew, even in the midst of having horrible things happen to them.

"Most of the horrible things done to them were by religious people who needed their congregations to be filled with people who were scared of God and who would come every week to hear about how bad they were and how they had to try harder to please God… and of course, give at least 10% of their money to the church– they called it a temple. They said their religion was the only way to please God and that everyone else was excluded from Him.

"But these first Christ-followers knew how good God really was and how He loved everyone. They knew that Jesus loved everyone, that He was the savior of everyone, and that God accepted and included everyone… that we were all in His family. They called that good news. Our word 'gospel' simply means good news!

"Then, after about 400 years, some misguided people, in an attempt to make people behave right, started perverting the truth. They started organizations that paid them good salaries, and they started teaching 'fake news'– lies to control people and get their money. It was religion all over again. Sadly, that continues today."

"So, Pops, are all churches and their leaders bad people?"

"Oh, no, Jack! Not at all. They're good people, well-meaning people. They love God. They sincerely want to serve Him and do the right thing. They have just believed the fake news, the lies that people before them believed… and most of them are in the dark. They've never questioned what they've been taught… even though it doesn't make sense to them.

"They think they know things about God… things that actually aren't true. They believed fake news about a fake god. But, as Jesus said to religious people about 2,000 years ago, none of them know the real God, His Father. Only Jesus knew what He was really like, and Jesus started telling them. He came to dispel the fake news and tell them the Good News.

"Jesus loved those religious people. God surely loves them. I love them. Your mom and dad loved them. Your dad really wanted to help them. That's why he read, studied, and did so much research. That's why he wrote his little book… to help them, and especially to help you!"

"Is it a long book with a lot of big words? Maybe I should wait until I'm in college or something to read it."

"Your dad wanted to make it easy to understand, Jack. He wanted it to be so that fifth graders, especially sharp ones like you, could get it. So, he made it so that you could just read a little bit at a time and think about it and ask God to show you if it's true or not."

"I know my dad talked to God a lot. I think He must have listened to God a lot too, because He was always writing down things God said to him and then telling Mom and me about it."

"He did listen to God, Jack! And we all can! Jesus called his Father 'Papa.' That's what your dad and I call him. Papa talks to us all the time… and He always encourages us. He never puts us down, condemns us, shames us, or makes us feel guilty in a bad way."

"That's what Dad told me!"

"He was exactly right, Jack. I'll give it to you tomorrow on your birthday, and then maybe we could start reading it together. That sound ok?"

"Sure!"

Jack was excited to see something his dad had written and Fred knew that Jack was continuing on his greatest adventure ever– knowing the only true God, Jesus's Papa.

They made their way back to the convertible, hopped in, and Fred burst into singing the last phrase of the state's official song, "And the skies are not cloudy all day!"

Turning Eleven

Fred knew that all birthdays were special, but that some tended to be more meaningful than others. Turning 21, or 40, or 65 were meaningful milestones for he and his wife and he remembered fondly how turning eleven had special significance for his own son years ago.

He noticed that his grandson Jack, like his dad, was becoming a little more independent. He had chosen a band instrument to get started on. He was noticing girls in a different way.

Eleven can be momentous year for many boys, and it certainly was for Jack Miller. He found himself thinking often about this being his first birthday without his parents. That alone was memorable. Because of their sudden demise, it was his first birthday living with his grandparents in a new city.

It was his first birthday apart from his childhood friends in Houston, and his first with his new friends in Kansas. During the course of his special day he thought about all these things.

While the great sadness was never far from the surface of his thoughts, he also looked forward to the party that Nana and Pops had planned for him.

The party– at Jack's request– was at a local arcade. After an hour's worth of enjoying various video games, ping pong, foosball, a variety of pinball machines, and carnival-type games of chance, the group of boys had birthday cake and soft drinks at the arcade.

Jack got some fun presents from his friends and his grandparents had a cool party gift to give each of the other boys.

Then the three Millers made it back to their home and were welcomed by a lonely Mikey who, as always, became instantly happy upon seeing his family.

No one was hungry, but when asked, Jack was ready for his presents. He was thrilled to get a "limited access" cell phone, an envelope with tickets for him and a friend to go to a KU basketball game, and some new clothes.

He caught on to the nuances of the cell phone quickly and was very appreciative of the day with his friends and all his gifts, but he was most interested in getting the promised book from his dad. Not wanting to seem ungrateful or rude, once he sensed that the regular presents were complete, he said, "Hey, Pops…"

"I bet I know what you're gonna ask. You'd like to get the book from your dad that I told you about, right?"

"Yes, sir!"

Fred went to his office and came back with a 6x9 paperback book with the title "Grace Is…"

Jack took it in his hands like it was a delicate piece of fine china. Opening the cover, in his dad's handwriting, he read the following:

To my son, Jack: *I reckon it's about time you started learning to see what really is! In order to do that, you'll need to understand what Grace Is. This book includes a lot of what I've been learning the past few years. It's taken me a long time change my mind about all the fake news I had learned from religion! This isn't really a kid's book. It's for a bright, inquisitive, sensitive, compassionate young man. That's you! ~Love, Dad.*

Jack's eleven-year-old heart was swirling with a mixture of sadness, joy, and anticipation as he leafed through the pages. His grandparents watched with similar feelings.

"Thanks for everything today, Nana and Pops. I really appreciate all you do for me. I think I'd like to go to the man-cave for a while if that's all right."

After hugs all around, the birthday boy, with his ever-present Labrador, sketch book, cell phone, and new book from his dad, bounded out the back door and into the man cave.

Chocolate Covered Faces

Emotionally and physically exhausted, the 70-year-old grandparents settled into their favorite living room chairs. Fred had poured them each a glass of Merlot and they sat in silence for a while, both lost in their own thoughts.

"He seemed to have a good time today. Don't you think, honey?"

"I think so, Suze. It was obviously bittersweet, as are a lot of things in this era of our lives, but all things considered, he seemed to enjoy all the boys and the games."

"Don't sell yourself short, Chief Warrant Officer and planner extraordinaire. You made sure all the boys were included and everyone got their turns at the popular things."

Lifting his glass and touching hers, he said, "Well, here's to a long continuation of pretty good teamwork, my dear."

After unplanned naps, watching recaps of various football games on TV, and some busy work, they eventually decided they should check on Jack.

"He's been up there a long time, Fred. Shouldn't you go and see how he's doing?"

"Why don't we call him? Let's make good use of that present."

Jack was startled at the ring of his new phone and after a brief moment of forgetfulness, he remembered how to swipe the appropriate pop-up and said, "Jack Miller speaking."

Fred smiled as he remembered how his son always answered in a similar manner. "How's it going, Jack?"

"Good."

"Whatcha been doing?"

"Uh, I've been sketching something I thought about from Dad's book."

"Cool! How 'bout you and Mikey coming back to the house now and we'll have a snack before we hit the hay?"

"Could I stay just a little longer, Pops? I've got this idea that I want to finish before I forget it."

"Do you remember how to set the alarm on your phone?"

"Yep."

"Well, set it to go off in twenty minutes and then come on in. Will that give you enough time?"

"I hope so."

"Ok, see you in twenty."

Fred turned back to his sports show and about twenty minutes later, the boy, dog, sketchbook, and cell phone arrived promptly.

"I'm proud of you for coming at the time we agreed on, Jack. That habit will serve you well in life, just like it did your dad. How do you like his book?"

"When I read it, it sounds just like him talking! I remember the way he said things and all. Pops, do you think I'll ever forget what his voice sounds like… and Mom's?"

"No, partner. I still remember what my mom and dad sounded like, and they've been gone a long time. Besides, we have some old family videos and we'll get those out one of these days."

"I'd like that, Pops."

"Now, how 'bout showing me and Nana what you drew."

From the kitchen they heard Nana say, "I'm fixing oatmeal raisin cookies and chocolate ice cream. Why don't you guys bring the sketchbook to the table and we can look while we eat?"

Before he opened his sketchbook, Jack wanted to explain what he had been thinking. "In the beginning of Dad's book, he wrote about dancing and how he liked to play with his band for dances and watch people have a good time as they moved around. He said that God is like a dance."

"He talked about Papa, Jesus, and Sarayu doing this circle

dance that was always full of motion and how there was love going around all the time and how much fun they had. He called it 'joy.'

Fred and Susie both smiled from their own joy in seeing Jack's understanding of God.

"He said that we could think of God as not just dancing, but as God being the dance. I thought that was cool. So I drew this:

"Wow, Jack! That's great!" His grandfather exclaimed.

"Yes it is!" Susie genuinely complimented him. "I think you are really starting to see what really is!"

"So, Jack, how do you see knowing about God's dance and the three of Them including you in it affecting you in the things you do?"

Looking at his grandfather like he was thinking: it's so obvious, don't you get it? Jack said "Well, if I know They're always here with me, even though I can't see Them, and if They're God and powerful and all that, and if I'm with Them, that means that no matter what happens, it's gonna be ok, because we're all together. Don't you see that in the picture? Look…"

As they looked closer, Fred and Susie could see nine distinct images in what seemed to be perpetual motion. They each counted again and again came up with nine.

"Jack, you're gonna have to help this old man here, what's the significance of nine?"

Again looking at his grandpa like he wanted to say 'duh' but didn't, Jack started counting with his fingers one at a time: "Papa, Jesus, Sarayu, Mom, Dad, me, you, Nana, and Mikey… don't you see? We're all together and happy and dancing and all that… just like you said we will be one day."

Both Pops and Nana used their napkins to wipe away tears of joy, and for the moment, had no words to express their happiness at Jack's vision of love and community.

The corners of his mouth started to form a little smile that soon turned into a big grin as Jack looked back and forth at his grandparents. Eventually the smile turned into a laugh that wouldn't stop.

Wondering what in the world he was thinking, Fred and Susie turned to look questioningly at each other and then they saw it. They both had smudges of chocolate under their eyes where they had wiped away tears with napkins that they'd previously used to wipe chocolate ice cream from their lips. They looked like football players ready to play under the lights.

Now they were all three laughing so hard they were crying even more. Fred couldn't resist. Using his fingers, he wiped some more chocolate ice cream on his face. Jack joined in and pretty soon even Nana looked like a clown.

Mikey ran around the table barking, wagging his tail, and wanting in on the party, too.

After a while, the hilarity subsided and Susie said, "Oh, my. I wonder what Jesus, Papa, and Sarayu were doing while we were doing all that!"

Without hesitation, Jack said, "I think they were wiping chocolate on their faces too!

Uncovering Fake News– The Biggest Lie of All Time

After their big birthday celebration, the Millers slept in the next morning. Once they'd eaten a late Sunday brunch, Susie suggested that the guys and Mikey take advantage of the Indian Summer they were having by going for a ride in their convertible. Fred knew without her having to mention it that she could use some alone time, besides, he was always up for an adventure with the top down.

They'd just pulled out of the lane leading to the Grace Community when Mikey, as usual, stood on his hind legs, front paws on the side of the car, ears flapping in the wind, tongue hanging out, and tail wagging as if to say, "this is what I've been waiting for!"

"I sometimes wish I could do what Mikey does. Wouldn't that be fun, Jack?"

"Uh, actually, I never thought about that, Pops…"

"Oh, well… seems like it would be fun for me," Fred smiled. "Where you want to go, partner?"

"Could we go down to the river? Sometimes when we've driven over the bridge downtown I've seen people on the path by the river bank and it looks like a cool place."

"Let's do it!"

Fifteen minutes later, they parked the Really Is next to a variety of vans, pick-ups, sports cars, and old beaters in a gravel lot between the railroad tracks and the Kansas River. They joined a kaleidoscopic group of families, singles, college students, couples, various dogs, and little kids all enjoying the beautiful afternoon and idyllic riverside park.

Jack wanted to explore the paved nature trail that followed the river bank for a couple of miles until it reached the downtown Vermont Street Bridge. There was a dense wooded area with huge old trees from the path to the railroad tracks about a block's length to the south west… a perfect area for Mikey to explore.

Fred groaned after a few minutes when the pooch came back soaking wet and generously covered with mud from an inlet that he had frolicked in.

"What's the matter, Pops?"

"I was just picturing what the back seat of my convertible will look like after Mikey's been there on the way home."

"Oh. Yeah..."

Fred resolved not to let it spoil his, or Jack's, afternoon. He trusted Jesus to work it all out for the best and decided not to even try to restrain the dog... not that he could have anyway.

They enjoyed watching some large fish feeding close to the shore and swans and geese landing on the water– foraging and then flying off to greener pastures. Occasionally, other birds and wildlife would catch their eye as well as the wonderful maple trees still carrying some strikingly beautiful red, yellow, and orange leaves.

After traversing about a mile and a half, Fred suggested that they sit on one of the benches and rest a bit. They made sure Mikey stayed close by.

"What's that big building just past the end of the bridge, Pops?"

"That's the newspaper. It takes up about a city block. Been there since long before I was born. The part we can see is fairly new, but they've printed the news there for about 150 years."

"Do they print fake news?" Jack asked.

"I'm sure they have, Jack. But probably not intentionally. They do a good job. Most people wouldn't print or pass something along if they knew it was fake, and newspapers have reporters who research things and try to make sure they get the truth."

"My dad sure found a lot of fake news about God, didn't he?"

"Yes, he sure did."

"Where did that all start, Pops?"

"Ah, that's a story. How much time do we have?"

"Maybe you could give me a condensed version, Pops." Jack wasn't sure that was possible, but he was interested.

"In the very beginning of the Bible, we learn about the first people God created. Remember their names?"

"Adam and Eve?"

"Yep. God created them, and all of us, in His image. You know God exists as the Father, Jesus, and Sarayu. So even though God is really a spirit, He created them with His attributes– to be like Him. And they were.

"They were with God all the time and everything was perfect.

Everyone got along, nothing went wrong. They had fun and it was great!

"And then evil came along and lied– gave them fake news. The Bible said evil was in the form of a snake… who, in effect, said that God was holding out on them. It said God wasn't as good as they thought. It said they couldn't trust God. That was fake news and they believed it."

"Could the snake really talk, Pops?"

"I don't know, Jack. Some people think everything written in the Bible is literally true, and other people think that some things were stories that were told to make a point. The stories may not have actually happened, but the message they tell is true. A lot of the stories that Jesus told were like that.

"Jesus told a story about one man having a log in his eye and another having a little speck in his eye. We know that's just a story that He used to make a point."

"How do we know the difference?" Jack wondered aloud.

"We don't, always. We look at other parts of the Bible that talk about similar things. We look at history– writings and documents that archeologists have found from the same era. We look at how other people have interpreted things in the past, and most of all we ask God to explain things to us.

"The Bible was never intended to be a history book, although there are historical things that happened that are recorded in it. Some line up with other historical records, others seem to be more general.

"The Bible was never intended to be an 'owner's manual' with rules and do's and don't's about how to live. Although there are things we can learn to put the odds in our favor that good things will happen, there's no guarantee. All kinds of things like weather, other people's decisions, accidents and the like can thwart even the best laid plans."

"Like hurricanes?" Jack asked, knowing the answer.

"Yeah… anyway, the Bible was never intended to be a theology book that lays out all the doctrines that a person should believe. Common sense shows us if that was the original intent, it failed miserably because there are over 40,000 denominations and tens of thousands other individual churches and ministries who each have different ideas about doctrine!

"The Bible is a love-letter from God to us and its sole purpose is to show us Jesus and His unconditional love, forgiveness, grace, acceptance, and inclusion for all people. The Bible says that Jesus is the exact representation of the Father God. Jesus said that if we'd seen Him we'd seen the Father. The Bible all points and leads us to Jesus and His love.

"Everyone who has an interest in God and who reads the Bible has ideas about God. Most of those ideas we get come from someone else. Many Bibles have notes on each page that explain what the passages mean... in someone's opinion. There are hundreds of translations and versions of the Bible, and then each translation can be published by different groups that each have their own idea of what things mean. It can really be confusing.

"What's worse is that most of those groups who have their own way of interpreting the Bible believe that they are right... and everyone else is wrong!

"So what each of us has to do is listen to Sarayu, the Holy Spirit of Christ, who lives in us and who talks to us, and ask what is right and what is wrong. I also find that we virtually have to decide on some very basic issues that we then use as sort of a filter to read the Bible through."

"Like what, Pops?"

"Well, you know that your mom, dad, Nana, and I all believe that God is good, that He's for us– not against us, that He loves us unconditionally, that He's already taken care of our sins and taken care of our relationship with Him, and that there is nothing bad about Him. Since we have that mindset, or filter, then when we read the Bible and see it say something that could be contrary to that, we have to start asking some questions."

"What kind of questions?"

"Well, is that an accurate translation of the original words the Bible was written in? Has anything been added or deleted? Then what's going on in that particular situation, time, and place? Who was this written to and what did the writer want them to know? Is there some other meaning that people in the past have believed that is different from what it seems to say?

"I may look at several different translations of the passage, and see what other people have said about it. I look at the original Greek words and see how many different meanings they have that could be different from what the English translation is. Then I ask Sarayu to help me know what God wants me to believe about it. I'll know because something inside me resonates when something is true. That's Sarayu!

"You know that I'm a teacher, Jack. I teach people what I've learned about God, but I have no power… no human being has the power to help anyone else see the truth about what really is. The Holy Spirit is the only one who can reveal and verify what's true.

"Jesus said in John 8:12, 'I am the light of the world– whoever journeys with Me shall not walk in darkness, but will radiate the light of life!' And the moment you meet– actually discover Christ in you, you experience His life, His hope, His freedom, His joy in the midst of the darkness! You realize you are free!

"But as long as we believe fake news, then we think we are separated from God and that we have to find our way to God by doing the right things and not doing wrong things. We think God's love is conditional– that He only loves us when we do well.

"As long as a person believes the fake news, that they are separated from God and that God's love is conditional, limited, and exclusive, that person won't be able to see or hear love, grace, and the finished work of Jesus for them and everyone.

"Such a person will read the Bible and incorrectly see rules and regulations mandated by an angry, distant, detached, punitive, record-keeping god who is just waiting to punish and cast away people for not doing what he demands. At best, they will see Jesus as the good God who came to save us from the bad god.

"Fake news has made life really hard for most people, Jack. They believe horrible things about God that just aren't true.

"A long time ago, an old man named George McDonald said something like 'Many good souls will one day be horrified at the things they now believe of God… they can make little progress in the knowledge of God… while holding evil things true of Him."

"So, Pops, you're kind of like a teacher who teaches good news, not fake news. Right?"

"That's about the best description I've ever heard of what I do, Jack!"

Just then they were startled by the loud honking of a flock of large, colorful geese threshing about somewhere several yards away down in a marsh by a river inlet. Hurrying over to see what was going on, they found Mikey having the time of his life running back and forth trying to catch one of the big birds... but each would fly away before he could get to them.

"Here, boy! Come here, Mikey! Leave those poor birds alone!" Jack ran back and forth trying to catch his friend before he did any damage, and finally wrestled him to the ground. The geese settled a few more yards away. They apparently were used to such startling interruptions.

Fred filmed the excursion on his iPhone to show Susie when they got home, and the threesome thoroughly enjoyed their mini-adventure...even though Jack was now covered with dirt and mud from his pooch.

As they started to make their way back to the path, Mikey didn't want to leave a place where he was sniffing and exploring a little further off the beaten path. As they went to see what he was looking at, they found what appeared to be part of the foundation of an old building that was covered with a heavy undergrowth of vines, dried river mud, assorted plants, and pieces of ceramic or old pipes that had been smashed over the years.

As Jack explored the sight, he said, "Hey, look, Pops! Here's an old brick with writing on it. Let's clean it up and see what it says."

Moving back to the paved path where a river inlet afforded them easy access to water, they used sticks and little rocks to clean the brick to where they could read: Bell Brothers Piano Company. Lawrence, Ks 1893.

"I haven't thought about them forever! Back in the late 1800's, there were companies all over the United States that made big old upright pianos, Jack. Some were very ornate and pretty– and they all weighed a ton! I saw some of them when I was in school at KU. There was a store downtown called Bells Music.

"The owner was 90-years-old when I knew him and he had married Bonnie Bell, the only child of one of the Bell Brothers.

He and Bonnie never had any children, but they transitioned the piano manufacturing company into a store that sold new pianos, sheet music, band instruments, televisions, records, and record players... anything musical. I bought a new trumpet there once.

"He told me that the Bell Brothers had once had a big old brick building down by the river where they made pianos, but I never knew where it was. Now I know... it was right here!"

"But you can't even tell there was a building here, Pops... and we're quite a ways from that street up there. There should be a street here if there was a building, right?"

"Back then the streets weren't paved and the riverbank may have been in a different place, Jack. Rivers change their size and course over the years-mostly because of how much it rains and what we humans do to them.

"For example there have been some lakes created upstream that affect the river here, and as you can see over there, we have a dam now. It wasn't here 120 years ago. And in places like this where there have been different bridges across the river, sometimes the builders dredge out a place or force the water to go a slightly different direction.

"You know, this is a good example of how fake news can spread."

"What do you mean, Pops?"

"Well, it's probably been over 100 years since the Bell Brothers had a building here that made pianos. So anyone born in the last fifty or sixty years wouldn't have any idea it was ever here."

"Can you Google it, Pops?"

"Sure." In a few seconds, Fred started scrolling through links. Wow! I can't find anything! That proves my point!" What do you mean, Pops?"

"Well, a writer or historian or teacher could say, 'There have never been any businesses closer than two blocks away from the river at 6th and Kentucky streets in Lawrence.' They could insist that's true... because that's all they can see, there's nothing on the internet about it, and there's no one around who can remember anything different.

"But I know different. I know that's fake news, because I talked to Mr. Bell's 90-year-old son-in-law 50 years ago and he told me about the company. And you just found some bricks and the remains of the wall of their building... right here!

"Sometime I'll take you to the Watkins Museum downtown and I'll bet that maybe we can find some old pictures or writings or newspaper stories about the Bell Brothers Piano Company in 1893!

"OK, what was I talking about before I got so sidetracked?"

"Uh, fake news and the Bible, I think." Jack answered, not sure of the connection.

"Oh, yeah... I got carried away for a moment, didn't I?" He smiled.

"A whole lot of people believe the lie that God is angry, that He has to satisfy His 'justice,' He must punish people in hell paying back evil with evil, and that only a few people will ever get to heaven. But first of all, that's not true--it's fake news. Second of all, people didn't always believe that!

"A few people believed those lies when the first church started, but they were by far the minority... mostly former Jews who were reluctant to give up their religion. There were six major schools that taught the people who would lead the churches after the first generation died off. Only one of them taught that awful belief about God.

"It didn't really gain much traction until the 12th Century with a guy named Anselm who took the Greek legal system and incorrectly said that's what God's justice is like. Then in the 1500's, a European lawyer named Calvin made a very big deal about it, and it eventually became popular in America through a preacher named Jonathan Edwards in the 1700's.

"So starting in the 1100's, people were being taught this fake news, but they didn't have the internet or the ability to go to museums and libraries and read about what the church initially believed when it started and flourished for the first few hundred years. As a result, everyone started thinking that the lies were what people always believed. But it wasn't.

"Now, with the internet and the instant availability of writings of the leaders of the church for the first few hundred years, and with mass availability of books and letters from that era... we know the truth.

"But… it's very hard for people to give up what they, their parents, and grand-parents have believed was always true– just like with some of the Jews in the first church.'

"Once people hear that one thing in the Bible is not true and is different than they thought, they begin to wonder if they can trust it at all… and that's very hard for some people to handle.

"It would be like you having a history book at school that tells a lot of right things about Lawrence in the late 1800's and early 1900's, but also said no businesses were within two blocks of the river downtown. Once you found out that was wrong, you might say, 'If I believe that, then I can't believe anything else in my history book is correct.'"

"But, Pops, it might just be that one thing that was wrong but everything else could be correct."

"Exactly! So an honest person would go, 'Ok, now that I know God is good, is for me and everyone, is not angry and punitive… I don't have to throw out all the Bible. Instead, I can look at the rest of the Bible and see how it lines up with my new belief.'"

"That makes sense, Pops. So you're teaching people that they have believed lies and you're teaching them what has always been true… but they didn't know it?"

"Yep."

"Aren't people glad to know that God is good and He's not mean and angry and gonna get them?" Jack asked.

"Oh, Jack." His grandfather sighed. "Some are… and their lives have changed wonderfully because they can now trust the God they believe in. But… some resist the truth. They even call us hateful names and even try to hurt us. The hurting now is mainly by the words they say, but not so long ago, they actually burned people alive for teaching the truth."

"Oh…" Jack said thoughtfully. "But you continue to teach it anyway?"

"How could I do anything else, son? When you know that God is good, that God loves everyone unconditionally, that God has already forgiven all our sins and accepted and included everyone, that God is for us, not against us… how could I teach lies instead of the truth? Not only would I be teaching lies, but I would be discrediting and misrepresenting our good God who loves us all!"

"So you do it even when people are mean to you and say bad things about you?"

"Yes, Jack. People aren't the enemy. They just believe lies. The truth, Jesus's unconditional love, will one day set them free. I just want them all to be able to experience and enjoy that freedom sooner rather than later, because I know the damage it does to a person."

"Pops..."

"Yeah, Jack?"

"I'm gonna have to think about all this. I might want to sketch some things."

"No problem, Jack! Maybe when you're older and are interested in researching these things—like your dad did—you can read some of the books that he and I shared.

Realizing that was his cue that today's lesson was finished, Fred wisely put a cap on his teaching, tousled the boy's hair, and they made their way back to the convertible with lighter conversation.

All Good Things Come From God

Mikey was still filthy and caked with mud. As they got to the parking lot, Fred wondered what he would do with the dog and his prized convertible. As he was thinking, a college-aged guy approached him and said, "He's a mess, isn't he?"

"Yeah, not sure what I'm gonna do. I didn't plan for the possibility of having a river rat in the back seat on the way home!"

"I've got just the thing! We knew we'd have a lot of trash after our fraternity picnic, so I brought some 30-gallon trash bags. You can have a couple."

The young man ran over to his car and returned with trash bags. He stretched them out and tucked them in the right spots of the Really Is and said, "You guys are set!"

"Thanks, my friend!" Fred shook the boy's hand and expressed his genuine appreciation.

As they drove off, Jack commented, "That was good... getting that trash bag."

"Sure was. You know where that came from?"

"Uh, from that college guy…" Jack was starting to think his grandfather might be getting a little forgetful.

"Actually… all good things come from God, Jack. We're all made in God's image and everything good comes from God. It may seem like it's our idea or that someone else is just a good person… but in reality, anything good like that comes from Jesus motivating us to do just what He would do."

"I'll have to think about that, Pops."

"No problem, son."

After they got home, Fred had time to rest a little while Jack sketched and Susie got things ready for their Sunday evening Grace Community.

After dozing off for a bit, Fred was awakened by the sound of his cell phone ringing. At this time on a late Sunday afternoon, experience told him that someone was calling to say they couldn't make it to the gathering that night.

As he looked, "Unlisted" showed up on the caller ID, and Fred assumed it was a charity wanting a donation, but for some reason he chose to answer.

"Mr. Miller?" Fred couldn't place the voice, but it had a vague familiarity to it.

"I'm so sorry…"

Still groggy from his nap, Fred tried to gather his thoughts and really concentrate. Hadn't he received a call like this a few months back, he wondered?

"Who's calling, may I ask?"

Click. The phone went dead.

Trying to search his mind, he couldn't associate the vaguely familiar voice or think of any reason someone might need to apologize to him for.

Old Mack Donald

That evening they had another gathering with their friends. Soon, the adults went their separate ways and the three Millers (plus Mikey) were cleaning things up in the kitchen.

"You grownups got pretty excited tonight. I heard everyone

clapping and hollering and all!" Jack commented.

"It's hard not to feel that way when we are reminded about how good God is and how much He loves us and has done for us," said his Nana.

Then she asked, "What did you and the boys do?"

"We just hung out. I showed them some of my sketches. Oh… and I told them about Old Mack Donald."

"What?" Pops and Nana asked at the same time.

"You know, 'Old Mack Donald.' You told me that 'Old Mack Donald' said, 'Many good people will one day be horrified at the things they now believe of God… they can't really do well as long as they believe evil things about God.'

"You were really paying attention, Jack!" His grandfather beamed with delight. "His first name was George… George MacDonald… who lived over 100 years ago– so I guess we can call him 'Old' MacDonald, for sure!"

"So, how did that come in with your conversation with the boys?" Nana inquired.

"Well, Brandon was just talking about a sleepover he had with another friend– a guy from our baseball team… and they, uh… did something they weren't supposed to do. The other guy's dad caught them and made his son take his pants down and he whipped his legs with a leather belt. Brandon thought he was gonna get whipped too.

"Then the dad told them they should know that God is always watching them and He knows every bad thing they do and He has a book that He writes it all down in. He said that God has a really bad temper and if boys don't do what's right, that one day God will do much worse to them than whip them. The dad said he was whipping his son now to teach him to do right so maybe God wouldn't punish him so bad later.

"Brandon asked me if that was true and I told him God wasn't like that at all. I said that's fake. I told him what you said Old Mack Donald said… that one day we'll be horrified about the lies we believe about God."

"What did Brandon say?" Nana asked gently.

"He said he thought I was right and that his mom and dad were a lot nicer and didn't argue very much now that they knew about

God being good."

"And Robbie?" She inquired.

"He started to do that shaking thing with a strange look on his face when Brandon talked about his friend getting whipped… like he was remembering something bad. But I just put my arm around him and told him not to worry, that God wasn't like that and I didn't think his dad would do that anymore."

"Oh…" Susie and Fred said together.

"I don't think he will either, Jack. You are a really good friend to both of those boys. You and Jesus together are really helping them."

"Yeah" Jack said, matter of factly. "I like it when we do that. I think I'll go draw some now if that's okay."

"Go right ahead, we're almost done here. We'll be in later to tell you good night.

After Jack had gone to his room, Susie said, "My apologies for giving you a hard time about teaching theology to Jack. You seemed to make a real impression on him."

"That would have been Jesus" Fred said with a grin.

Part 6
An Unlikely Minister

Transitions

Jack's last semester in elementary school turned out to be a pivotal one regarding his young heart and mind's experience and acceptance of God's compassion. He was also learning about His unconditional love, forgiveness, acceptance, grace, and justice.

He and his grandparents were still heavy-hearted about the loss of Freddie and Rachel. There were often times when deep sadness would suddenly come over them, seemingly out of nowhere. Tears still dampened pillows at night.

As the brutal north winds, occasional heavy snow, and ice storms transitioned into warm, but still heavy, March winds and April showers, Jack's understanding of the way the only true God (as Jesus calls His Father) relates to us transitioned as well. He went from believing the lie that God is cold, distant, aloof, not involved, and always judgmental into experiencing the warm, personal, hand's on, no-condemnation relationship that brings new life in Christ just as spring brings new life to the outdoors.

He wasn't the only one for whom eternal hope sprang afresh that spring.

The Holy Spirit of Christ used Fred's weekly meetings with William Kelly at his confinement in the Douglas County Jail to resonate with the Holy Spirit in William. Hope eternal began to spring forth in what society's eyes would judge as a hopeless situation.

Rather than address William's upcoming trial (and the likely outcome of being life behind bars) Fred focused on helping Will get to know, experience, and enjoy Christ in him in the now.

At one such meeting, Will told his new spiritual mentor, "Fred, I've come to terms with the fact that I'll die in prison... one way or another. I got peace about that and I know that the moment I croak, I'll see Jesus face-to-face and all my guilt and shame and condemnation and mistakes will be gone. I'm sure grateful for that.

"I actually think it best that I stay in prison, 'cause I sure make a mess of things on the outside. At least I cain't hurt nobody no more in here.

"But sometimes I cain't sleep 'cause I worry about what's gonna happen with my boy, Pat. I ain't seen him for five months now. I don't know where he is or what's gonna happen with him. I worry about people hatin' him because of my screw-ups. I worry about him getting' in with the wrong people like I did. I worry about him gettin' hurt…"

"Listen Will, that's what everyone does. We all worry and there's one major problem with all of our worrying."

"What's that?"

"When you worry about something that might happen in the future, do you think about Jesus being there, being with your son, helping him as he goes?"

"Nope. Never give it a thought."

"Here's the deal, Will. Jesus, who is in you, is in Pat, too. He just may not know it yet… just like you didn't. And Jesus– God– lives in the present… what's happening right now. He's already taken care of your past and has your future in eternity taken care of too. Where He lives is in the right now… with us. So when you or I worry and come up with all sorts of things in our mind about what might happen… it can seem very real to us… but Jesus isn't in those scenarios… because they aren't real– they are just fantasies, make-believe.

"Will, most of the stuff we worry about never happens. And it doesn't do us any good to worry about it."

"So, what do we do?"

"A guy named Paul, the Apostle Paul, who was a murderer and did a lot of really bad stuff to people, met Jesus one day. God showed him that Jesus already lived in him. Paul had hated Jesus, made fun of the church, killed people, hurt people, and took their jobs away from them. He was 'bad' man.

"So Jesus had to take some time to get this guy, Paul, to start changing his mind about God and Jesus. They went away to a desert for a few years and Jesus started showing him the very things I'm showing you!"

"Jesus liked that dude!?"

"You bet! Then Paul learned how not to worry… and he had a lot to worry about! Like you, he was in jail and he thought he would die there… one way or the other. Some people who have studied that stuff, believe that his cell was a hole in the ground with no bathroom and no running water. The cell was shaped like an upside-down light bulb. They would lower his food down to him in a bucket. The dirt floor in the bottom of that hole was his toilet."

"Damn!"

"Yeah. And Paul knew he was probably gonna get the death sentence. So he worried. But Jesus taught him and then he wrote some words to help us. Open your Mirror Bible to page 324– that's the fourth chapter of a letter Paul wrote to a church over in Asia a long time ago.

"Philippians 4:4-8, 'Joy is not a luxury option; joy is your constant! Your union in the Lord is your permanent source of delight; so I might as well say it again, rejoice in the Lord always.'"

"Pastor Fred, I don't always know what all them fancy words means, but I do know that since you've been telling me about how good God is, I cain't believe sometimes how happy I am, even though I'm behind these bars… and know I always will be."

"I'm so glad for you, Will! And that's exactly what Jesus and Papa want for you. That's good stuff, my friend! Now, let's go on, 'Show perfect courtesy towards all people! The Lord is not nearer to some than what he is to others!'"

"Pastor Fred! I've been telling that to the other cons here… that God loves them just as much as He loves preachers and do-gooders and all. Most of 'em don't believe me, but a couple of guys are askin' questions and I read to them out of this here Bible, and they like it!"

"See Will… your life isn't over, you're just getting started in a new career!"

They both beamed… it was as if Christ, the Light of the world, was lighting them up real-time.

"Okay, verse six– this is where he talks about worrying: 'Let no anxiety about anything distract you! Rather, translate moments into prayerful worship, and soak your requests in gratitude before God!' What's that mean to you, Will?"

"I reckon he's saying not to get all worked up about somethin' that might not even happen, cause that takes your mind off of what's real, which is God bein' with me right here now. And when I tell God what I need, be thankful for what I already have... somethin' like that."

"Exactly like that, Will! Did you ever read the Bible or have someone teach you before?"

"Hell, no! I ain't never read no book, let alone the Good Book. Never was much for readin', I just couldn't understand nothin'. I never went to school much, and I finally quit after the 8th grade, cause I couldn't understand nothin' they was talking about. I didn't like them teachers and the kids making fun of me. I can hear 'em now, 'Billy's stoopid. Stoopid Billy." He looked down and sighed.

"Well I can tell you, William Kelly, that you are anything but stupid. You are understanding what you're reading in the Bible... which a whole lot of people aren't yet able to do!"

"I always thought if I just had a chance, I could do somethin'... but everybody always laughed and said, 'Billy's stoopid.'"

"No more, Will. Let's look at a couple more verses here before I have to go.

"Philippians 4:7– And in this place of worship and gratitude you will witness how the peace of God within you echoes the awareness of your oneness in Christ Jesus beyond the reach of any thought that could possibly unsettle you. Just like the sentry guard secures a city, watching out in advance for the first signs of any possible threat, your heart's deepest feelings and the tranquility of your thoughts are fully guarded there.

"What's that say to you, Will?"

"Says that when I think about Jesus and how He loves me and likes me... even though I've screwed up big time, I'm protected from those bad thoughts and worries just like I'm protected here behind bars from someone on the outside coming in and hurtin' me. It's like He's a guard over me... takin' care of me."

Fred wanted to burst out in praise. The Holy Spirit was revealing Jesus and deep truths to this unlearned man who had absolutely no religious training whatsoever.

"Just like Jesus to do that," Fred thought.

"Good! That's exactly it, Will. Now, here's the last verse for today– Philippians 4:8. 'Now let this be your conclusive reasoning: consider that which is true about everyone as evidenced in Christ. Live overwhelmed by God's opinion of you! Acquaint yourselves with the revelation of righteousness; realize God's likeness in you. Make it your business to declare mankind's redeemed innocence. Think friendship. Discover how famous everyone is in the light of the gospel; mankind is in God's limelight! Ponder how elevated you are in Christ. Study stories that celebrate life.'"

"I got to do them a few words at a time. Is that okay?"

"Sure. That's what I do, too."

"Okay, he's saying that when we know God's opinion of us… even a jerk like me… His opinion is so good it just blows you away, right?"

Fred nodded.

"There's some more big words there, but it means, believe God when He says I'm right with Him… and it ain't nothin' I done to get right with Him. Jesus had my back. He took care of it.'"

"Yep."

"Then He wants me to look at other people as friends… not look at them like enemies, or try to figure out what I can steal from them. And it looks like God is putting on this big show in the theater and He's shinin' the spotlight on each of us and we're all stars! I reckon if we stop to think about them things, we won't be wasting our time worryin'… is that kinda it?"

"That's exactly it!" Fred exclaimed.

Just then, the guard came to get Will and they each expressed their gratitude for being together again. As Fred made his way back to the outside through the myriad of sliding doors behind and in front of him, he kept thanking Jesus for this opportunity and kept thinking, Will could help a lot of people behind bars. Changed lives change lives.

What Did You Do Today?

That evening at dinner, as was their usual custom, one of the Millers would say, "So, what happened in your day?" After listening, another would say, "What about yours?"

When the question was posed to Fred, he mentioned some mundane things, then said, "I had a really good visit with William Kelly at the jail today."

"What was good about it, Pops?" Jack asked.

"I think I told you that I gave him a Mirror Bible a few weeks ago, and he really understands it! It's clear that the Holy Spirit of Christ in him is explaining things to him… and he's telling other inmates about how God loves them, too!"

Jack was certainly surprised at that revelation. Susie asked, "Fred, why are you surprised that he understands it? We've seen that happen over and over during the years– how the Spirit opens people's eyes and Jesus' light illuminates truth to them."

"Of course we have!

"So?" she quizzed.

"William told me today that he didn't go to grade school very often and the kids there called him stupid. He quit after 8th grade. He's barely literate."

"Oh, my…" she exclaimed. "And he understands the Mirror Bible. That would be Sarayu's work, wouldn't it?"

"No doubt."

Jack interjected, "If the kids called him stupid, he probably didn't want to be at school. I wouldn't. One time last semester, a bunch of kids younger than us– third grade, maybe– were laughing and pointing at a kid who dropped his tray. I couldn't see who the kid was, but they were calling him stupid. I felt really bad for him. If that happened to Mr. Kelly, that's part of his story, then, isn't it?"

"Good thinking, Jack."

"I bet he misses his son. Does he talk about him, Pops?"

"Yes, he does. As you might imagine, he feels like he's really let him down and he knows he'll never be able to make it up to him since he'll be in jail the rest of his life. He hasn't seen Will since the day of the, uh, incident."

"Could you help Pat go and see him, Pops?" Jack asked, hopefully.

"Hmm… that's a good question, Jack. I don't know if the system would let me be involved. Let me think about how to go about that."

Soon, Jack went off to sketch, Susie picked up a book she was reading, and Fred went to his office to pray. After feeling like he had clear direction from Jesus, Fred called Mrs. Belt, the school secretary.

'Pastor Miller' came up on her screen and she answered right away. "Hello, Fred. Is everything all right with Jack?" She had diligently kept an eye out for Jack, as she knew his situation and wanted to help her old friends however she could.

"Fine, Ellie. No problem. I'm not calling about him. Actually, I've been visiting William Kelly, Pat Kelly's father, in the county jail, and I think he would really like to see his son. I know he's in the custody of the state and in a foster home… I think in Topeka.

"I sure don't want you to overstep your bounds or ask you to do anything unethical. But if there's a way within the system that you could help me pursue, I'd sure appreciate it."

"So you've been visiting William Kelly. I wondered what's happening with him. There are so many rumors, you know… seems like a new one every day. Fred, I could see him and the man he clobbered through the office window… I still have nightmares about all the blood and people screaming and everything. Actually, if I'd have used my brain, I would have figured that you were probably trying to help him. Have you had any luck?"

"There's no luck involved, Ellie. Everyone has a story, you know. And after you dig a little and gain someone's trust, they open up to you and start telling you about their hurts and what happened to them when they were little… and pretty soon you can start to put the pieces together.

"He's not denying what he did and he knows he'll spend his life in jail… or worse. But God loves him and I'm trying to help him learn more about our good God."

"Well, if God could love William Kelly, then I guess God would be good… way better than me, that's for sure. Anyway,

I'll call some folks tomorrow and let you know what I come up with."

"I knew you would! Thanks so much, Ellie!"

"Pastor?"

"Yes?"

"You should know somethings about the boy... Pat Kelly. Of course, you can't ever say I told you."

"Of course."

"He's a very troubled little boy. He's in the fifth grade, but functions at a low first grade level. He has a lot of anger. Unfortunately, some of the other kids make fun of him, and that brings out the anger.

"Before he left here, one day he spilled his food at lunch and a bunch of third grade kids who didn't know him called him stupid and he flew in a rage and hit one of them. You know the rules. He got suspended and the other boy lost his recess for the day. Some things aren't fair."

"Excuse me, Ellie... did you say the other kids called him stupid?"

"Yes."

"Oh..."

"Those words can really hurt kids. Can't they, Pastor?"

"More than we can imagine, Ellie." Fred thought, almost overwhelmed with sadness.

"We called his parents to come and get him, but couldn't reach them. They aren't involved at all. They never came to parent teacher conferences, never responded to requests to sign forms like for field trips... so Pat didn't get to do some of the things the other kids do. They never paid for books or meals.

"There were times when no one came to pick him up from school and a teacher or aide dropped him off. I had to take him home when he got suspended for hitting. They lived in that little run-down trailer park that's just on the edge of our school population boundary. We're all afraid to go in there, so we just let him out and hoped for the best. It just breaks my heart, Pastor."

"Sure breaks mine. You're a really good person, Ellie Belt. We've been through some things like this together over the years, haven't we?"

"We've seen some bad things, Pastor… but I never saw a murder a few feet from my office window…"

"I'm so sorry, Ellie. Can I pray for you?"

"You know you can, Pastor."

"Lord Jesus, You know Ellie. You live in her and You know the wonderful, tender heart that You gave her. You know how she cares for all the kids and how she works behind the scenes to help them all. Lord, help Ellie to know how much You love her… and all the kids. And Lord, help her to really know that You've got this… You're in charge and You're working it out for the good. Amen."

"Thanks. You really think something good is gonna come from this?"

"Already is, Ellie. I've seen it."

"I don't suppose you're gonna tell me."

"Not right now, but one day you'll know."

"Pastor, thanks for helping these folks… and me."

"Sure, Ellie. I'll look forward to hearing from you."

Fred ended the call, took a deep breath, let it out slowly, and prayed, "Jesus, as always, this is going to have to be you doing it all. I don't even know where to start."

I got it Fred. You're doing fine.

Evening Information

Jack went to school and Fred and Susie each had their routine for the day, but Fred stayed near the phone, thinking he'd get a call from Ellie Belt.

About 8 p.m. that evening, his cell phone rang.

"Hi, Ellie."

"Sorry I didn't call you during the day, Pastor, but I didn't want anyone else in the office to hear me… you understand."

"Sure I do."

"Well, Pastor, this is a little bit complicated. Mrs. Kelly is still in jail on the drug charges. She has two older kids by previous men, and they had Pat together. Each of the kids are in a different foster home. She's most likely gonna get a harsh sentence because she's a repeat offender who was on parole when this happened. In addition to catching her in the middle of a drug deal, when they searched her home, they found a large quantity of drugs for sale, weapons, and stolen items.

"Since they haven't been in their trailer for several months– or paid rent– the landlord, following the laws, confiscated everything the police didn't take, cleaned the place out, and re-rented it. There's no home for anyone to go back to if they could. Pat has been in three different homes since the incident. He's been in trouble at the schools he's gone to, and he's in danger of not being able to stay with the family he's currently with.

"There is a provision within the guidelines for a child in foster care to visit incarcerated parents, but there are several restrictions. The child has to want to see the parents and vice versa. Right now that's not the case with Pat or his mom.

"Then the foster parents or a case worker in the system has to facilitate everything. His current foster parents are wanting to get rid of him… not help him. The system is short-staffed and I was told that the likelihood of his, or any case worker, wanting to add something like this to their case load would be virtually nil."

"Wow. So we're at a dead end, huh?"

"Not exactly."

"What does that mean, Ellie, my friend?" She could feel his smile over the phone.

"There is a provision that an attorney involved in the case, or a licensed Pastor who already has jail clearance can intercede if all the parties are agreeable, and if said Pastor has a clean record— especially regarding any dealings with minors."

"Well, there's no problem on my part… but getting all the parties to agree–who would all the parties be?"

"Both parents, the current case worker, the child, the current foster parents, and then the parent who is requesting the visit has to be in good standing to receive visitors at the facility where he's incarcerated… and it has to be at a time the jail says will work within their parameters."

"Okay… where do I start?"

"Call the case worker tomorrow between eight and five. I'll give you the name and phone number." She did. "Write this down, too." She gave him the regulation and information regarding this "pastoral intervention" possibility.

"Fred, please don't tell her... or anyone... that I gave you this information. I would get in a lot of trouble."

"I know, Ellie, and I promise you I won't. Fortunately, I don't have to lie. We have what's called 'Pastor/Parishioner Confidentiality' privilege. Thanks, Ellie. This means a lot."

"I know, Fred. Thanks for helping these folks. They're fortunate to have you."

"Bye, now."

God Works All Things Together

Over the course of April and May, Fred Miller was amazed at the work of the Holy Spirit in the William Kelly situation. Just like dominoes falling one-by-one, Pat Kelly was moved to a new foster home in Topeka, where, as 'fate' would have it, the foster parents, Simon and Marianne Conroy, who previously lived in Lawrence, had attended Fred and Susie's church two decades ago. Now they had an eight-year-old son, Liam, who was in third grade at Shawnee Heights Elementary school.

They had remained friends and used the Millers as references when they decided to be foster parents. They were happy to have Fred, Susie, and Jack come to visit with them, and even happier to help with facilitating Will's re-connection with his incarcerated father.

The Conroy's had fostered numerous children over the years, at times thinking they might adopt one or more, but it had never worked out. Simon had a small house painting company comprised of several retired school teachers. The business afforded him some flexibility to help with special needs that came up from time to time in fostering.

The jail authorities facilitated Susie's initial and on-going visits with Mrs. Verna Kelly. While she wasn't yet as receptive to spiritual things and often cancelled meetings, she did want to see her son again. Susie was able to get her to sign the consent form, explaining that, in her opinion, it could help her cause if she also signed the form allowing Pat to see his dad.

Susie didn't feel compelled to relate to Mrs. Kelly that such a visit hinged on her own signature.

The case worker, who personally was appalled at the vicious and murderous attack by William Kelly on his victim, nevertheless, wanted to facilitate estranged family members in their attempts to maintain some sort of contact with each other.

Before broaching the topic with William Kelly, Fred waited until he had all the signatures and agreements in hand along with the assurance of the proper authorities that William Kelly was eligible for a family visit. Of course, he continued to visit William twice a week and from time to time they would converse about Pat.

Fred took Jack with him on a couple of occasions to visit the Conroy's, and he played with Pat and Liam in the spacious back yard.

They even had a group outing where the Conroy's and Pat Kelly met the Millers at the Kansas City Zoo and spent the day together. A good time was had by all.

The week after their trip to the zoo, Fred again made his way through jail corridors to meet with Will Kelley. After greeting each other, Fred asked a question that he already knew the answer to. "When's your birthday, Will?"

"It's tomorrow."

"I know getting out would be the best, but other than that, what would be the best thing you could ask to have for your birthday?"

"Oh, man… just to see my boy… to hug him and tell him how sorry I am for all this mess. But the odds of that would be just about like me gettin' outta this place. Ain't gonna happen."

"Will, Jesus has a birthday present for you."

Expecting to hear a Bible verse about something Jesus had done for him, Will asked, "What's that?"

"Two o'clock tomorrow, Pat's coming here for a visit. You get an hour with him in an open room– no looking through a window and talking on a phone."

Will stared at him with a totally blank expression for several seconds and finally said, "Don't mess with me, Pastor Fred. I thought I could trust you."

"You can trust me, Will!"

As Fred told him about various meetings with different people, including several times with Pat and his foster parents, Will started to believe, but still had a very concerned look on his face.

"What'll I say to him? After all I've done... and not done for him. After the way I've made such a mess out of everything... I don't know what I could even say."

"Will, you've told me how you've found yourself talking to other guys here about how much Jesus loves them and how He's for them... and you've told me you didn't know where those words came from. Remember, we both agreed it was Jesus talking... using your voice and everything."

"Yeah!" he smiled for the first time.

"Tonight you talk to Jesus. Thank Him for making this possible. Ask Him to talk to your boy, and He will, I know."

"Does... does he want to see me?"

"Yes. This was his choice. I've talked with him several times and made it clear that if he didn't want to see you, we'd drop it and you'd not even know it was a possibility. He misses you, Will, and he's scared for you."

"Man... I never thought I'd even get to see him again... 'cept maybe at my trial or something. I been thinkin' that's the last time I'd ever see him."

Will thought for a few moments, then said softly, "I cain't promise him nothin'. I cain't tell him I'll do better. I cain't give him nothin' to look forward to. I cain't..." Then the tears started to come.

Fred waited until his friend composed himself, then gently said, "Pat knows that. He just wants to see you."

"We ain't even got much stuff to remember. Most of the time I just let him run and did my things... which was never much good."

"Will, he remembers a time you took him to a carnival. That was fun for him. And he talks about when you went swimming with him in a creek, and when you played pinball machines with him. He remembers the good times, Will."

William Kelly was lost in thought with a faint smile on his lips when the jail attendant came to tell Fred that his time was up.

"Will you be here with Pat tomorrow, Pastor Fred?"

Too emotional to talk, he nodded his head yes.
"Fred… thank you."

'Stupid'… Again

That evening at dinner Fred explained to his grandson the details of what would happen tomorrow. While Jack had been to Topeka three times to meet Pat and his foster parents and their family, and gone to the zoo as a group, he hadn't spent much time alone with just the two of them.

"Nana and I will pick you up from school before lunch tomorrow, then we'll go to Topeka and pick up Pat and have lunch at Dairy Queen. We'll go to the jail then and you and Nana will wait in the receiving area while I take Pat to see his dad. When we're done, we'll take Pat back to Topeka and that will be it."

Jack thought for a moment and then said, "What will I talk to him about? The few times we've been together, Liam has been there too– along with you guys. I don't really know him very well and he doesn't say much."

"Why don't you ask Jesus about that tonight, and if you want, we can talk some more about it tomorrow?"

"Okay."

"Oh, and Jack, remember you told me that some time ago in the lunchroom that some kids called another little boy stupid and they got in a fight?"

"Yeah."

"That boy was Pat Kelly."

Jack and Susie both gasped as a myriad of thoughts went through their minds.

"I know you'd never call another kid stupid, Jack." His grandmother said. "Maybe knowing that about both him and his dad will help you better relate to him tomorrow."

"Yeah."

After doing the dishes, Jack went off to sketch while Fred and Susie watched the Royals, but mainly talked and prayed.

"How you feeling about this, dear?" Susie asked.

"Suze, it's been so obvious all through this that Sarayu is

moving things here and there and putting everything in place. I shouldn't be worried about anything."

"But you are."

"Of course I am! How about you?"

"The same. I know not to worry and to trust God. I can teach others that, but sometimes, you know…"

"I know…"

The next morning as Fred, Mikey, and Jack prepared to walk to school, Jack put his sketch book on the kitchen table and said, "Nana, would you be sure to bring this sketch book in the car when you come to get me from school?"

"Sure, I'll take care of it."

They made their way through the woods to the nature patch without much conversation, then Jack offered, "Pops?"

"Yeah, Jack?"

"I thought of something I could talk to Pat about in the car."

"What's that, son?"

"Well, I thought I could show him some of my sketches and tell him about them, then I thought maybe I could tell him that I know how he feels missing his mom and dad and all, and tell him that I miss my folks too."

"That sounds good."

"I've got a couple of drawings I could show him about how sad I get, but they also show hope and show how good you and Nana are and how much I like being with you. I could tell him that I hope things turn out well for him, too."

Tears were streaming down Fred's 71-year-old face and he was unable to speak.

Jack could tell they were tears of joy, and just said, "I knew we were gonna be ok when you were talking at Mom and Dad's celebration service. I was really sad, but I just knew we'd be ok."

Sensing their emotions, Mikey moved in between the two and took turns nuzzling their legs.

Fred tousled Jack's hair and put his arm around him for a moment and whispered, "Thank you, Jesus."

The morning flew by for Jack… not so much for Fred and Suzie. Their trip to Topeka was uneventful and they arrived at Pat Kelly's foster home a few minutes early.

Pat's foster parents were very happy for him to have the opportunity to visit with his Dad. Having the benefit of experiencing children visiting their incarcerated parents in the past, they were able to coach him about how it might go.

Jack made small talk with Pat and took him to the back seat of Susie's car. They had a quick lunch at a nearby DQ, loaded back up, and before they reached the I-70 turnpike going East back to Lawrence, the boys were talking and Jack was showing and explaining some of his sketches.

In twenty minutes they exited the K-10 loop around the West and South parts of Lawrence, then took the East exit that was just a couple of miles from the Douglas County Jail.

Neither of the boys had been to a jail before… although Pat had certainly heard about them as both his parents had been frequent guests of a variety of state and local correctional facilities. Many of his parent's friends had done some time as well.

Pat was apprehensive, but as he did in most every situation, tried to mask his true feelings with a gruff bravado and tough-guy projection.

After encouraging him, the three Millers escorted Pat to the massive front doors and entered in the stark concrete, tile, and steel edifice and proceeded to the entry desk.

"Hi, Pastor Miller. Good to see you again." The administrative officer said.

"You too, Barry. I have the appropriate signed documents here and I can testify that this fine young man is Patrick William Kelly." Fred slid a folder in the small opening of the protective bullet-proof glass window.

"We got our faxed copies this morning, but thank you for bringing these. Everything is in order. If you'll give us your I.D. and leave all other items with your family, you and young Mr. Kelly here can proceed through these doors."

Susie and Jack sat down on an uncomfortably hard metal bench and watched as Fred and Pat waited for the first set of heavy doors to open. The accompanying, very loud sounds of the remotely controlled doors enhanced the stark and repressive nature of building and situation.

They waited in the 4-foot square space until the first doors clanged and bolted shut behind them, and several seconds later, the identical set of doors opened in front of them. Then they passed successfully through a metal detector and each was given a visitor's badge. A young prison staff gentleman accompanied them through another half dozen double door locks, two separate elevator rides, and down a long, stark concrete and tile hallway. Surveillance cameras were conspicuously filming them everywhere where they went.

In a few minutes, they were led into a simple room that had three chairs and were told that they could have a seat.

Eventually massive doors at the opposite end of the room opened and a staff person escorted William Kelly, feet shackled, into the room.

Immediately Pat jumped up, and said, "Happy Birthday, Dad!" He ran to his dad, hugged him for all he was worth, and started sobbing. Overcome with emotion, Will lifted his boy up and held his face close to him and they both hugged and cried for several moments.

The officer stood guard at the now-closed door, and Fred was very aware that what appeared to be mirrors on each of the walls were actually two-way windows that held officers who were monitoring their every move should some attempt at a hostage situation develop. None did, but they had protocol to follow.

Fred opened the conversation by saying, "I'm really honored to be here with you two –jail rules required a responsible adult be with a minor on such visits, but unless you need to ask me anything, I'm just gonna move my chair over by the wall and let you two have this time to yourselves."

"How you doin', Dad?"

"Okay. You know I'm safe here and the food's okay and as long as you keep outta trouble, the law's nice to you. Not much trouble you can get into in solitary when you only get out for an hour a day... unless there are special visits like this.

"I'm ok, Pat, but you sure don't ever want to have to come here. Best to keep your nose clean and be out where you're free, know what I mean?"

Nodding his head, the boy said, "I miss you..."

"Yeah, me too. You okay with the people you're with? I hear

they's nice folks."

"They're good. The first four or five places I went to wasn't so nice. They was real strict and seemed like all they wanted was to make some money by having me there. But these folks, they's real good."

An awkward pause seemed to stretch a little too long, so Fred, praying as always, interjected, "Pat, you want to tell your dad about the trip we had with your foster parents to the Kansas City Zoo last Saturday?"

"Yeah. Dad, it was really cool! They had all these animals that made funny sounds and all."

Pat got more and more animated as he mimicked the actions and sounds of the chimpanzees, elephants, seals, gorillas, ostriches, kangaroos, and others. They both shared laughs and became engrossed in the experience.

After some questions about school, siblings, and general happenings, Will Kelly indicated that he had some things that were important to him for Pat to hear.

"Look here, boy. What I done was bad. Real bad. I never really meant to kill your ma's boyfriend, I just kinda went nuts. Been drinkin' and never should have been there anyway. But you know all about that. I did it and I'll have to pay the price for it and that means that we won't never get to be back like a family no more.

"I wish I'd done things different. I wish we'd had a normal family. I wish I'd done right by you. But I didn't… and I'm not gonna have a chance to make up for it now. I'd have to have somebody show me how anyway… never learnt how to do it right."

Pat listened silently as he stared at the floor. Occasionally he glanced up and saw his dad's anguished expression.

"I never knew how to love no one 'cause no one ever loved me. Least it seemed like that. My folks never knew no better. I never knew what love was 'til I got here.

"You know the Good Book says that all the time the Lord is doin' his thing when nobody can see Him. He's pulling' strings here and workin' deals there and workin' things out so different folks end up together.

"I wish I wasn't here in the slammer. But you know what? If I wasn't here, I'd still be doin' the same dumb stuff and nothin' would get better. But since I been here, I learnt somethin', boy.

"Fred here brought me this blue Bible. It's got a lotta big words in it, but that don't bother me none. I got this voice inside me, I call Him the Spook. It's like the holy ghost or somethin' like that… I ain't good with fancy words. But it's spooky, you know, havin' someone inside your head talkin' to you. He tells me what it all means and I been able to tell some of the other guys here.

"The deal is that God ain't nothin' like I thought. I had this idea that God was really ticked at me cause of all the bad stuff I've done. I thought there's no way in hell God could have the time of day for William Kelly. I thought one day I'd really be in bad shape cause I'd die, then God would make me pay big time. That's what I thought, boy.

"But looky here, now. Pastor Fred, he done told me the truth! He told me God loves me… Me! God loves me, even after all the crap I done. He told me God even likes me and that Jesus hung out with guys like me all the time and had a good time with 'em.

"Fred told me that Jesus done took care of all my sins. He don't even remember 'em no more! They's all forgiven. He told me 'bout grace. That means when you screw up, God don't punish you, instead He loves you and gives you good things and likes to hang with you.

"I know that now, boy… and I'm different. I don't even think the same way as before. Used to be I was always figurin' out how to swipe something from somebody, how to get to them before they got to me… always looking for the angle.

"Not no more! I ain't even interested in that no more! I can see that everybody's got a story. They all had stuff happen in their life that wasn't no good. They all hurtin'. And I see how God… He hurts right there with 'em. He's with people even when they mess up big time like I did.

"That's something else, boy… something else. So you listen here. Yer ole man loves you… I just never knew how to show you… didn't know what to do. But God, He really loves you and He knows what to do.

"He's right there inside you now, and if you start listenin' to Him, He'll talk to you "Especially cause He ain't telling me how bad I am and He ain't callin' me stoopid or nothin'. He just tells me how I'm His boy and He loves me and He's gonna take care of me no matter what and He ain't goin' nowhere.

"Look here, boy, that's what your ole man wants you to know. God loves you, too. Just like He does an ole screw-up like me. God's in you, too, and He wants to talk to you. Fred, here, he'll learn you how to talk to God and how to hear what He has to say. He loves you boy, and He ain't goin' nowhere, and He'll work things out for you, too, so you don't mess up like your ole man has.

"You got that?"

"Sort of. The foster people been tellin' me that. So has Jack... he draws pictures and stuff and he showed me some pictures of dead animals and stuff... and animals at the zoo, all behind bars, and how they want to get out and run and be free and how God helps us do that and teaches us how to stay out of trouble and get along. I... don't get along good sometimes..."

"Look here, boy! Yer on the right track. I never knew none of this stuff when I was a kid. Hell, I didn't know it six months ago!

"But you know what, one day, in the next life in heaven, you and me... we gonna be there together and we gonna be with Jesus and God and there's not gonna be any trouble and no one's gonna call us stoopid or nothing like that. Nobody's gonna rat on us for nothin'. It's gonna be all good. I don't know how, but it is!"

"Dad?"

"What?"

"Will Ma be there too?"

"I reckon she will, boy. And she'll be changed just like us. We'll all get along, boy!"

"What about Butch?"

"Who's Butch?"

"Ma's boyfriend... the one you took the bat to and killed him."

"I never knew his name. Pastor Fred says we'll all be there. There's a song about it in the good book. Tell us that, Fred."

"It's called the 23rd Psalm. It goes something like this: The Lord is my shepherd; I have all that I need.

"That means just like Will here in jail. He maybe doesn't have everything he'd like to have, but he'll always have all he needs.

'He lets me rest in green meadows; He leads me beside peaceful streams.'"

"That sounds nice, don't it, boy?" Will said.

"He renews my strength. He guides me along right paths, bringing honor to His name."

"That means God gets you back up when you get beaten down. When you start to go the wrong way, get in with the wrong group or somethin', God will guide you and show you how to get outta there and back on track.

"Even when I walk through the darkest valley, I will not be afraid, for God is close beside me.

"That's like with both of you right now," Fred said. "No need to be afraid, because God's with you and He's taking care of both of you.

"Your rod and your staff protect and comfort me."

"Pastor Fred told me that means that when someone calls you stoopid or tries to take somethin' from you, you don't have to go hit 'em. God's got your back. He protects you and takes care of everything. So you trust Him and don't go fightin' and you'll be better off, right Fred?"

Nodding affirmatively, Fred continued with the scripture, "You prepare a feast for me in the presence of my enemies.

"Here's what your dad was getting at. He and Butch were like enemies, right? Well in heaven, God's gonna work all that out so that people who were enemies before, are gonna be at this big party together and have this big feast and sit next to each other and hang out.

"You honor me by anointing my head with oil. That's something they did in the old days. My cup overflows with blessings. Surely your goodness and unfailing love will pursue me all the days of my life, and I will live in the house of the Lord forever."

"That means that God is gonna take care of you big time. He's good and He loves you and His love never fails, no matter what bad thing you do. You may have to pay the government for that bad thing… like your dad is here in jail, but God has forgiven him and blessed him and is good to him and God's love never fails. God never punishes you for bad things you do.

"You all, and us, and Butch… we're all gonna be in that great place forever and no one will cry anymore. No one will do any bad stuff. They won't need any jails then."

Fred looked up at the jail attendant and realized the man was really listening to everything he said and had a big smile on his face.

The attendant was a little startled at Fred looking at him, and he quickly turned away and checked his watch. Then he said, "Time's about up fella's. Two or three more minutes here."

"Ok, boy. I'm sure glad you came to see me and I got to see you. I'm sure glad!"

Pat hugged his dad and said, "Me too, Dad. I miss you."

They hugged for a while and then the door opened for the attendant to take Will Kelly back to his solitary cell.

He grinned at his son and said, "I'm 34 years old today… had 34 birthdays, and this is by far the best! Remember boy, God loves you, He sure does. So do I."

The massive doors rattled and closed behind him. Fred and Pat stood to face their doors and waited for them to open. As they started to walk through them, he felt Pat's hand reach up and take hold of his.

"Thank you, Jesus, for this precious little boy," Fred prayed silently.

Neither spoke until they were back at the front entryway. And Pat never let go of Fred's hand until then.

The foursome piled into the car and started out on the trek back to Pat's foster parents. After a brief silence, a little voice said, "Can you show me some more of them pictures?"

By the time they got Pat back to his foster home, Liam Conroy was home from school and the three boys went outside to play while Fred briefed the group on the day's happenings. Everyone was pleased and relieved that there were no challenges, and they were all especially encouraged by Will Kelly's new understanding of Christ's love, grace, forgiveness, acceptance, and inclusion for him and everyone.

Simon and Marianne also informed Fred and Susie that they would like to pursue adopting Pat, depending on the outcome of each of his parent's trials and the interest of any other family members.

The Millers encouraged them on their endeavor and assured them that they'd be supportive and helpful in any way that they could. They all knew there were a lot of potential hurdles to overcome.

On the way back to Lawrence, Jack asked to hear about the actual jail visit and Fred recounted as much as he could to his wife and grandson. They could see God's hand all over the event and the Kelly's lives.

Fred also explained that he had been in contact with Will Kelly's court-appointed attorney, a bright young woman whose intellect and enthusiasm helped make up for a great lack of experience. She was only two years out of law school and had never defended a murder case.

At Will's request, he was going to plead guilty, and there was no plan to plead insanity or mitigating circumstances to avoid prison. There was a slight possibility that since he was pleading guilty, and since he'd been drinking before the crime, that he might get a 2nd degree murder sentence, which would include the possibility of getting out after a number of years. He certainly hoped to avoid the possibility of being executed by hanging, which was the Kansas provision for 1st degree murder.

While Kansas law reinstated the death penalty in 1994 and the law was still in effect and there were currently 10 inmates on death row, no one had actually been executed since 1965.

However, for someone sentenced to death, there was always the possibility the winds of justice would change and executions would begin again.

After arriving home that afternoon, Fred was ready for a nap. Susie had some things to do before preparing dinner, and Jack was happy to play with Mikey in their spacious back yard… after wearing himself out with the "trusting axe."

He found his anger being directed at the unfortunate life situation young Pat Kelly had been dealt.

Summer Time

Jack graduated from elementary school the last Wednesday in May, but it didn't seem like a milestone event for him since he had only been at Windsor Elementary for a year.

He had seven customers for Miller's Mowing, baseball season was ready to start, and he enjoyed swimming at the downtown pool with some of his buddies.

Fred continued his involvement with the Kelly's. Mrs. Kelly was given 30 years in prison as a repeat offender, being a felon in possession of a weapon, a parole violator, and multiple other charges. She would be eligible for parole in 20 years.

As the court system worked through Mr. Kelley's guilty plea and his attorney's request for 2nd degree charges with a possibility of parole, the community had ample news to gossip about over the summer months.

Fred was Will's only character witness, and they were all pleased to get the desired verdict. Pat Kelly was at the sentencing with the Conroy's and was given a few moments to see his dad before he was taken away to the Kansas State Prison in Lansing to begin the next stage of his life. He could be released in 12 years or less.

Fred arranged in advance to line Will up with a prison ministry program and set up monthly visits. They stayed in contact with Pat and the Conroy's, who were working towards adoption. Since both parents would be in prison well past the time their son would be 18, and there were no other relatives in the picture, the possibility of adopting Pat looked promising.

Section 7
The Unforced Rhythms of Grace

Instrumental Change

Middle school was not as traumatic for Jack as it was for many kids, maybe because, after experiencing the trauma of instantly losing his parents the summer before 5th grade, most anything else life could throw at him would pale in comparison.

Of course he had some growing pains, some puberty-induced relationship issues, some insecurity with the change from elementary school regimen, but for the most part, it was uneventful.

He and Fred both missed their daily warm weather walks to and from school, especially the opportunity it provided for them to be with Mikey… his one great connection to his former way of life. But car-pooling with some friends was a good experience in its place and weekend walks were always a special treat.

'Miller's Mowing', Jack's lawn care business, proved to be just as good as Susie predicted when she first taught Jack how to manage his allowance money. Each year, he added a few new customers and by the time he started high school, he had 20 regulars. He saved most of the profits for a future car purchase.

Jack continued to play baseball in the summers, but he didn't try out for the school team because everyday practices and Saturday games wouldn't work with his other interests.

Fred was still able to play catch and teach the finer points of our national pastime to his grandson, even as he started his 8th decade. Susie came with Fred to all the summer games and they enjoyed the times afterwards at the Dairy Queen with other parents and grandparents.

Jack continued to draw, exhibiting and even selling some of his sketches at local art fair events. He maintained a special relationship with Mr. Garcia, his 5th grade art teacher, who worked privately with Jack and continued to encourage him to develop and refine his ability to express emotions in his art.

Socially, Jack's closest friends were those in the school band

and his baseball buddies. He also had an ever-changing group that came with their parents to the Grace Community.

While he enjoyed and excelled in playing trumpet, it was never a passion. His middle school band experiences were pretty much standard fare– a few concerts a year where the band played marches, show tunes, and watered-down versions of classical repertoire. He enjoyed playing in the pep band for sporting events, but wasn't particularly interested in the few times they tried marching in preparation for high school.

Then came his freshman year, the first in high school. He was in the marching band and enjoyed the games and trips out of town, but it still wasn't as wonderful to him as it seemed to be to other students.

He decided to try out for the jazz band and was thrilled to learn he was the only freshman to be chosen. He liked jazz much better than classical music, but still had a restlessness… something was missing.

Fred noticed that any time they had music playing at home or in the car, Jack was constantly drumming on some surface with his fingers and hands, and even moving his feet as well. He was full of rhythm.

One evening after dinner, he casually said, "Jack, have you ever thought about playing drums?"

Surprised, Jack said, "All the time! I wish I'd have started out on them. I can hear drum stuff in my head, you know, much more than trumpet stuff."

"Well, why don't you?" his grandfather asked.

"It's too late, right? I've spent a lot of Mom and Dad's money on lessons and music and my new trumpet I got last year. That would all be wasted, wouldn't it?"

"Nothing's ever wasted. God is always working out everything for the good. Every good gift is from Him. If He's given you the gift, talent, and ability to play drums, then do it… explore what He's given you and let Him lead you."

"Wow… I've *really* been wanting to. I think about it sometimes and wish I was playing drums, but I've kinda felt like that was selfish and wasteful…"

"You know, Jack, scripture tells us that God gives us the desires of our heart. You can look at that a couple of different ways. Most people take that to mean that if they really desire something, pray hard and long about it, work hard to do good and not make God mad at them, that He's sort of obligated to give them whatever it is they desire.

"I don't see it that way. God's not like a divine slot machine or like a big waiter in the sky that we can summon and coerce and work the system so that He has to come through for us... not at all.

"He's our friend, our loving Papa, and He delights in us. The way I understand it, the better we get to know Him, the more we experience and enjoy being with Him and being in Jesus's, Papa's and Sarayu's Divine Triune circle dance of love, joy, and everything good.

"And God, who knows all about us and how we're wired, He knows what we like and what fulfills us... He actually gives us... instills in us... the desires of our heart. I think God knew that rhythm, playing drums, and all that it entails, would be a wonderful thing for Jack Miller... so He put that desire there. That's what it means that, 'God gives us the desires of our heart!'"

"So I should be grateful that I want to play drums and thank Him for giving me that desire... and not feel bad for wanting something like that?"

"That's exactly right, son!"

"Wow!" he said as he became pensive and thought for a moment.

"Pops, what if I want something... that's bad... if I want something bad to happen to someone? Did God put that desire in my heart?" He knew the answer the minute he said it. "Never mind, I can trust Sarayu to show me, right?"

"You got it! Tell me, Jack, is there someone you want something bad to happen to?" His grandfather asked.

"Not someone real... but sometimes I think about maybe if there was someone who caused my folk's death... I have bad thoughts about them," he admitted, shamefully.

"Those thoughts are normal for us humans, Jack. I have them too. Don't feel bad about them or be ashamed. Shame only comes from the evil one... not from Jesus, Papa or Sarayu. Remember, there is no condemnation for anyone who is in Christ... and that's you!

"Any time we need help forgiving someone for anything, Christ in you... and in me... will help us, and most likely, we'll be amazed.

"Now, back to music, remember that you wouldn't necessarily have to quit playing trumpet altogether. Just because you have a greater desire, you may be able to continue there, just with less emphasis on it. Or, maybe you'll one day let the trumpet go. Either way is ok. How 'bout we talk to Mr. Williams about it? He's a great band director and he might have some insight."

"That would be great, Pops! What do you think, Nana?"

"Whatever you guys come up with will be fine," she smiled. But inwardly she was hoping that a drum set would surely be placed in the man-cave and not in her living room.

Mr. Williams, a drummer himself, had mixed feelings when Fred and Jack broached the subject. Even as a freshman, Jack was his best trumpet player in the high school band, and his director knew all too well that a great trumpet player raised the level of any concert band exponentially.

A pragmatist, he also knew that he had some other good trumpet players... but not a single good jazz drummer.

"We only have a couple of weeks left in this semester. Do you have a zero-hour scheduled next semester, Jack?" he asked.

"No sir."

"Well, we don't publicize this much, but we offer a class called Advanced Music Studies where serious students can come in an hour earlier than usual each day and work with me on whatever we agree would be mutually beneficial to the student in preparing for a possible music major in college.

"I'll agree to work with you on playing jazz drums. We have a set here you can practice on, and we'll see where it goes from there. But I would stipulate that you continue to play trumpet in the concert band for at least the rest of this year."

That seemed like a win-win-win situation to everyone.

At dinner that evening, the conversation centered around Jack's new opportunity. Fred gave Jack a list of some groups that had great drummers and suggested that he Google them, pick out some he liked, then study them.

After dinner that evening, Fred chuckled inwardly as he noticed Jack sketching a drum set while watching and listening to 311's drummer, Chad Sexton. It seemed he had an emerging passion.

Christmas is Coming

Jack couldn't wait for Christmas break because the three Millers decided to go to Houston for several days after Christmas.

The renters who had lived in Freddie and Rachel's house since their passing had just moved and the house needed some attention before new renters came in January. Fred and Susie thought Jack would enjoy staying a few days there and reconnecting with his childhood friends while they cleaned, painted, and touched up things.

Since the house was mortgage-free, Fred and Susie put all the rental profits along with insurance money from their truck in a special investment fund for Jack that he could one day use to buy a home, or for whatever he wished.

Jack had stayed in touch with his closest friends in Texas, and they had made plans to be together every day that he would be in Houston.

He was so excited about the trip that he didn't think much about Christmas and his Grandparents didn't mention it much.

On Christmas day they got up for a late breakfast and after cleaning up, they moved into the great room where the Miller's old artificial tree occupied its customary place.

He did notice that there weren't very many presents under the tree, but assumed that the trip to Houston would be his main present.

As per the Miller custom, each would find a gift with their name on it, then starting with the oldest, they would open them one at a time so everyone could enjoy the experience.

Jack had thoughtfully purchased a couple of nice presents each for his grandparents, and he received his usual every-holiday-gift sketch book, plus tickets for him and a friend to go to a KU basketball game. He knew those were hard to get and was very appreciative. He also got some new clothes.

"Well, that's about it for this Christmas... we have a lot of packing to do to get ready for our trip tomorrow, so we should get started."

Jack was a little disappointed in the paucity of gifts, but he kept focusing on the trip to Houston, which was a very big deal to him.

Fred spoke up, "Okay, I have some things in the work room that I need help in getting out and loading up. We'll need them to work on the house there. Could you two come and give me a hand for a few minutes?"

Not giving it a thought, Jack agreed. The three made their way from the back porch through the two-inch covering of Christmas snow they'd received a couple of days before and entered the barn/man-cave building.

When they got inside, Jack started for the tool room when Susie said, "You know, I haven't been up in the man-cave since before you came to live with us, Jack. Could we go up and you show me what you've done with it?"

Susie led the way up the stairs, and turned on the light to the spacious hang out. Fred followed on her heels... thus they were both positioned to see the full effect of Jack's surprise when his eyes fixed on a new six piece, pearl-white Slingerland drum set with bright, shiny Zildjian cymbals.

Mouth hanging open, eyes wide with surprise, the young man stared in shock for a moment before he jumped in the air and shouted, "Sweet!"

Now as tall as his grandparents, Jack embraced them both at once in a big bear hug and cried tears of joy.

"I had no idea! Actually, I was thinking our trip to Houston was my main Christmas present."

Moving behind the shiny assortment of ride, crash, and hi-hat cymbals, bass, snare, floor, and mounted tom-toms, he sat on the black leather throne, pulled a pair of sticks from the leather stick holder hanging on the bass drum and tentatively tapped on everything.

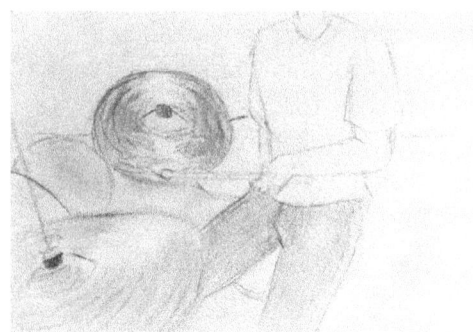

"Jack," his grandmother said, "I have one more gift for you."
He stopped tapping to listen.

"I'm giving you the gift of my absence so that you can have more fun with your new present and not have to worry about your grandma's ears." She smiled.

They both grinned as she hugged him.

"I'm with her. Have fun!" Fred said as the two took their leave.

"Wow," Jack thought as he wailed away for all he was worth. "This is better than taking the ax to the tree out back!"

Back to Texas

Early the next morning Fred picked up their rental SUV for their first trip back to Texas since Hurricane Harvey. With the three Millers, Mikey, tools, cleaning equipment, luggage, and a couple of coolers with food for the week, it seemed best to have a bigger vehicle that would also give them plenty of individual space.

Jack had a growing list of tunes featuring drummers on his play list, and spent much of his travel time listening, sketching, and playing with Mikey.

Fred and Susie enjoyed road trips together, taking turns driving, reminiscing, commenting on things they had been reading and watching, and generally enjoying each other's company.

Their two-day trip was uneventful. They spent the night on the south side of Dallas, had an early breakfast, and rolled in to Houston about noon.

After stopping for a fast-food lunch, they drove west to Conroe.

They were unprepared for the wave of sadness that suddenly encompassed the three of them as they entered Jack's former hometown. It was as if the "Hellish Darkness" descended with an unholy passion. Looking in the rear-view mirror, Fred could see the angst on Jack's face. Mikey sensed it as well.

Tears streaming down her cheeks, Susie reached over and grabbed Fred's arm, even as he was driving. He managed to pull off the highway and stop at the edge of a large parking lot while they regained their composure.

No one spoke for a few minutes. Finally Jack said "Let's go to my house" and they resumed the journey.

The last time they were here, the town was hardly recognizable. Signs had been blown down, cars were left overturned, boats were capsized in people's lawns… it was a disaster area.

Now everything was rebuilt and several new buildings seemed to be flourishing.

Along with his great sadness, Jack was a little disappointed that things weren't exactly as he remembered they were four years ago before the flood. And he was also anxious to see his boyhood home… he also wondered what his emotions would be when he saw all the reminders of his mom and dad and their family life pre-Hurricane Harvey.

Jack was clearly excited to see his old neighborhood and his despondent mood changed suddenly. He was ecstatic as they pulled into the drive of his former home. There was a big banner tied between two stakes in the front yard that said, "Welcome back, Jack!"

Someone had drawn stick figures of a boy and a dog and written, "You're not in Kansas, anymore, Mikey!" There were signatures of several of his old buddies on it along with a note telling him whom to call to facilitate their reunion.

Fred and Susie each breathed a sigh of relief.

Not wanting to be rude to his grandparents, he asked them how he could best help them, and wondered when it would be alright to contact his friends. After unloading the SUV and getting settled, Fred suggested he call his friends and enjoy the rest of the day with them but to let him know if he would be going anywhere out of the neighborhood.

Susie had already been in touch with the moms and was assured that his old friends had maintained their integrity and would not be enticing Jack into uncomfortable situations.

Within a few minutes of his call, a group of young teenagers showed up at the front door. Everyone talked at once, there were lots of hugs and fist bumps and high fives, and within minutes it was almost as if they hadn't been apart for a little over four years.

Jack's core group who had put together their little elementary school newspaper were still together. Colin, Grayson, Erwin, and Clara had remained close friends, and there were a couple of other guys from his baseball team and three girls whom he barely remembered who seemed to now be part of the Houston group.

He and Clara had stayed in touch and it was obvious to Fred and Susie that there was a special spark between the two gangly, relationally awkward, high school freshmen.

After a while, they made their way down the street to one of the kid's home. Jack looked back and waved at Fred and Susie as he joyously embraced the opportunity to be with his special friends.

When Fred and Susie re-entered their son's former home, the 'Hellish Darkness' again grabbed their hearts and minds. It was like an unbearable heaviness weighed on them. Each had to sit for a few moments and turn to Jesus for His ever-present help. After a while, at about the same time, they came out of the funk and hugged for a long time.

Jack was elated over being with his old friends and excitedly told his grandparents a lot about his day and what his friends were up to. Mikey enjoyed running around his old haunts.

However when bedtime came, Jack's emotions started to run rampant again.
"Nana" he called from his bed.
His grandmother came to his room and asked "What is it Jack?"
For the first time he requested "Do you think you could lie down with me til I go to sleep? Mom used to do that when I had a bad day."
She laid on top of the covers next to him, stroked his hair, and like she had done 40 years earlier with her own son, spoke comforting words until she heard his breathing change and saw that he was asleep.
It was a sweet…and bittersweet time for Susie Miller.
Over the course of the next four days, the elder Millers worked methodically at preparing their furnished rental home for the new renters who would arrive the next week. Jack helped with the more physically demanding jobs.

They gave Jack a lot of leeway with his old friends, but also made sure that he kept in touch with them. One day Jack was home for a quick lunch before two of the parents were taking the group to a beach in Galveston about an hour from Houston. Susie made sure he used plenty of sunscreen and gave him all the obligatory warnings about water safety. They were waiting on the front porch as the two vans pulled up, already loaded with kids.

Jack seemed to know just which one to go to and was off before Nana could go over her safety tips one more time. As they watched them drive away, a tall twenty something man came walking down the sidewalk, looking their house over. He seemed startled to see the older couple on the front porch.

"Can we help you?" Fred hollered.

"Uh, no… just out for a walk," he replied in a rather unusual voice, then kept on walking.

Fred didn't think anything of the encounter, but Susie said, "Have we seen him before? His bright red hair seems to ring a bell somewhere, but I just can't quite place it."

Racking his brain, Fred said, "It was bright for sure, but I don't seem to remember him. Maybe he looks like someone you've seen in Lawrence some time."

"Probably so," she said, not giving it any more thought.

Jack made it home safely from the beach outing and the sunscreen seemed to have done its job. "I'd forgotten how fun Galveston Beach is!" he exclaimed. "We don't really have anything like the ocean in Kansas."

"Don't we know!" Fred agreed. Jack talked about how nice it would be to come back more often.

On the eve of their next to last night in Houston, Jack was home for dinner. They ordered pizza and talked non-stop about his friends and their activities.

"What do you have planned for your last day and tomorrow night, Jack? Anything special?" Fred asked.

"Uh, actually, tomorrow night, Grayson and this girl, Cait, asked if Clara and I wanted to go to a movie with them," he blushed.

"Oh, that sounds like fun," Susie answered. "They all seem like such nice kids!"

"Sounds good to me," Fred chimed in. "Where is the movie and how will you get there and get home?"

"Uh, I don't know yet. I'll find out and get you the details. Will that be ok?"

"Sure. Just like at home, we wouldn't want you riding with someone who doesn't have a license, and I'd like to visit with Clara's mom just so I can be assured that you all will be safe and everything." Nana stated, sweetly. Jack knew that beneath her sweet demeanor was a very insistent requirement that everything was on the up-and-up.

While some of his friends complained about over-bearing parents, he was grateful for their standards. He knew of kids who'd lied to their parents about situations then paid the price for it.

It turned out that Clara's older brother, who was home on leave from the Air Force, would be driving them to the local theater and bringing them back to Clara's house just two blocks away, where her parents had a finished basement that doubled as the hangout for Clara and her friends.

They agreed that Jack would be home by midnight and the plans were all set.

While Jack had girls who were friends in Lawrence, he had never had a girlfriend, and had never been on an actual date. He was very much looking forward to the evening, but also had a stomach full of butterflies.

At dinner with his Pops and Nana, he bashfully asked some questions that they were happy to answer. Fred had already taught Jack to always hold a door open for Nana and other ladies, to wait to sit until after they were seated, to always walk next to the street with the lady to his right, and some other basics.

"Jack, you'll want to pay for Clara's ticket to the movie and for any snacks that she has there. You could ask her when you go in to the theater if she'd like anything then... or later on. Assuming that she doesn't order one of everything in the place," Fred smiled, "get her what she wants and, of course, don't complain that it costs too much."

Nana interjected, "Don't take any calls on your cell phone, unless it's from us– that would only be if there was an emergency, and I wouldn't recommend that you do any texting while you're with her either. When someone does that, they are sending the message that whoever they're texting is more important than the person they're with."

"I never thought of that. Thanks. Uh, Pops... I didn't bring very much money with me. I didn't even think about it."

"No problem. Here's $40. I think that will cover everything."

"Thanks, I'll pay you back when we get home... I mean, back to Lawrence." He didn't want to make the mental transition that this house in Conroe wasn't still his home.

When it was time to walk to Clara's house, with a straight face, Fred said, "Nana and I would like to walk with you and make sure that Clara meets our approval before you go to the movie with her."

Jack's jaw dropped, eyes widened, and countenance fell immediately. "Gotcha!" Pops said.

They did a little mock boxing amidst Jack's sigh of relief.

Standing on the front porch and watching their grandson walk down the street gave rise to both Fred and Susie's hearts swelling with pride at the special young man he was becoming... actually always had been... and they were noticeably touched when he turned to wave at them just before turning at the corner and going out of sight.

The elder Millers put the finishing touches on their work and caught up with some friends through social media, and Fred turned in after the 10:00 sports on tv. As usual, Nana settled back with her current book and would be up when Jack got home.

This particular evening, around 11:30, her mind went back to that eventful night four and a half years ago when she sat in the same stuffed chair in the same living room at the same time, thinking it was past time for her son and his wife to arrive home from helping flood victims.

Just as tears started to well up in her eyes, Fred came out from the bedroom, anticipating a flashback. Taking her hand, they moved to the couch and held each other without speaking for several minutes.

"It's hard not to remember that night, isn't it, Suze?"

"Especially being in this place at this time, and especially since Jack is... all we have left."

"He's been such a blessing, hasn't he? Obviously, I want Freddie and Rachel back and wished that evening would never have happened. But other than that, I wouldn't trade anything for having Jack in our lives. What a gift Papa has given us."

"He's really special, isn't he, honey?"

"Papa... or Jack?" Fred teased.

"Both! You know what I mean," she grinned.

They were startled at the sound on Susie's phone that indicated she had a text. Looking quickly she read, "We're watching a movie that's almost over...would it be ok if it was 12:15 when I got home?"

"Sure. Thanks for asking," she typed.

Right at 12:15, the front door opened and a very happy fifteen-year-old bounded through the front door.

"We had a great time! Everything was super fun and I only spent $30! Would it be ok if I used the other ten for something in the morning and waited to pay back the $40 when we get back to Lawrence?" Jack asked.

"Sure. You can tell us all about it tomorrow… but we'd better hit the hay now. We have a long drive ahead of us." Fred answered.

"What time will we leave tomorrow?"

"Nine. I don't want to fight rush hour traffic, so we'll have breakfast, pack up, then leave around nine. That way we'll get to Oklahoma City at a good time to spend the night there."

"Could I eat kind of early? Uh, I'd like to run a quick errand then."

"Sure. See you in the morning." Fred tousled his hair, Nana gave him a hug, and they went to their separate rooms.

"What do you think that's about?" Susie asked her husband.

"Flowers, my dear. Betcha ten bucks it's flowers."

"Hmmm."

A Bouquet for Clara

Jack went to his bedroom and immediately got out his sketch book and started to draw. Even though it was long past his regular bed time, he was wide awake and on a mission.

Memories of the week with his friends, and especially the good time he had on his first date were tumbling through his mind like pin balls darting around a game, occasionally hitting something that would light up and make an exciting sound.

He forced himself to concentrate and started drawing. When he finished he looked at his phone and it showed 3:15 a.m. "Woah!" he thought. "I've got to make sure I wake up on time."

With his mind racing, he got in bed, wanting to fall asleep. Mikey, as always, was lying on the floor next to him and Jack eventually dozed off with his hand on Mikey's head.

He didn't have any trouble at all waking up when the alarm on his cell phone went off at 6 a.m. He took a quick shower, got dressed, packed his things for the trip home, and was grateful that his grandparents were up for breakfast by 7:00.

The three shared thoughts, impressions, observations, and recollections of the previous week's events and each marveled at how quickly the time had flown by.

Jack had mixed feelings. He really enjoyed being with his Texas friends, especially Clara, but he was also really looking forward to playing his new drum set and learning from Mr. Williams.

As they finished breakfast, Fred asked, "So, what's this errand you need to run and will you need me to take you anywhere?"

"Actually… if you could, that would be great. There's a grocery store that's only about a mile from here. Would you have time to take me… now?"

"Sure, let's go." Fred caught Susie's eye and winked as he followed Jack who was already in the garage.

There were only a few cars in the parking lot at this early hour, so Fred parked close to the front door. "Would you like me to go in with you?"

"No, thanks. I'll just be a minute."

In just a few minutes, Jack came bounding out the front door with a bouquet of pretty spring flowers wrapped in light green cellophane.

Jumping in the car, he said, "These are for Clara!"

Fred smiled and said, "Nice. She'll like them! Did you get a little card to go with them?"

"Yeah, but I have a picture I drew that I'm gonna give her… it's way better than a card you get in a store." He said, matter of factly.

They drove in the driveway at about 7:30 and Jack said, "Could I help load things up now and maybe take these to Clara a little after 8:00? I don't want to get there too early, but I told her I'd come and see her before we left."

"Sure, why don't you give the flowers to Nana and she'll know just how to keep them looking good until you take them to Clara."

Jack bounded in the living room, calling, "Nana? Could you help me, please?"

As his grandmother emerged from the kitchen, Jack approached her with the flowers and she said with a pixieish grin, "Oh, for me? You shouldn't have!"

"Uh, they're for Clara," he said, a little embarrassed.

"I know that! Just messin' with you, boy!" she laughed.

Relieved, he asked her if she could keep them in a good place while he helped his Pops load the SUV.

Just as they were putting the last of the things in the vehicle, the alarm went off on Jack's phone. Silencing it, he said, "Gotta get my picture and flowers and head over to Clara's. I'll be back and ready to leave by 9:00, if that's ok?" he asked.

"Of course. Tell Clara and her folks 'goodbye' for us."

Jack skipped a few steps as he headed down the sidewalk. Fred and Susie watched him go from the driveway, and weren't bothered at all when he didn't turn to wave as he went out of sight.

'Til We Meet Again

Jack bounded up the front porch stairs to Clara's home, rang the doorbell, and as if she'd been waiting by the door (which she had), the door opened and his sandy-haired, freckle-faced friend appeared with a winsome smile.

"Hey Jack! What you got there?"

"Some flowers. I saw them in the store the other day when I went with my grandparents to get some things for the house. They were so bright and pretty… they reminded me of you," he blushed… as did she.

Taking the bouquet in one hand, she hugged him around the neck with her other hand and said, "They're beautiful. Thanks!"

They stood awkwardly in the entryway for a moment, then Jack said, "I also drew a picture for you." Unrolling the sketch that he had tucked under his arm, he handed it to her.

"Let's sit down so I can lay my flowers down and get a good look at this."

She put her bouquet on the coffee table and they sat on the living room couch a foot or so apart. She took the drawing, held it in front of her, and let out a little gasp.

Using every bit of the 9x12 sheet, Jack had managed to capture a very realistic picture of him and Clara sitting next to each other at the theater, watching a movie. You couldn't tell what was on the big screen in front of them, but you couldn't miss the smiles on their faces… and the fact that they were holding hands.

"Oh, Jack. This is… wonderful! How late did you stay up drawing this?"

"Well past my regular bedtime, for sure!" he smiled. "But I knew what I wanted… I had it in my mind and just had to finish it for you."

"I remember you drawing little things back in grade school, but this is really good– I mean… I like it very much!"

Just then, Clara's Mom appeared in the doorway from the living room to the kitchen and said, "I have some pastries and juice, can I bring you two some?"

"Sure," they said in unison… and smiled at each other.

"Mom, look! Flowers!"

"Oh, my… those are very pretty. How 'bout I put them in a vase and bring them back out for you?"

"Sure, Mom!"

Her mom brought the muffins and cranberry juice in and set them on the coffee table, along with the bouquet, and said, "What pretty flowers… that's very nice, Jack!"

"He drew me a picture too, Mom…uh, I'll show it to you later," she said, holding it close to her.

"I'll look forward to seeing it. Nice to see you again, Jack. Tell your grandparents bye for me, and have a great trip back to Kansas."

"I will, Mrs. Carter. They said bye to you too."

Telling Clara that he'd have to keep an eye on the time, Jack set his phone on the coffee table and they talked for a few minutes about fun things that had happened the past few days, agreed to keep in touch, and Jack tentatively said, "Maybe you could come to Kansas and visit sometime."

"That would be nice."

Just then, Jack's alarm went off. Sheepishly silencing it, he said, "I promised Pops I'd be back before 9:00. He wants to leave then and he likes to be on time." He smiled.

They both stood up and walked towards the front door and Jack awkwardly said, "Well, goodbye…"

Clara responded with, "Let's say, 'til we meet again.' That's much better than, goodbye, don't you think?"

He grinned and she caught him by surprise as she stood on her tiptoes and kissed his cheek. "I'll text you." She smiled.

"Yeah, me too." He gave her a quick, awkward hug… like his baseball buddies did after someone hit one out, and left with a big smile on his face. Not aware that anyone was watching, he skipped a few steps before walking briskly down the sidewalk. Just as he reached the corner to turn and go to his old house, he looked back and saw Clara waving to him from her front porch. Waving back, he thought his heart might burst.

They quickly finished loading the car and left the house ready for the new renters. In an hour, Houston wasn't even a blip on the horizon behind them as they headed North to Kansas. But it was very much in the horizon of Jack's mind. He had some music going on in his ear buds and was simultaneously drawing and playing with Mikey's ears.

Seeing Nana turning from her front passenger seat and attempting to talk to him, he took the ear buds out and asked her to repeat what she'd said.

"I heard a ding on your phone. I think maybe you got a text."

"Thanks, Nana."

As he clicked and opened the text, he got a huge smile as he saw that Clara had sent him a picture of her flowers in a vase on a little table, with his sketch framed and placed next to the vase. What touched him most was the accompanying red heart emoji.

Not wanting to rush to a quick reply that might not be appropriate, he thought quite a while before responding with, "The flowers are pretty... just like you." He included a similar heart emoji. He waited a few moments, took a deep breath, prayed: *Jesus, I hope this is ok,* then hit send.

A few moments later came Clara's reply– a big smiley face... and a big heart.

Jack decided to leave it at that and wait to text her something about a different subject later on, when he thought the time would be right. Soon, his lack of sleep caught up with him and he dozed off and slept until they got to Dallas.

He and Clara sent a variety of texts, some with pictures from each other and the two day trip home went by quickly.

The weather changed progressively from 70 degrees in south Texas to the 30's in Kansas and there was still a skift of snow on the Flint Hills as they got closer to Lawrence, which they reached mid-afternoon on the second day.

After unloading and unpacking, Jack got two $20 dollar bills from his lawn-mowing profits, took them to his Pops and said, "Fast pay makes fast friends, Pops!" After asking his grandparents if there was anything else he could help with, Jack and Mikey went to the man-cave for a session with his new drums. He proudly sent Clara a selfie of him and his set.

Spring Semester

The Millers started their new routine of getting up an hour earlier due to Jack's zero-hour class. He was super excited about going to school, which was a marked change from the previous semester. It seemed he had a purpose.

Jack had a natural talent for drums, and that, combined with lots of practice and encouragement from his musician-grandfather, precipitated a rapid progression in his drumming.

He still loved his art class and enjoyed playing trumpet, especially in the 18-piece jazz group. He felt a little awkward being first chair as a freshman with juniors and seniors behind him in the trumpet section, but everyone was accepting and he soon felt at ease. He did have frequent thoughts of playing drums in the group, but kept them to himself.

Fred took advantage of the availability of KU's jazz combos and big bands, as well as taking Jack to most every concert in the area where jazz and rock groups were featured. Of course, Fred enjoyed the experience as much as Jack, so he didn't view it at all as an inconvenience. Sometimes Nana accompanied them, but not often.

Jack loved the fact that his 75-year-old grandfather liked most of the same music as he did, and it didn't bother him to be accompanied by a white-haired senior citizen to a Victor Wooten performance at a local college-age venue. He especially loved the drummer, "Future Man."

As the semester progressed, Mr. Williams actually gave Jack the opportunity to play drums on a few songs with the jazz band... then his enthusiasm started to really take off.

Soon it was time for the end-of-the-year variety of concerts that each of the many high school music groups provided. Jack played trumpet in the concert band, and mostly with the jazz group, but he also played drums on two of the 15 or so tunes at that group's concert, including their rousing closer– a medley of big band tunes that had several drum solos.

At the cookies and punch reception after the jazz band's concert, Mr. Williams casually approached Fred for advice. "Chief, you've had a lot more experience with high caliber groups in this arena than I have. Any suggestions for improvement?"

Never wanting to interfere with local teacher's leadership, Fred made it a practice not to offer advice unless it was solicited. When asked, though, he was usually ready.

Making sure they were out of ear shot from the others at the reception, Fred stated, "The group was excellent. You're doing a great job with them! I love that you expose them to a variety of styles. And... you have several good trumpet players. You might consider having Jack play drums all the time," he offered.

"I was hoping you'd say that!" Mr. Williams said. "Barring any ringers moving into the district for next year, that's my plan. I'm available this summer to give him private lessons, if you think he'd be interested. I'll also be leading one of the jazz groups at the KU band camp for a couple of weeks, and that's something you might consider as well."

There was no need to convince Jack. He was immediately all in. They agreed that he would continue to play both trumpet and drums, and he continued to practice both... but with a much stronger emphasis on drums.

The two-week summer music camp started the second week in June. Students came from Kansas and several surrounding states, and the competition was several notches higher than at Lawrence High. Out of town students could stay in the dorms, Lawrence students could stay at home and attend for considerably less money... Jack opted to stay at home and commute.

Fred took him to the campus every day and sometimes stayed to listen to different groups and visit with old friends from his music days. The first week ended with multiple concerts. Jack was the drummer in the 3rd (of four) jazz groups, which played Saturday evening.

He was the 5th chair trumpet player (astounding for a freshman) in the top concert band, which culminated the week's concert series with an outdoor performance in an idyllic setting on the side of Mount Oread. As the audience viewed the band, they could see miles into the Kaw Valley to the south and the setting Kansas sun to the west.

With the sounds of the excellent music, the audience's appreciation and encouragement, the director's comments about the experience with the students, and the sight if the picturesque setting, everything combined synergistically to create one of those special moments that Fred and Susie enjoyed and etched into the memory vault of their hearts for future recollection.

They enjoyed the concert as much as Jack did and they talked about various aspects of the first week of camp on their way home, and continued as they enjoyed ice cream and oatmeal raisin cookies in the back yard afterwards.

"What's your biggest impression of what happened during the week, Jack?" Fred asked.

"You know, I've been thinking about that," the boy replied. "At the first concert band rehearsal Monday morning, hardly any of us knew each other, of course. We played a couple of marches and another piece that I'd heard before. Then we had some time to go to the practice rooms before the afternoon rehearsal.

"I didn't want to make a fool of myself, so I thought I'd run through the other songs in the folder. There was this one called the 'Frescobaldi Tocatta.' I'd never heard of it and don't know what a Tocatta is!" He smiled.

"So I played through it, but it didn't make much sense to me. That afternoon we played it with the full band and it wasn't very good. I thought maybe the conductor would drop it. But each day it started getting better and better. Then when we played it tonight, I got goosebumps!

"It was like this wonderful music that I really hadn't heard before. I looked around a little and it seemed like the other kids were feeling the same thing… it was like we were all playing over our heads and everything fit together to make something we never knew would be there. Does that make sense?"

"Sure does."

"While the audience was clapping for it, I just had this thought that Papa sees us people the same way. He sees the talents, abilities, likes, and dislikes that we have, and He knows what we're capable of way before we do. He's really patient and He's always working things out for the good... even when things don't look too good to us.

"Then... bam! One day everything comes together and it's better than we ever thought, and we realize Papa, Jesus, and Sarayu were working on that all the time and They could see in advance how good it would be."

"That's amazing, Jack... amazing! God has given you spiritual insight far beyond your years. That's a very special gift. Sometimes people who hear things like that from God are called mystics– you might Google that sometime and learn a little about it."

"Mystics... sounds like a cool name for a band," Jack smiled.

Long Distance Relationship and Trinity Trio

After Jack's two-week band camp finished, the summer before his sophomore year in high school consisted of baseball practices and games, lawn mowing, some trumpet practice, a couple of Royal's games, day trips with his grandparents and lots of drumming. Susie was indeed grateful for the man-cave in a separate building from their house.

He and Clara texted often and occasionally FaceTimed each other. His grandparents expected one or the other to start dating someone in their hometown, but so far that was not the case.

Clara also had musical ability, singing being her first love. She participated in various vocal groups at school and loved being in musicals and group performances. Playing flute in the school band was also fun, but didn't compare to singing for her.

They often talked about when they might get together again and were hoping that might happen the next Christmas.

There were lots of nice girls in Jack's circle of friends in Lawrence and by now, couples started to form and many of his friends were dating, if not as couples, at least they were pairing up at group functions. Jack seemed content to have his long-distance relationship with Clara and wasn't easily attracted to occasional subtle advances from Lawrence girls.

Besides, he was on a mission to start a band. He'd become friends with two boys who were a year older than him. Buddy King and Dave Garlow were both in the high school jazz band. Buddy's parents had started him in the Suzuki piano program when he was three years old and by now, he was somewhat of a prodigy.

While Buddy was an excellent classical player, much to his parent's surprise, jazz was his main interest. He also started playing guitar at an early age and was one of those rare individuals who was very accomplished on two vastly different instruments. He had a great ear and could quickly play most anything he heard.

Dave initially started on trumpet and he and Jack were section mates. By 7th grade, the band director needed a tuba player, Dave offered to try, and made the switch rather easily. He really started to bloom in 8th grade when he had the opportunity to learn bass guitar.

Jack enjoyed playing with them both in the school group and talked to them about forming a little trio. They readily accepted the offer.

The man-cave was a perfect place for the boys to play without drowning out all other activities on their homes. They started periodic sessions during the summer, and by the start of Jack's sophomore year, had become a good little group.

With Fred's help, they started playing for free at various events in the community, and then turned that exposure into some paying gigs, which even enhanced their love of playing together. At Jack's leading, they named their group the "Trinity Trio." The name had special significance for Jack and the other two were ambivalent.

The existence of their group provided a ready-made rhythm section for Mr. William's Lawrence High big band and jazz combo the next two years. He would often feature the trio as part of the band concerts.

The Divine Triune Circle Dance

One September Saturday afternoon, Fred suggested that he, Jack, and Mikey take the Really Is out to the lake at the old farm. Jack always enjoyed going there, but especially liked it now that Fred used the secluded area to begin teaching Jack to drive.

Fred drove on the two-lane rural county highway and exited to the gravel road leading to where his family's old farm had been. Pulling over and stopping the car, he changed places with his grandson and gave Jack the wheel.

Being in the country was always special to Jack, although he didn't think he'd ever want to actually live that far away from everyone. With the top down and wind blowing in his face and no worries about traffic, Jack especially enjoyed having control of a sports car like the Really Is.

He wasn't desperate to have his license like some of his friends were, but realized that the convenience would be nice.

When they got to the clubhouse where Fred's family home had been, he practiced parallel parking between two trees on the edge of their old orchard. Eventually they moved ahead to the lake.

Mikey was in and out of the water, chasing wild-fowl and an occasional squirrel as Fred and Jack sat on the elevated bank overlooking what had become a very special place for the two of them.

"Your trio is really getting good, Jack! You guys are as good as many of the groups I had in my Army bands over the years, and you're still in high school!"

"Well, Buddy and Dave are older… and Mr. Williams has been a big help to us." He deferred.

"In this old musician's judgement, you are advanced well beyond your years. Just sayin'" he smiled.

"You might be a little prejudiced, Pops!" Jack suggested.

"There could be a little of that, too," he admitted.

"So, tell me what's behind the name?"

"What name?"

"Trinity Trio."

"Oh, sure. You know I've thought a lot about how you've explained Jesus, Papa, and Sarayu to me ever since our first trip from Houston back here…

"You've told me how They are so close, so united, so together, that people say the three of Them are One. I love that description that says They are so close that when one cries, the other two taste salt."

Fred nodded assent. "Me too."

"I see a real similarity in a jazz trio. I guess it could be the rhythm section of a pop group or country group or Latin band or even a polka band!" he chuckled.

"The thing is that when the three are playing together, there's one total sound. You hear the group... not just three individual instruments doing their own thing. Each has their own function and role to play, but they're interconnected... they're one.

"The reason I like a jazz group to best define them, is that they are always creating! A country group or rock group or pop group, whatever, just memorizes an arrangement and plays it exactly the same every time. They even take other group's songs and cover them, playing them note-for-note the same way.

"While jazz groups have an idea of how they're gonna do a song, nothing's set in stone, and creativity is celebrated big time! The very nature of jazz– improvisation– means creativity, and of course, the Trinity is always creating!

"Most of the time they are all three playing together– at the same time. They're playing the same song, in the same key, at the same tempo, in the same style, with the same feel. Each of those could change, but when it does, they all immediately change together. Even though they have that template to work within, they are allowed, and encouraged, to create something new each time!

"Just like in the Trinity each has a specific role, I see it like this in the trio: the bass would be like Papa– the solid foundation, the root of the chord, the key element that sets the tone for everything. You know Jesus said that He only did what His Father told Him to do and only said what Papa told Him to say– the bass is like that with the trio. In a sense, we get what chords to play, what tempo, what style, from the bass that undergirds everything.

"The piano is like Jesus: the full range of everything there is comes from the chords and the melody. Every note in the song is created by the piano chords. All the notes are there– some are pretty, some are strident, some sound like different cultures– there's everything from the lowest A in the bass to the highest C at the top.

"And while the chords change, at the end, they always resolve to whatever the tonic chord of the song is... like Jesus is always working out everything for the good. We're all in Him, and one day everyone will be restored to our original identity... the restoration of all things. That's like when a song is finally over, the bass plays the tonic, and the piano plays all the notes in the chord. It's all good!"

"That's a perfect illustration, Jack! Just perfect! Now, how about the drums?"

"That's the Holy Spirit. Sarayu is continually leading– explaining– pointing things out, giving emphasis to something, getting our attention in different ways. He, or She, can be simple, complex, loud, soft, pulsating, laid back. He can change the tempo in an instant, can move things in a different direction, whatever... but it's always within the framework of the chord structure and key the song is in. The drums are the power source.

"There's a framework, but within that framework, there's almost endless room for expression. Like you could take a simple song like 'Take Me Out to The Ball Game' and play it in 3/4 or 4/4 Maybe even other time signatures, I guess! You can play it fast or slow, in a major key or minor... or pentatonic.

"You can give it a Latin feel, or swing, or country or rock. The combinations are almost endless!

"Once in a while one instrument will take an extended solo and the other two will lay out, but even then they'll occasionally contribute a little supporting thing for emphasis. They always know where the soloist is... even if they change tempo and get way out there," he smiled.

"So everyone gets to shine, no one cares who gets the credit, they continually support each other and are always working together for the common good of the trio.

"Rather than think about a simple song like 'Take Me Out to The Ball Game,' I prefer to think that with the original Trinity Trio, Their theme song, the one They start and end with, is a great love song. Their ever-flowing song… music… is a love song that describes and conveys Their pure, unconditional, agape love that always does what's best for the other person!

"Of course it's the most fun when you're actually playing in a trio, but I like watching and listening to other trios too, seeing how they relate to each other and support each other and feed off of each other."

"Wow, Jack! I've been in music all my life and never saw that connection… you've really captured a great way to get a grasp of what the Trinity is like! Maybe I never got it because I'm a trumpet player and we're not part of the rhythm section…" he mused.

"Pops, you know how much you like Dixieland groups, right?"

"Yeah, but I think I've failed in getting you to share my love of that style," he grinned.

"Oh, I like it… just not all the time! But think about this– here's what I've seen in the videos you've shown me. Each Dixieland band has a rhythm section– piano, bass, and drums, right? Or something like that… maybe they have a guitar or banjo instead of piano, maybe it's an upright bass or sometimes a bass guitar or even a tuba, but there's a trio of some sort that's the foundation of the group, right?"

"Of course."

"Well in a Dixieland band, you have a trumpet that usually plays the melody, maybe a clarinet that plays higher above the trumpet…sometimes playing harmony, but also adding little fun things in between the trumpet phrases. Then there's a trombone who plays lower, sometimes harmony, but he adds fun little incidental things too– just different than the clarinet."

"That's pretty much it. They each have a part to play, and they do it together. Of course, they sometimes have solos too." Fred noted.

"Yeah, but all the time the rhythm section is playing behind them… supporting them… giving them direction and foundation."

"That's exactly right!" Fred said.

"There's something more, Pops."

"What's that?"

"Well generally with a Dixieland band, or a standard jazz group, there's a little introduction to the song...maybe by the piano...that's Jesus 'speaking' things in to existence. Like He says, 'Here's what we're gonna do next'... the others catch that introduction, then join in and everyone plays together once or twice through the song. Then they each play solos, and finally they come back together for one more time. Sometimes they'll have a cute little ending, right?"

"Yes. What else?"

"Well, I've noticed that sometimes after the solos, they'll all play together two or three times through the song before they stop. Usually each time is a little louder than the other. And sometimes maybe the trumpet and trombone will play a little harmony riff over and over again and the clarinet will solo above that real high and real loud... and it just keeps building and building and building and then there will be a big, climatic ending... maybe they slow down a little... maybe they hit a big full chord and hold it for a few seconds which the drummer goes nuts... things like that."

"Of course that's all true, good observation, son... but is there something more you're getting at?"

Jack wanted to say, "Dang, old man, are you that dense..." but he didn't have to, his look conveyed what he was thinking!

"What?" Fred asked. "I'm obviously missing something!"

"Pops! The rhythm section is the Trinity... constantly playing Their love song, constantly expressing love and moving in Their Triune circle dance of love, joy, peace, patience, kindness, goodness, faith, compassion, grace, and mercy... always together and always under control. You've said that so many times I could say it backwards!" he smiled.

"Yeah, I get that!"

"Don't you see, Pops!? The horn players are us! Because They love us so much, They invited us and included us in Their group! We get to participate in the Divine circle dance of Their love! They give us talents, abilities and skills... and They include us in what They're doing! We get to be one with Them, part of the group!"

Fred's countenance was half stunned, half overjoyed. Tears

started streaming down his face and he couldn't speak.

"But, wait…there's more! If you buy right now we'll send you two special CD's and all you have to pay is the extra shipping and handling." Jack mimicked their favorite satire on the "Butt Weights" that end many TV commercials.

"Seriously, look at this: They include us, and we have the choice to participate… or not. If we join Them in Their deal, we have freedom and we can shine and enjoy everything and be part of something greater than ourselves!

"But if we say, 'OK, Trinity Trio– you're playing a fast Kansas City Jazz version of Take Me Out To The Ball Game in the key of Bb, but I'm gonna play a slow ballad, I Left My Heart in San Francisco in Eb– it's not gonna work out very well!

"They set the tempo. When we join Them, it's easy, great, it flows! But if we insist on doing it our way and we get ahead of or behind Them… if we go too slow or too fast, it's hard! There's friction and tension. It's not easy.

"I love the Message version of Matthew 11 where you've taught me that Jesus is speaking to religious legalists who set up their own rules for supposedly gaining and maintaining favor with God… and as a result, they're worn out, burned out, and not productive or successful. Remember what Jesus says to them?

"In Matthew 27 Jesus resumed talking to the people, but now tenderly. 'The Father has given me all these things to do and say. This is a unique Father-Son operation, coming out of Father and Son intimacies and knowledge. No one knows the Son the way the Father does, nor the Father the way the Son does. But I'm not keeping it to myself; I'm ready to go over it line by line with anyone willing to listen.'

"See, Pops! None of these wanna-be musicians know Papa or Jesus. They don't know that there's the best rhythm section ever that's inviting them to join the group, and that the members of the trio will include them and patiently show them note-by-note how to play well and enjoy the experience! Jesus goes on to say: Matthew 11:28-30 'Are you tired? Worn out? Burned out on religion? Come to me. Get away with me and you'll recover your life. I'll show you how to take a real rest. Walk with me and work with me—watch how I do it. Learn the unforced rhythms of grace. I won't lay anything heavy or ill-fitting on you. Keep company with me and you'll learn to live freely and lightly.'

"See– that's an invitation to musicians to leave their do-it-yourself way of playing and join the best, most supportive, perfect rhythm section ever! Isn't that cool?"

Composing himself, and letting Jesus speak as him, Fred looked Jack right in the eyes and said, "Jack, you know that most all grandfathers are proud of their grandkids and they like to brag… and exaggerate their accomplishments to their friends… and you know how proud I am of you in every area of your life.

"But I want you to take me very seriously now, I mean every bit of what I'm about to say, and I'm not exaggerating at all. Listen now…

"Jack, you have developed an amazing way of showing people what the Trinity is like. People have been trying to do that for 2,000 years without much success, really. And you… at 15 years old…"

"About to be 16!" he interjected.

"You have the best insight into the Trinity that I've ever seen. This could only have been revealed to you by Sarayu. I'm a musician with over 10 times the years of experience that you have.

"I'm a pastor… arm-chair-theologian who loves the Trinity and have made it my life's mission to help people see Them and Their Divine Triune circle dance of love… and I've never even thought about what you just described! I'm amazed… and I'm so proud of you!"

"Thanks, Pops. I think Sarayu used you to teach me all this… and gave me Jesus's eyes to see and ears to hear. It's a team effort. It's like we're playing in their band… and it's super fun!"

"Well, yeah!"

Ever the pragmatist, Fred asked, "So… now, what do we do with this?"

Again barely concealing a *duh* and resisting a face palm, the 15 year old said, "We tell people about it, Pops!"

"Oh, yeah… uh, that's what I was hoping you'd say!"

They both chuckled.

"I was thinking Pops, maybe my trio and I could do some

standard songs… love songs that have a good message. We could do a little video of each song, and you could narrate the Trinity Trio concept, and we could sometimes add some horn players and singers, and you could explain how the Trinity has already included us all in their group…

"Maybe we could put them on Facebook and YouTube. Maybe we could even take the group and do interactive concerts using this same concept."

"Son, you've got this 75-year-old musician who thought he was past his days of contributing anything but exaggerated old stories… to now be super excited about how God can use this… and we can have a lot of fun doing it. And, we can do it together… that's even better!"

Offering his hand to Jack, they shook hands and Fred said, "I'm in!"

"Me too, Pops!"

The two Millers enjoyed the rest of their time at the lake watching Mikey, the ducks and geese, and periodically coming up with additional thoughts about their Trinity Trio project.

Eventually they called it a day and Jack got to practice driving some more before they got to the blacktop.

That evening as Fred and Susie got in bed, she said "Honey, I've noticed lately that The Hellish Darkness' doesn't come around as often. I'm so glad."

"Me too, Suze. Papa uses time and His love to heal all wounds, doesn't He?"

"Yes…but I still ache to see Freddie and Rachel. And I ache that Jack has to put up with us instead of having them with him."

"He only has to put up with you. He likes me…" Fred said.

"You'll never quit messin' with me, will you, old man?"

As her husband chuckled, she said "Thanks for the humor. That time it helped. But don't quit your day job."

"Hmmp."

Music, Music, I Hear the Music

Music in general, and the Trinity Trio in particular, continued to be a big force in Jack's high school life. The group continued for a year even after Buddy and Dave graduated from LHS, as both decided to attend the University of Kansas and stay in Lawrence.

They played for more and more events and at a variety of venues, oftentimes adding some horns and occasionally a singer. Through Fred's connections and behind-the-scenes work, they played an ever-increasing number of times at local venues and for private parties, conventions, wedding receptions and the like. They sold some of their fledging recordings and had quite a social media following, especially on Facebook and their YouTube channel.

A serendipitous bonus was Clara's singing.

As she and Jack continued their long-distance relationship, she continued to study and progress in her vocal endeavors, and she too, had a genuine interest and affinity for jazz.

With her parents and his grandparent's blessings, the two made semi-frequent trips to Houston and Lawrence, spending time together and with friends at each place. Jack introduced her to the Trinity Trio and at first, Dave and Buddy were reluctant as most band mates are when a group member wants to have his girlfriend sing. However, they were pleasantly surprised and then supportive of her as they heard her musical talent and feel for the genre.

Clara made extended trips to Lawrence the summers before their junior and senior years, each time spending a few days at the Miller home before and after joining Jack at the university two-week summer camp. There they lived in the KU dorms and participated in the various social aspects of the camp as well as being in a number of musical groups. A special treat before their senior year was Clara being the vocal soloist in the top jazz big band where Jack was the drummer.

They even explored some long-distance digital recording where she would sing in Houston as the Trinity Trio played in Lawrence. They then mixed the combination down to a finished product that to the untrained ear, sounded like it was all done at one location.

After one such long-distance endeavor, Fred was listening to Jack as he did some mastering work. "This technology is really amazing, Jack! In my day we never dreamed of it!"

"It's cool, but it will never take the place of being together," Jack responded.

"How's that?" Fred asked.

"Well, when you use a digital recording– or even use a synth for sounds, there's no relationship, no give and take, no compromising, no working with, no playfulness. It's rigid and non-forgiving.

"Oh, it may be technically 'perfect' and 'right'… but for me, no matter how 'perfect' it might be in that way, there's no relationship! It's sterile and it seems like 'perfection' is all that matters. You have to get everything exactly right to be comfortable with it. If you mess up in the slightest, you're on your own. You have this never-changing, unforgiving 'click-track' going in your ear and when you get off, it's up to you to get back right.

"It's like lip-synching, it's fake.

"But with live musicians, with the real deal, the other members of the Trinity Trio can go with you and even work out your mistakes for the best. If the singer drops a beat and comes in too early… the Trio just adjusts and goes with her!

"I see that being the difference between religion and a relationship with and in the Trinity. Religion, like the law that undergirds it, is inflexible. It can make it obvious when you mess up, but it has no power to help you. On the other hand, in relationship with Jesus, Papa, and Sarayu, relationship is more important than rules and being exactly right. They take your lemons and make them into lemonade!"

"Yeah… that's it, all right! I'll work something up to narrate for another recording. But we'll have to have an example of someone messing up and the rhythm section making it right."

"There's no lack of those!" Jack grinned!

Part 8
Ultimate Reconciliation

What's Next?

As Jack prepared to start his senior year, he was faced with several decisions. Where (or if) to go to school, what to study, and what career to point towards were standard fare for all high school seniors. However, Jack had some additional wild cards in the mix.

Pops and Nana were all the family he had, so to go to school somewhere other than KU would mean being separate from them, probably for the duration... short visits home, notwithstanding.

Clara was very much in the picture. Their relationship had flourished, and while neither wanted to be married right away, both indicated that they wanted to go to the same school, study music together, and see how things would work out.

That meant that one of them, at a minimum, would need to pay out-of-state tuition, which would be sizeable.

They both looked into KU and the University of Houston. Each had comparative strengths and weaknesses.

They found out that Jack could establish residency by living in his parent's home Conroe for a year which would mean that starting his second year, he would pay in-state tuition. The tuition benefit, along with the nice, furnished home being there for him in Houston was attractive.

Jack and Clara applied and were both accepted into the school of music at U of H, and each set out to enjoy their senior year of high school.

They each made a couple of trips to the other's home and their schedules worked out for both Jack and Clara to attend each other's senior prom. They were cementing their relationship more and more with each passing season.

Prior to the spring of Jack's final year in high school, he turned his Miller's Mowing business over to a sophomore boy who was in various band groups with Jack and who had proven himself to be reliable and trustworthy. They worked out a very fair price for the business, which included mowing equipment and a sizeable list of loyal customers. His friend would pay him a percentage of each week's mowing revenue for the summer until the payment was paid in full.

They also negotiated a lease on their furnished rental home in Houston that would end the following July, giving them time to make necessary repairs and get it ready for Jack to move into in August. That trip, of course, would provide another opportunity for Jack and Clara to be together.

Soon it was almost time for Jack to officially move back to his boyhood home.

Leaving his grandparents and their home in Lawrence where he had been for the past eight years wasn't an easy thing for Jack. He deeply loved them, and greatly appreciated their love, generosity, care, and support… especially in the darkest time of his life.

He liked Lawrence, his friends there, and especially the Trinity Trio. They had a little "final tour" group of performances at various places where they had regularly performed the last few years and it was fun to see the fans once again.

It was also bittersweet to part with his mom's car that he had driven since he turned 15 and got a learner's permit. It was now 10 years old and wasn't especially good for transporting a drum set. With Pops' help negotiating, he traded it for a new Subaru Forrester that would serve him well as a drummer, and for his trips back and forth to Kansas. By saving his profits from Miller's Moving and the money he made playing with the trio, he was able to pay cash for the monetary difference after the trade-in allowance for Rachel's former car.

Due to Freddie and Rachel's financial foresight and the life insurance policies they had in place at their untimely death, not only had Fred and Susie not had to use their savings to support Jack during his eight years with them, but there was ample money for a good education– including higher degrees if he so chose– and all the accompanying living expenses… and he had a nice mortgage-free home plus another account that held the profits from renting it the past eight years.

The financial management tool that Susie taught him with his first allowance had become such a regular part of his life, that he was well-grounded to be on his own from that standpoint. One of his favorite things each month was finding a charity to give his 10 percent, or more, to.

Fred and Susie were confident and fully assured that Jack was prepared to be on his own. Due to their flexible schedule, they were also prepared to fly or drive to Houston as needed to help when called upon.

Now almost 80, they were still in good health, but not as able to do all the things they had enjoyed the past eight years with their grandson. Walks had to be of shorter duration and playing catch was limited to more of a softball-type exercise.

On one beautiful, early summer evening, Jack asked if he could take the Really Is for a spin and go hang out with some of his friends.

With the top down, music from 311 blaring, and wind in his face, Jack was enjoying the moment immensely. He was looking forward to seeing some friends, but also thinking about soon being able to be with Clara every day when they were at college.

He was stopped at a light in the middle of town. It changed from red to green and he started to drive through the intersection, not looking to the left or right because he knew that traffic would be stopped.

Except one car wasn't. A new KU freshman, starting summer school before her freshman year, was texting and oblivious to her red light. Her car hit the Really Is just behind the driver's seat, spinning the convertible around like a top.

Jack immediately hit the brakes and tried to steer the vehicle, but the effort was futile. Fortunately, the car didn't flip over, but it did hit the median full-force all along the ride side, coming to an immediate stop.

Shaken, but not hurt, Jack got out of the car and ran to where the girl's car had stopped after hitting a parked car. Her airbag deployed and it was hard to tell if she was hurt or not.

Jack called 911, as did other motorists who had stopped to help.

Staying next to the driver's side of the girl's car, he could hear her crying, got close to the airbag, and spoke to her, saying, "It's ok, the ambulance is on the way. You'll be all right. Jesus is with you and He's taking care of you. Just trust him, I'm praying for you."

While she continued to cry… but softer now, Jack heard her say, "Who are you?"

"I'm a friend that Jesus sent. You'll be ok."

"Thank you."

Soon the police, ambulance, and mandatory fire truck arrived. With some difficulty, the medics were able to extract the young lady from her car, but it wasn't possible for Jack to tell if she was badly hurt.

She was obviously distraught, however, and kept wailing, "My parents! My parents! What are they gonna do to me?"

Jack wanted to assure her that Jesus was with her and that he wasn't upset, but she was surrounded by a cadre of medical personnel, and just as he was about to see if he could speak to her, one of the officers approached Jack and asked him what happened. He explained as best he could, and fortunately, his testimony was corroborated by a couple of witnesses who were driving behind him. They saw the entire event enfold.

The officer took Jack's information, checked the Really Is, and said, "Sure looks like she's totaled… too bad, too. She's a real classic. We'll call the tow company."

"Someone from the department will contact you… probably tomorrow. You're not planning on leaving town in the next few days, are you?"

"No, sir."

"Ok, if you're positive that you're not hurt, you're free to go. You can get anything out of your car that you want."

"Thank you, officer."

Jack got a couple of things from the badly damaged car, went to the sidewalk, and immediately called his grandfather.

"Pops…"

"Yeah, Jack? Everything ok?"

"I'm ok, but your car's not. Can you come get me at the corner of 23rd and Iowa?"

"Be right there. Trust Jesus, He's with you."

"I know, thanks."

Jack went back to the officer who was chalking off the scene of the accident and said, "Excuse me, sir?"

"Yes?"

"I'm concerned for the girl whose car hit mine. She seemed to be really concerned that her parents would come down hard on her. I want her to know that I'm not upset. Can I find out her name so I can go and see her at the hospital?"

"I can't give you that information, son. Tomorrow or the next day someone from the department will contact you with the insured's information so you can provide it to your agent. I'm afraid that's all I can do."

Jack thanked him and prayed for her.

Soon, Pops and Nana showed up in her car. Jack ran over to where they parked and said, "Pops, the policeman said he was afraid the car is totaled. I'm so sorry. It wasn't my fault. This girl ran through a red light and hit me… but I should have been paying better attention. I know how special the Really Is is to you… and, I don't know… I don't know what to say."

"Are you okay?" His grandfather asked.

"Yeah, I had my seat belt on and got jerked around a little, but I'm fine. I'm concerned about the girl that hit me, though. But… the Really Is…" he lamented.

"Jack… it's a car, a piece of metal and plastic that we've enjoyed, but that's it. I'll get another car… probably a convertible. I want you to let it go. No worries about it. Did you get your stuff and the registration and insurance out of the glove box?"

"I got my stuff, but didn't think about the other things."

"Why don't you go get them, and you and Nana go on to the car. I'll just make sure everything's all right with the police and then we'll go, ok?"

As Jack made his way to the Really Is, he realized this would probably be the last time he saw it, and he wondered how his grandfather was really feeling.

Within minutes, Fred was back at the car with Jack and Susie.

"Pops, I'm so sorry. I just don't know…"

Fred interrupted him, "Jack, listen to me… I'm not upset in the slightest. I'm overjoyed that you are okay… don't even give it another thought, really! Okay?

"Yes, sir."

"Jack..."

"What is it, Nana?"

"He means it... no worries about the car, really."

"Thanks... both of you."

Jack assumed they were going home, and when his Pops didn't turn at the right place, he asked, "Where are we going, Pops?"

"To the emergency room. We want to make sure the girl is okay and assure her that we're not upset. She's probably from out of town and her folks won't be able to get her right away."

"I thought that too, Pops, but the police officer told me we couldn't find out who she is until tomorrow or the next day."

Pops just smiled.

Nana shrugged her shoulders as if to say, "Don't ask me!"

Soon they parked at the city hospital's emergency room entrance. Always the gentleman, Fred held the door for his wife and grandson to enter first, but then he immediately went ahead of them and assumed control of the situation.

As they got to the emergency room desk, he motioned for the two of them to have a seat while he visited with the attendant. They watched as he pulled out his billfold and handed her something, then heard her say, "That will be fine, Pastor. Let me see if she can have visitors yet."

The lady then turned her duties over to another person and made her way into the E.R. ward.

As Fred sat down in the waiting area with his wife and grandson, Susie said, "We've certainly been here a few times over the years, haven't we?"

"Yep... sometimes with good outcomes, sometimes not so good..." They both thought of different times when they got calls to come quickly. While it wasn't their favorite thing to do, they always were glad to help family members... and those who were in the E.R.

Soon the attendant came back and indicated that Fred was to come to her. Jack and Susie couldn't hear the muted conversation from where they sat. In a moment Fred came over and said, "Nana and I can go in, but it would be best for you to wait, Jack."

Without asking if that was ok, Fred directed his wife to the doorway and they left the room. There was an E.R. nurse waiting for them.

"Hi, Pastor Fred, Susie."

"Hi Janet. Wish we didn't have to see you in these circumstances so often."

"Yeah, I know. It's great you got here right away. They're about to sedate Robyn and take her to surgery. You can go in and pray with her, though." She led them through a maze of desks, pods, hallways, beeping monitors, and constant activity.

As they were walking, Fred asked, "Janet, what's Robyn's last name? You know, at my age, I don't always remember."

Looking at her chart, she said, "McAlister. Robyn is spelled with a y."

"Thanks, have you all contacted her parents?"

"Yes, they live in Kansas City. They'll be here within the hour, I think."

Soon they came to the room and Janet led the couple into the side of a bed where a young lady with tubes in her arms and nose lay hooked up to a variety of machines. Her face was bruised and there was some caked blood in her hair. Her eyes were closed.

Leaning close to her head, Fred gently said, "Robyn…"

"Uh…"

"I want you to know that God is with you, and you're gonna be okay. Trust Him, okay?"

She opened one eye and softly said, "Are you Jesus?"

"No, Robyn, but He sent me. He loves you very much and He's in control."

"Is He mad at me?" She mumbled.

"Oh, no! He's madly in love with you. Always has been, and He's making sure you're ok."

"My parents… they're gonna be really pissed…"

"I'm gonna meet them when they get here. I'll talk to them. Don't you worry, now. You listen to Jesus. He wants to tell you how much He loves you."

She closed her eye and mumbled, "Jesus…" Then she seemed to breathe easier and be at peace.

At the moment attendants appeared at the door with a rolling bed and informed the Millers that they needed to rush Robyn to surgery.

They watched while they transferred her to the bed and got all the cords and tubes situated accordingly. As they rolled her past Fred and Susie, Robyn opened one eye again and said, "Thank, you, Jesus."

Fred and Susie went back to the E.R. waiting room and told Jack they had been able to be with her before she went to surgery and that her parents were on their way.

"What should we do now, Pops? Check about your car?"

"Jack," Fred said firmly, "Let the car go. No need to even think about it anymore. I'm not.

"Here's what I'm thinking, there's gonna be a couple of distraught parents come through these doors in a few minutes and they'll be briefed and taken to the E.R. surgery waiting room. I believe we should be here to meet them and help them if we can.

"He's right Jack. You can go back home if you'd like, but Pops and I should be here."

"I'm staying," Jack said, beating himself up that he hadn't thought of that.

"You thinking bad thoughts about yourself, boy?"

"Yeah, Pops."

"Where do you think they come from?"

"Not from Jesus, I guess."

"That's right. You don't have to take those thoughts. Reject them. Ask Jesus what He's thinking and go with that."

Jack let out a deep breath and said, "I'll be back in a moment."

He walked outside, took a few steps on the sidewalk, and sat on the curb.

"Jesus, what are you thinking?"

You've done everything right, Jack. I'd love you just the same even if you didn't. This girl's parents need help now. Focus on them.

"Thanks, Jesus."

Going back in, he went to his grandparents and said, "Should we wait here or somewhere else?"

Smiling, his grandfather said, "Let me check."

He talked to the attendant again, she wrote something down and gave it to him and pointed to the doors on the left. "I've been there many times… you won't need to show us the way. Thanks for being so helpful."

The three went down a long hallway, made a couple of turns, and eventually came to a comfortable waiting room. No one else was waiting there, so Fred turned the TV off, and offered to serve Nana and Jack from the beverages and snacks that were nicely arranged on a table with some fresh flowers.

"Pops, we don't know this girl… or her parents. How did you get in the ER to see her and find out her name and everything?"

"Once they know you're a pastor, people tend to trust you. We happen to know one of the nurses who was on duty… we've been here a lot. She mentioned Robyn's first name and I told her that at my age I wasn't good with names anymore and asked for her last name."

Susie just shrugged her shoulders. Jack smiled in amazement. "You've been around the block a few times, haven't you?"

"Yeah, this ain't my first rodeo." Fred smiled.

Some minutes later a mid-fortyish couple, looking very harried, came to the waiting room, glanced at the Millers, and sat at another table.

Fred got up, extended his hand, and said, "Are you the McAlisters?"

Startled, the man said, "Yes, have we met?"

"No, I'm Fred Miller. I'm a pastor here in Lawrence. This is my wife, Susie, and our grandson, Jack." They all nodded.

"Has Robyn been to your church?" Her father asked, as if he would be astonished if she had.

"No, my grandson just happened to be close to the accident scene and called and asked us to come. We thought maybe we could be of help."

"Did you see Robyn?"

"We did. I was with her for a few minutes before they sedated her and took her to surgery."

"Oh, thank you." Her mom said. "I was so afraid she'd be all alone and we couldn't get here soon enough. Thank you. Thank you."

During the course of the next couple of hours, Fred and Nana kept the McAlisters engaged and helped them not dwell on their concerns.

Susie offered to call any people for them if that would help, and she did call Robyn's roommates and freshman doom supervisor.

Eventually a surgeon appeared in the room, some blood splattered on his gown. He said, "Hi, Pastor Fred… I'm Dr. Hull. Are you folks the McAlisters?

"She's going to be fine," he assured them. She has some broken ribs and some nasty bruises. Her spleen was ruptured, but we took care of that just fine with surgery, and she'll be ok.

"There was a good deal of bleeding, as there usually is when a spleen is ruptured in a car accident. So we had to take care of that. We gave her an infusion of blood. She's young and healthy, so there shouldn't be any lasting health problems, but she'll be sore from the surgery and the operation.

"She'll be here a few days and we'll monitor her closely. As soon as we feel it's right, she'll be dismissed. I recommend that she take it easy for a few weeks. We'll go over all that with you before she leaves the hospital."

"When will we be able to see her?" Her mother asked.

"In a little while, we'll move her to a room in I.C.U.. You can be in there with her, but she won't come out from the anesthesia for several hours. She'll be pretty groggy for a while. Sometime tomorrow or the next day, we'll move her to a regular room upstairs. Then she'll perk up pretty rapidly, but still be very sore. Any other questions?"

"No, thank you very much. Thanks for taking care of our little girl…" Mrs. McAlister said tearfully.

"That's what I do. You all are in good hands here with Pastor Miller and Susie. They seem to have a direct line to God. Amazes me over and over again!" He smiled at the Millers and took his leave.

After reassuring the McAlisters that they wanted to help however they could, and leaving his card, eventually Fred, Susie, and Jack left to go to their car. Five hours had passed since the accident and it was close to midnight.

They were silent for a while on the way home, then Jack said "Pops?"

"Yeah, Jack? Except it better not be about the car," he smiled.

"You did good, Pops. Real good."

"That Jesus is something, isn't He? It's amazing what He can do with an 80-year-old guy, isn't it?"

An hour or so after he went to sleep Jack awoke, and upon going to the kitchen for a drink, he saw that his grandfather was still up. "Whatcha' doin', Pops?"

"Checkin' out prices of convertibles. Want to look with me?"

"Oh, Pops, I'm so sorry, I…"

"Damn it boy" he interrupted loudly. Jack was shocked.

"I mean" he said much more softly, "quit beating yourself up, Jack. I'm gonna get a new ride outta this deal. Let's enjoy this, ok?

"Excuse me," Susie interrupted, coming out of the bedroom. "I just thought I heard Pastor Miller cussing—like the old days.

"It must have been a bad dream, Nana. We were just having fun looking at new convertibles. Want to join us?"

Turning her back and going back in the bedroom they heard her mutter "Cussers and liars. A fine job I've done with them. What's a pastor's wife to do?"

She couldn't see the huge grins on their faces, but she knew they were there. "All wives, moms and grandmas have eyes in the back of her head," she thought, concealing her own smile.

Over the next couple of days, Jesus did work everything out and Jack made a couple of trips with his grandparents to the hospital to visit with Robyn.

On one of those visits, they talked a little bit about the wreck.

"I honestly can't remember anything about it. The only memory I have is of talking to Jesus… which is strange, because I've never been religious or anything."

"What did He say to you?" Jack asked.

"He told me that He loved me. I asked if He was mad at me. He said, that no, He was madly in love with me. He told me not to worry and that everything would be alright."

"Wow… that's pretty cool."

"Yeah. Have you ever talked to Him? Do you think I'm weird?"

"I talk to Him all the time. If you're weird, then I am too!" he laughed.

Jack knew that Jesus would continue pursuing Robyn and one day she would come to know.

The rest of the late summer was pretty uneventful. Jack was preparing to transition to college life in another city, albeit one where he would be with friends and live in his old house and old neighborhood. That didn't seem to be such a big deal.

Perhaps the hardest part of this transition for Jack was the process of losing his best friend, Mikey. Now at an advanced age, Mikey was no longer able to go upstairs to the man-cave or go for walks. He had some internal health problems and limped noticeably. He still perked up whenever Jack came home from school or a social event, but it was clear his days were numbered.

After talking things over as a family and consulting with Dr. Oldham, they agreed it would be in Mikey's best interest to have him put down. They decided to do that a few days before Jack would actually move to Houston.

The afternoon before the planned procedure with the vet, Fred said, "How 'bout we take a little spin in our new convertible…the Really Is 2.0? I was thinking maybe we could take Mikey and go out to the lake at the old homestead and let him see the geese one last time."

They had to help Mikey in the back seat, and rather than put his paws up on the side of the car so the wind could blow on his face, he was only able to lay in the back seat, but his expression showed that he was happy nonetheless.

Jack did most of the driving on excursions like this. His grandfather was still able, but deferred for a number of reasons… not the least of which was the enjoyment he got from seeing Jack's delight at being behind the wheel.

Shortly after getting on the two-lane country road, Fred sang out his familiar, "Home, home on the range" and Jack quickly joined him in their duet which ended with a robust two-part harmony on "where the skies are not cloudy all day!"

After a nice drive in the country and going through the gates, they pulled up as close to the lake as possible so Mikey wouldn't have to go too far.

Sure enough, as they crested the old railroad grade that formed the bank of one side of the lake, a flock of startled geese honked loudly and flew up out of the water and landed on the ground at the far side of the lake. In earlier years, Mikey would be off after them. This time he just watched, but his tail wagged as if he was recalling fun times of yesteryear.

Fred and Jack sat on the bank with Mikey between them.

"We've been coming out here a long time, Pops."

"Yep. And your dad came here with me, and I came with my dad before that. Lots of good memories," he sighed.

"Nana and I have been thinking about your going back to Houston. We're so proud of you and so glad that you'll be in a good place with friends and have Clara's family two blocks away. But…"

"But what, Pops?"

"You know, son… things don't always work out the way we hope."

"Yeah, I think I had that class… eight years ago."

"Yeah… we all did. I was thinking about you and Clara. Nana and I love her very much. She's a wonderful girl and we couldn't be happier if things work out for you too. We'd be very proud."

"But… they might not. Have you thought about that?"

"A little. I know things change when you go to college and get older. I've already seen friends who were couples at high school graduate and then break up. I don't want that to ever happen, but I know it could."

"Nana and I want you to know that should things not continue to work out with you two as a couple… if you want to go to a different college, if you want to come back here and live with us and go to KU, or even not go to school… you are always welcome. You're never an inconvenience and everything we have is yours… including our being together. There would be no shame to going to Houston, trying it, and finding out it's not what you want."

"Thanks, Pops. I always figured that was true, but I appreciate your saying it.

"So you'd really be okay if I didn't even go to college?"

"Yes… have you been thinking about something else?"

"Actually, I have. I really always wanted to be in a circus. I didn't want to scare you and Nana, but I've been secretly working on sword swallowing and fire eating. I'm pretty good. There's a Ukranian Circus that performs in Eastern Europe that's offered me a job." He did a pretty good job of keeping a straight face.

"Let me know how that works out for you. We'll still be here if it doesn't," Pops smiled wryly.

"Seriously, I do know that it might not work out with Clara, but I sure haven't met anyone else that makes me feel like I do with her. She's cute and smart and a great singer. She has a good sense of humor and that playful personality. She's good and honest and wants to do the right thing.

"You know we talk about God a lot."

"I didn't know that."

"Yeah. Her folks never really bought in to the church thing. You know they're good people and they believe in God, they just don't know much about Him… Them. But she told me she always knew there's a God… and knew that He had to be good. She never bought in to some of the weird things her friends believed at different churches."

"That's good!" His grandfather-pastor said.

"Yeah."

After a while, they made their way back to the "Really Is 2.0" and loaded Mikey into the back seat for his final ride back to their home.

So Long, Good Friend

There were just a few days of summer left before Jack would move to his boyhood home in Conroe and start a new and exciting chapter of his life as a first-year student at the University of Houston.

This was to be both the saddest of these days, the strangest, the most unusual, and ironically, the most grace-filled.

After breakfast, Susie said goodbye to Mikey. She'd sworn and laid down the law two decades ago that there would be no more pets in the Miller household. That was before her son and daughter-in-law tragically died while rescuing flood victims during Hurricane Harvey, leaving their only child– and her only grandchild– to come to live with her and Fred. She couldn't say no to Mikey coming with them.

Over the last eight years, she and Fred had come to love and be attached to Jack's best friend, constant companion, and primary connection to his past.

It had been hard on all three to see the loving lab's decline over the past year, and with Jack leaving for Texas, today was the right time to take Mikey to the vet for the last time.

Tears filled her eyes as she saw her 78-year-old husband pull out of the garage in his convertible with her 18-year-old grandson and his best friend in the back seat. As they pulled out of the Miller lane and on to a main street, the wind started to blow on them and Jack gingerly held Mikey up so the wind could blow on his face.

He stuck his tongue out briefly and his tail wagged slightly, but that was about all he could muster. Jack cradled his head in his lap and stroked his ears, tears streaming down his cheeks.

One look in the mirror showed Fred's face was wet as well.

They stopped in the parking lot of Dr. Gary Oldham's Veterinary Clinic, turned the car off, and stood by the Really Is 2.0 for a moment. With his eyes open Fred prayed aloud, "Lord, Jesus– thank you for providing this wonderful friend to us. Thank you for the fun we've had and the love and grace Mikey has shown to Jack, Nana, and me. We believe we'll be reunited with him, Freddie, and Rachel one day and we thank you for all of that. Amen."

They checked in at the clinic and took their seats, Mikey in Jack's lap. In a few minutes, Dr. Gary "Ears" Oldham came through the stainless-steel double doors and compassionately approached them.

"Hi, Fred, Jack. Mikey's been a special friend, hasn't he?"
They nodded affirmatively.

"Have you said your goodbyes?" he asked.

"Yep," Jack said haltingly. "We're ready."

"Thanks for giving me the privilege of taking care of him these past eight years. I'll take very good care of him now. Do you want to see him after we're done?"

They'd already decided that this would be their goodbye, so Jack handed him to the Dr. and said, "No, we're ready to go."

"Ok, guys. See you later."

Ears carried Mikey lovingly in his arms, turned, and walked through the double doors.

Neither Fred nor Jack tried to hold back or cover up their tears. The other customers shared a bit of their grief. Fred went to the receptionist's desk and said, "How much do we owe you?"

"She handed him a statement that said, "Pastor's Discount. No Charge." It was signed "Ears" with a smiley face.

"Thanks," Fred told the receptionist. "Tell Dr. Gary thanks."

"From both of us," echoed Jack.

Getting in the car, Fred showed Jack the bill. "That's really nice, Pops."

"Yep. That was a good thing he did for us… and Mikey."

"All good things come from Papa, don't they." It was a statement, not a question.

"That they do, that they do."

They drove home in silence. Upon arriving, Jack went to his room, gathered Mikey's blanket, bed, and toys and put them in a plastic bag and took them to the trash. Then he got the Trusting Axe and had a long session on the old oak tree.

Eventually he made his way to the man-cave and wailed away on his drums. Finally he came back in and started a sketch to honor Mikey.

Grace: Unconditional Love in Action

They were pretty quiet at lunch and were rather startled when the doorbell rang.

"Are you guys expecting anyone?" Susie asked.

"No," they said in unison.

"I'll get it." Fred offered.

As he opened the front door, they looked up to see a 6'5" man dressed in jeans and a denim shirt. He had bright red hair tied back in a ponytail and a painful look on his 30 something face.

"Can I come in? I have something to tell you all." He asked in a high-pitched, south western Texas accent.

Each of the Millers had an uneasy feeling that they had seen this man before, and that what he had to say was going to be difficult. Little did they know…

"Sure," Fred answered. Sticking out his hand, he said, "I'm

Fred Miller."

"I know, Pastor. I'm Claude Montgomery. I'm from Houston."

"Claude, this is my wife, Susie, and our grandson, Jack."

"I know. Pleased to meet you. I seen you before."

"Please sit down, Mr. Montgomery," Susie said graciously.

As he sat, he groaned, "I'm sorry, I'm so sorry." Instantly, Fred recognized the high-pitched voice from various random phone calls over the last few years.

"What are you sorry for, Claude?" Fred asked gently.

"I'm from Houston. I was there eight years ago. I volunteered to help flood victims. One day I got paired up with your son and his wife. Their truck was bigger than mine and could go further in the water. We towed a little rowboat on a rope behind it.

"We got to be pretty good friends since we were together rescuing people all day. They told me about Jack and that he was with you guys. Freddie gave me a card and told me about their Grace Community and invited me to it. I wasn't too interested in it, but I liked them… a lot.

"We had lunch together with the Red Cross people and then went back together to rescue people in the afternoon. I was glad to help, and I couldn't work anyway. I'm a bass player… I play in bands and the club we were playing in was under water. I think we hit it off so well 'cause we found out we were all musicians.

"There were so many people that still needed help that we agreed to stay after we had some MRE's from the National Guard for dinner. A TV station was there and they interviewed Freddie and Rachel. They got word that a levee had been breached and water was pouring into another neighborhood, so we headed there.

"We probably brought seven or eight families back to the staging area before the water really started rushing in that neighborhood. The people in charge said that because it was dark and the water was coming in so fast, that whenever we got out of the truck, we had to have the rope tied around each of us so we wouldn't lose anyone. Freddie and Rachel were glad to hear that, 'cause they said they weren't great swimmers.

"I wasn't sure their truck was going to make it any farther, but we pulled up to a house that had a bunch of people on the roof and parked in what we guessed was their driveway and let the truck lights shine on the house.

"I used to be a life guard and a swimmer, and I didn't think I needed to be tied to the rope so I told them to stay in the back of the truck while I swam to the house and managed to get up on the roof. I told them to throw me the rope so I could tie it on to the house.

"Right when they threw it, a huge wall of water... maybe two feet high... came rushing in on them." He was now sobbing. "I never got the rope.

"I saw them go under and then it swept the truck and boat away. I was gonna dive in to help them, but one of the kids on the roof slipped off and I dove in to get her. We barely got back on the house before another big rush of water came.

"It was dark and I couldn't see where they went and I never heard them again. I knew if I'd have followed orders and had the rope tied around me, I could have saved them," he moaned in anguish.

"I called the guy in charge of our rescue group and told him what happened and asked him to send some people right away to look for them. He said there was no one there to send out to help us... and I didn't even know what street we were on. He said as soon as someone came back, he'd send them to try to find us.

"I kept hoping they'd swim up and yell at me... but deep down I knew they were gone. We watched as little cars bobbed up and down and washed past us. Trees and trash and all kinds of stuff banged against the house. It was like we were on a pier in the ocean and the waves kept crashing against us.

"Nobody came and we stayed on that roof all night. There were three little kids, their folks, and me. They were all shook up about their house and afraid the water would rise and get us. I was in shock about your folks. I let them down. We were all wet and cold and it rained all night. Sometimes the wind almost blew us off."

"Fred and Susie started feeling The 'Hellish Darkness' descend in waves as they listened. Jack was in shock.

"The next morning, the National Guard came in a big boat and rescued us. It was just in time, too, 'cause the water was almost over the roof.

"As soon as we got back I started asking about Freddie and Rachel, but nobody knew nothin'.

"I tried to go home, but my neighborhood was flooded, so I went to a friend's house, finally got dry and warmed up, then I crashed for about 20 hours. Man, I had bad dreams… I knew if I'd had that rope tied to me, they'd a made it… I just kept thinkin' if I'd have dived in, I could have saved them… I knew I could, but the little girl… I had to go after her.

"I couldn't sleep that night… or most nights since. I had Freddie's card with his phone number and I kept calling… but no one answered. I saw on the news a couple of days later that their bodies were found and identified.

"I went to the funeral home websites and found out when the service was and I went. I kept thinking the whole time that the funeral didn't have to happen… if I'd only done the right thing. I was the last one through the receiving line. You gave me your card, Pastor Fred, so I've known how to get in touch with you.

"I've kept it a secret, but it's been eating at me ever since. Several times it got so bad that I called you to apologize, but I couldn't say much more than 'I'm sorry.'

"I've drove to your old neighborhood and walked past your house several times. Once, a couple of years ago, you all were out in the yard when I went by. I wanted to stop and tell you, but I just couldn't.

"Lately, something in me said that I had to come here and apologize and tell you and ask for your forgiveness…" he sobbed, appearing as distraught as a human could be.

All the memories of that night flooded into the minds and emotions of Jack, Fred, and Susie. They were stunned.

Fred summoned every ounce of his will and prayed silently as strongly as he'd ever prayed, "Jesus, take over… please, Jesus!"

"The 'Hellish Darkness' seemed to instantly lift and he seemed to almost experience an out-of-body experience. A light seemed to engulf the room and everyone sensed the Presence of Peace.

He found himself getting up and walking to Claude Montgomery, putting his arms around him, and saying, "Of course I forgive you, son. This has to be very hard for you. I'm so sorry you've had to go through this."

As Fred hugged him, he hugged Fred for all he was worth, repeatedly saying, "Thank you, Pastor, thank you!"

As Susie and Jack watched this real-life drama play out just a few feet from them in the Miller's living room, their minds and emotions seemed like a tornado in action with mental images of watching the news and hoping, police coming to the house, the funeral, saying goodbye to Jack's home and friends, and a myriad of other painful memories. Neither was sure where this whirlwind was going to land… or how it would affect them, however they too experienced the light and Presence of Peace.

They both prayed for Jesus to live as them.

Jack fought off memories of envisioning doing bad things to the person who caused his parent's death, should he ever meet him or her.

Then, almost like a director had choreographed their movements, they simultaneously made their way to Claude and wrapped their visitor in their collective arms saying, "You're forgiven, Claude. Jesus loves you and so do we."

They maintained their embrace for what seemed like an hour, but in reality was only a few minutes.

Susie was the first to break the hug… and the silence. "Claude, you've been bearing guilt and shame for eight years and I can see it's taken a toll on you. If you had tied the rope to you like you were told, it sounds like you would have lost your life too… and no one would have saved that little girl.

Fred followed with, "I was in the army for 24 years, Claude, and we had lots of training about exactly how to do things, but you know, in the heat of a catastrophic moment, we never know what's going to happen. I'm praying that you'll be able to let God take those feelings of guilt and condemnation away from you and trust Him that He was working everything out for the best at the time."

While their guest was comforted by their words, he was unable to speak and continued to sob.

"Let me get us some ice tea… I'll be right back. Fred, you want to get some tissues for our friend?" As she proceeded to the kitchen, the others sat in silence. Each wondered what to say in this situation, knowing that it certainly didn't call for small talk.

Eventually Jack broke the silence with, "This has probably been on your mind every day for eight years… just like it has ours, hasn't it?"

"Oh man. I lost my old man early, so I know a little bit of what you're going through. But he drank himself to death and we could see it comin'.

"Y'all didn't know nothing.' I hurt so bad for you… but I just couldn't come to you and confess… 'til now. I just couldn't make you wonder anymore." He stared at the floor, unable to look at them.

Susie heard Claude's words as she stood in the doorway bearing a tray with four glasses of iced tea and lemon wedges. Placing it on the in table that separated them all, she said, "Mr. Montgomery, I can only imagine your anguish. As you know, the three of us have been in anguish for eight years. We call it The 'Hellish Darkness.'

"But Jesus has been there with us and He's helped us through this. I don't by any means want to diminish the enormity of our loss. Having said that, we've all three trusted that Jesus is working all things out for the good, and we know we will one day be united with Him… and Freddie and Rachel.

"What happened is done and in the past. Speaking for myself, I have no ill will against you and if there is anything to forgive, my forgiveness is total and sincere… just as Jesus's forgiveness for me, and each of us, is unconditional.

"I'm a nurse. There were a few times over 40 years of nursing when I thought I knew better than the doctors and I deviated from protocol. Once, a patient went into shock and nearly died. I don't know for sure that my mistake was what caused it, but that haunted me for years. My saving grace was knowing that God forgave me for all my misdeeds– even ones I didn't know about. I absolutely harbor no ill will against you at all."

Fred continued, "I feel exactly the same, Claude. While we'd all certainly like to have our son and daughter-in-law back, I sure don't hold you responsible for our loss. Jesus loves, forgives, and accepts us unconditionally, and He gives us His ability to do the same."

With each statement of forgiveness and acceptance, huge weights noticeably lifted off of Claude Montgomery.

There was silence for a couple of minutes, and although no one looked at Jack, he knew it was his turn to speak.

"Mr. Montgomery, when I first heard what you said, I was filled with rage. I wanted to attack you with every ounce of strength I have and scream 'why didn't you follow the rules?' Thank God that Christ who lives in me comforted me and told me it wasn't your fault. He reminded me that He loves you just like He loves me too, and there's nothing that needs forgiving.

"Pops told me early on that God works all things out for the good… maybe this is part of that. God wants the best for me… and for you. My stomach turned from rage against you to compassion for you in a few minutes. I felt the Presence of Peace. I know that's Jesus, because on my own, I'd a been all over you."

"I don't understand what you folks are sayin'– all this Jesus bein' inside you… or God stuff or whatever. But I felt the peace too. And I know real when I see it. You all seem real… real good. The best I'd hoped for was a polite 'thank you' and then you'd a thrown me out on my ass… uh, butt" he groaned.

"Ass is good enough Claude. Without Jesus, even at 78 years old, when mad enough I could still give a good ass-kickin'– at least in my mind I could," he laughed, and the ice was broken.

"So…" Claude asked Jack. "You been here with your grandparents all this time… you doin' alright?"

"You know, Mr. Montgomery…"

"Claude… I'm just Claude."

"You know, Claude, I am doin' alright. Of course, I wish the accident had never happened. Of course, I wish I'd have had these last eight years back in Texas with my folks.

"When you told us what really happened, there was like a tornado in my mind swirling with pictures of all that happened– the police coming, the funeral home, saying goodbye to my friends… and then that tornado dropped us back down here in Kansas.

"Things have happened here that I wouldn't have experienced in Texas. But most importantly, Pops and Nana are the real deal. There's no one better than them. We've done these last eight years together.

"We've cried and yelled and sulked… at least I have. We've questioned God, we've had pity parties with ourselves, playing the victim card. I've taken an axe to the big oak tree out back lots of times to vent my anger.

"But we're family. You said you don't know about this Jesus or God stuff. You want to know what Jesus and God look like? They look like my Pops and Nana. They are the real deal… and not just with me, but with everybody else. I could tell you stories."

"I'd like to hear 'em. Maybe if you ever come back to Texas, we could, uh…" he started to say hang out, but realized that would be asking the impossible…or so he thought.

"Actually, I'm moving back to Houston next week. I'll be going to school there. And you said you're a bass player… I'm a drummer. What kind of stuff do you play?"

"Everything. But I like jazz the best. Not much work for jazz though. I play in different trios that play in hotel lounges, that kind of stuff. It pays the bills, but don't pay enough for me to get married or nothing like that."

Ever one to compassionately look out for others' needs, Susie said, "Claude, have you had lunch?"

"No, Mam. And I should be goin'– I never expected you folks to even want me in your house after I told you what I did…"

"We just finished lunch, but I've got plenty left over and the guys and I can have some dessert while you eat and we can get to know you better."

Without asking if that was okay with him, she said, "Fred, help me in the kitchen, would you? Jack, you want to show Claude your drums for about ten minutes and then come back to the kitchen?"

Although he was momentarily taken aback with the thought of being alone with the man who possibly could have saved his parents, he heard Jesus say, *Do it… for Me, Jack.*

"Uh, sure. Give me just a minute, Claude. I'll be right back."

Jack went to his bathroom, closed the door, leaned up against the wall, and talked to Jesus. "Lord Jesus, I think I've forgiven this man, but I'm not sure I can just relate to him like another friend. Will you help me, please?"

See him through My eyes, Jack. See Him as I see him. See what really is.

As Jack thought about those words, he got an impression in his mind: *Claude is My son, too. I love him just like I love you. He doesn't know this, but I influenced him to come here because I've prepared your family to help him.*

Exhaling rather forcefully, Jack sat on the side of the tub, feeling the immensity of those words. Rather than see this man through his own eyes, he was to see him through Jesus's eyes. He was to be Jesus's ambassador of reconciliation. Woah!

Taking a deep breath, he left the bathroom, went to this man whom he hadn't known existed less than an hour ago, this man who was maybe responsible for the horrible death of his parents and the ending of life as he had always known it, and said, "Ok, buddy– let's go take a look at where I make music."

Feeling like he was in an out-of-body experience– something he never expected, Claude followed him.

"I got these drums for Christmas about four years ago. Then I started a trio with a couple of friends from school. We practice here and we've done some amateur recordings and stuff."

"Can you play some sounds for me before we have lunch?" Claude asked.

"Sure." In a few seconds they were listening to "All the Things You Are" as recorded by the trio. After the first chorus, a throaty alto with style and character sang beautifully. After piano and bass solos, the singer joined the group again and they produced a wonderful and very tasty stretch ending.

"Dude… that's *your* group? That's better than any of the trios I play with in Houston. And the chick… she's somethin' else, man."

"In a lot of ways!" Jack chuckled.

"She your chick?" Claude said with raised eyebrows.

"Yeah, man."

"Dang!"

Jack chuckled, then realized it was time to go back for Nana's second lunch and dessert.

As the two made their way down the stairs from the man-cave

and back into the house, Jack found himself talking music with this stranger much like he did with his band mates. "Only Jesus," he thought and smiled inwardly.

As the four gathered around the kitchen table, Claude had a couple of large sandwiches, several refills of chips and a generous portion of Susie's special potato salad.

Fred started the conversation with, "So, Claude, did you stay in Oklahoma City or somewhere last night on your way here?"

"No, man. We got off at 10 and I drove straight through. Just stopped for gas and the bathroom. I had to make time because I got to be back for a 6 P.M. gig tomorrow night."

Quickly doing the math, Fred replied, "Wow, so you have to leave in a couple of hours and drive straight through again, right?"

"Yeah, man."

"You can do that with no sleep?"

"Have to, man. You miss gigs and they get somebody else. There's lots a cats wantin' to gig, and fewer and fewer jobs. You do what it takes… or you get a real job, know what I mean?"

"Yeah, I do. I've done some gigging, but never had to depend on it for a living. I got that steady check from Uncle Sam every month for 20 years… and then the retirement. And I got to do music all the time. Other than the constant moving around and the Army's regulations, it was a sweet gig."

Inwardly, Susie was amused at how quickly her husband could morph into speaking jazz– as he did with most of his army men and women. It took him a while in the pastorate to learn that speaking jazz was like a foreign language to most people.

Being respectful of allowing Claude time to eat, the Miller's intermittently asked about Claude's life. They found out that he had studied at the University of Houston for a couple of years, and then quit to play music full time. Fred assessed that he must be a pretty accomplished bass player due to the engagements and groups he mentioned.

They also realized that he had no church background, but considered himself spiritual and was certainly open to learning more about Christ living inside him and God's unconditional love.

In addition, the three grieved at the toll that eight years of guilt, shame, and condemnation played on this man who had never talked to anyone else about it. They each knew that Sarayu had been working all this time in his life and brought him to them as a key part of his restoration.

After lunch and dessert, Claude spoke, "I need to be headin' out pretty soon. I'm gonna find a shady little spot where I can pull over and zone out for a couple of hours, then get some hot black coffee, put on some Miles Davis, and start following the sun."

"We've got a spare bedroom, why don't you nap there? Just tell me what time you want to be up and I'll come and get you." Fred offered.

"Oh, man... I couldn't do that... I mean after what I done and all. You people have really lifted a load off'n this cat, but that would blow my mind."

"Well, consider it blown. I won't hear of you sleeping in your car when we have a room right here."

"Uh, okay, I guess..."

He showed him to the guest room and promised to knock on the door in two hours.

Even with the stunning experience of unconditional love, forgiveness, and acceptance swirling in his mind– where he had expected the possibility of hate, shame, condemnation and shunning, the Texan was so tired that he fell right asleep.

Susie went to the garage work room and after rummaging a while, she found an old thermos. She got to work preparing a couple of different types of sandwiches, put some chips in a zip lock bag, and included some cookies and fruit. She put them in a grocery sack and set them in front of the front door so as not to forget them. Then she set out to make strong coffee.

While she was taking care of those things, Jack and Fred went to the backyard, moved their lawn chairs to the shade, and visited about the unexpected experience.

"Well, this has been quite a day. It was hard enough saying goodbye to Mikey, but I certainly never expected a visit like we just had!"

"You know, Pops... I think this is a gift from Papa. We've always wondered exactly what happened that brought about my coming to Kansas to live with you… and now, just when I'm ready to move back to Texas, we find out. It's like God is tying up a loose end for us, you know?"

"Seems that way, doesn't it, son?"

"Yeah… I was just thinking about telling Clara all about this… maybe I'll wait 'til I get there and we're together. Something this important should be talked about in person, don't you think?"

"Good insight, Jack. I'm sure she'll want to experience this with you. You're looking forward to seeing her, aren't you?"

"Dang, old man, you're getting more perceptive than ever!" he joked.

Susie opened the back door and said, "Come on in boys, it's time to wake Mr. Montgomery."

As they got up, Jack looked around and said, "C'mon Mikey, let's go in." Then a sudden wave of sadness hit him. Fred gave him a little hug and said, "He was a great friend, wasn't he? He was here for you in the hardest time of your life. Really, he'll always be with us."

Claude Montgomery thanked the Millers over and over, and was very grateful for the food and coffee that Susie had prepared for him. When Jack asked him for his phone number and email, Claude seemed to really believe that their sincerity was just that… sincere.

They each gave him a hug and Fred asked if he could pray for him. Without really asking for an answer, he looked up and said, "Jesus, thank you for bringing our new friend to us. Thank you for protecting him on the way here and for giving him a safe trip home. Help him to really know that You have forgiven him for everything in his life… just like You have with us. Help him to know that You live in him, You love him unconditionally, and You want him to get to know You. Thanks, Jesus. Amen."

"Thanks, all of you." Claude said, choking up as he got in his truck. Rolling down the window, he said, "How *do* you get to know Jesus?"

Jack responded immediately, "On your way home, Claude, just talk to Him. Tell Him you heard that He's there in you and with you, and ask Him to speak to you. Then listen. When you hear good things… things like He's there and He loves you and He's for you… that's Jesus. If you hear anything bad… like condemnation, shame, judging… bad stuff, that's not Jesus. He's good… real good. Never bad."

"Thanks."

As he started to drive away, Jack said, "Til we meet again, Claude."

The man whom they didn't know existed, who had just filled in the biggest mystery of their life, drove down the lane and left for Texas. Somehow, they all knew they'd see him again.

They each felt the ever-present sadness lifting a bit.

As Claude Montgomery got on I-70 West and headed towards Wichita and Oklahoma City, he said, "Jesus… if you're there, I want to know. Talk to me, man…"

New Old Clothes and Freddie's Last Letter

Conversation about their visit from Claude Montgomery filled a lot of their time the next couple of days. In addition, Nana and Pops planned special presentations to Jack before he left for Houston.

He had friends to be with "for the last time" and a "final" concert for the Trinity Trio, but his grandparents worked the schedule so they'd have some quality time as well. One of those times was after lunch three days before they would help him move.

Nana went to his room and said "Jack, I've waited for just the right time to give you something today, but everything had to work out just right to make it work!"

"For instance?" Jack asked playfully.

"Well, you had to grow up!" she responded.

"What criteria do you use to determine when a guy grows up?" He smiled.

"In your case, you'd need to be about 5'11"– give or take an inch, and weigh around 170 without a pot belly," she said confidently.

"Huh?"

"Just a minute." As she left the kitchen for a moment, Jack looked at Pops, who just shrugged as if to say "you'll just have to wait!"

In a few moments, she came back carrying hangers that held a couple of nice sport coats with matching slacks, an expensive looking dark blue suit, and a very nice tuxedo.

"What do you think?" she smiled.

"Wow... those look very nice, Nana! But I'm not sure college kids dress like that very much. And why would I have to be my height and weight to qualify to get them?

"These were your dad's. I saved them and thankfully you grew a couple of inches over the summer and they should be just right. You might need them especially if you play in some groups at school... or maybe start another trio or something."

Jack was stunned. He gingerly took the tux in his hands and lovingly felt its smooth material. "I think he wore this at their wedding. It looks like the one in the picture. And I remember him wearing those sport coats.

"Nana... thanks. I don't know what to say..." He wrapped his arms around her and hugged her for a long time as tears of joy streamed down both their faces. "Thanks... for everything"

"You're more than welcome," she beamed. "I had a feeling eight years ago that these might be meaningful. This last year I just kept hoping and praying that you'd have another growth spurt!"

"By the way, we got you some nice dress shirts to go with these, and there are a couple of your dad's tux shirts along with his bow tie and cuff links all laid out on your bed."

They followed him to his to his room as he surveyed the rest of his clothing bonanza. Holding up the cuff links, he said, "What do you do with these?"

"I'll show you, Jack," Fred said. "You haven't had any experience with those things, yet, have you?"

"No, but can I try them on?"

"Of course! What do you want to start with?" His proud grandmother asked.

"The tux!"

"I'll leave you boys alone to do that," she smiled. "Oh, and your dad's patent leather tux shoes and two pair of his dress shoes are under your bed. They might be the right size as well. If not, we'll get you a pair that fit."

Susie went back to the kitchen to put some things away as Jack proudly dressed himself, with Pops' help, in his dad's tux. In a few minutes, the handsome young man appeared in the doorway wearing a tux for the first time. His grin was a mile wide.

"Oh!" She gasped… you look especially like your dad wearing that!"

"Take a picture, would you please, Pops, and print it out?"

Fred knew what the outcome of this picture would be. He couldn't wait to see the eventual sketch.

"How do the shoes feel?" Nana asked.

"Oh, yeah…" He raised his pants legs to reveal white socks and shiny patent leather tux shoes.

"I didn't want to change socks, but I do know to wear black ones with this outfit!" He grinned.

"While you're wearing your dad's tux, I have one more thing to give you before you set out on the next stage of your life. Let's go into the living room."

Jack looked very out of character in his new tux sitting between his grandparents who were wearing shorts and casual summer attire, but he didn't mind.

"Jack, the first birthday you spent with us, I gave you a letter from your dad, remember?"

"Of course. I still have it." He looked puzzled.

"Well, your dad had another letter for you. He left me instructions to read it, and then give it to you sometime after your 18th birthday. I know that was a few months ago, but it seemed like Jesus wanted me to wait until right before you left to give it to you. I didn't know exactly when that right time would be, but now I believe I was to wait until after our surprise meeting with Claude Montgomery."

Taking the manila envelope that his grandfather handed him, Jack saw his dad's familiar handwriting: To my son, Jack Miller.

Jack opened the envelope and extracted a several page type-written letter, and said, "I think I'll change clothes and then go to the man-cave to read this, if it's okay."

"Figured you'd want to," Fred answered.

Jack changed back to his shorts and t-shirt, hugged his grandparents, and silently took the familiar path to his special getaway. As he opened the door at the top of the stairs, he found the air conditioning was already on and there were oatmeal raisin cookies and a glass of iced sweet tea awaiting him.

Dear Son,

One of the most meaningful things in my life is hearing from Papa. Most every day He tells me how much He loves me and delights in me. I've been writing down what He says to me and compiling the pages to give to you—because everything He says about me is equally true about you!
Hopefully these Notes From Papa will be a great encouragement to you like they have been to me!

Love,

Dad

Jack felt as though he was taken to a spiritual sanctuary where he was sitting on Papa's lap as he read:

To My most special child, in whom I so delight,
I want you to absolutely know us– Jesus, the Holy Spirit and Me. To truly know Us and relate to Us with no fear and no reservations and no inhibitions, you must know what really is!
Here's what really is:
Jesus, the Holy Spirit and I have always existed in Our Divine Triune Circle Dance of love, joy, peace and everything good. We are love, and love gives and includes. Love never excludes!
Before creation We conceived, We dreamed up every person who would ever be born and all of creation... everything! Our plan and will was, and is, to include everyone and everything in Christ... in Our Divine Triune circle dance.
We decided to create beings in Our own image and likeness with Our DNA– beings with whom We can fully love and relate to.
We knew in advance what would happen with Our creation. We knew that sin would cause spiritual and physical death. Death is the opposite of Us. We are life! We knew this

would result in all people having darkened minds and their not being able to see the truth about themselves and the truth about Us.

We knew all of that before creating anything, and We had a plan before creation to remedy and restore everything! Our plan is Jesus- who is grace personified!

Grace is the means that We used to restore everything to Us. Jesus came to earth at just the right time... fully God and fully human. And He succeeded in Our mission! He took care of everything in His finished work at the cross... once for all creation!

Jesus defeated, set aside, made obsolete and abolished the law that condemned humanity. He defeated, killed and destroyed sin, evil and death.

I forgave everyone's sin, (past, present and future.) I took it away, I don't count it against anyone or impute it to anyone, I choose not to remember it or bring it up to anyone. Sin is not an issue with Us.

You all died with Jesus, were buried with Jesus and rose to new life in Christ, being born from above with Jesus, in Jesus and as Jesus: pure, holy, innocent, right with Us, without fault, fully accepted and included in Christ.

At the day of Pentecost, Our Holy Spirit was poured out on all people and took up residence in all people! Adam's race died and was done away with. Only Our New Creation exists now! We are now revealing to you and everyone what is– what is already true. This is truly good news for everyone! Eternal life is knowing Us... Jesus, the Holy Spirit and I... knowing Us now and forever.

When a person doesn't know Us, they perish... they stumble all over themselves in the darkness of their own minds. Our will is that no one continue to perish and instead that everyone has eternal life... knowing Us! We will achieve Our will!

When a person knows what is, when they know Us... then they experience the eternal life that they already have! What has always been objectively true for and about them also becomes subjectively true for them.

Our love never fails and you can never be separated from Our love. No one can ever be separated from Us and Our love. Separation is a lie.

In this life and in the life after, Our white-hot consuming fiery love for you all is continually burning away the darkness and the lies that each of you have believed. Our love never fails... it is ultimately successful!

At times during this process, it may be emotionally and mentally painful when people experience Our white-hot burning and consuming love for them exposing, burning up and taking away the darkness and lies that they have believed about themselves.

This process can seem like punishment, but it's not... it is restorative love in action. It can seem like "hell," but it's not. It is love doing its necessary restorative work. At some point each person will have all their lies and darkness burned away and all there is left for them to see and believe is what really is... Us, and Our white-hot unconditional love for them and all people.

During this process, people can experience Our love for what it really is. That's "heaven." Or, as long as a person continues to resist and hang on to their darkness induced lies, they will experience the exact same process as "hell" and will perceive it as punishment.

Whichever way a person experiences Our restorative, purifying process, they will experience it in Our presence. We are never separate from anyone!

Eventually everyone will ultimately see what really is– love... not punishment.

One day everyone will ultimately see what is... and what always has been and always will be: Our pure, white-hot, unconditional love for everyone that never fails!

For now, you have the Faith of Jesus that all this is true! For now, you have the certain hope that this is what really is.

One day you will no longer need faith or hope because all there will be left is Our love... the greatest of all! We are love and you are the eternal object, focus and recipient of Our love.

We are totally for you!   *~Love, Papa*

Part 9
End of One Era and Beginning Of Another

Jack and Clara became an item starting their freshman year in high school and a couple their junior year– all while living hundreds of miles and four states apart.

During their five years in college together they talked a lot about marriage and became engaged their senior year, which came as no surprise to those who knew them and had already expected them to live out their lives together.

They enjoyed those years of freedom very much and were involved in a variety of events and organizations while generally being able to spend considerable time together.

Since they were both music education majors, they took many of the same classes and had a fun time competing for the best grades and scores on tests. It all seemed to pretty much even out.

While they each had some separate friends, they mostly hung out with a fun group of peers from the music department. Their degree pursuit required a large amount of practice time on a variety of instruments, which meant that the music building with all its practice rooms, snack bar, and social area was their primary weeknight social venue.

They were both involved in their own jazz group that had a growing number of fans, including their classmates—when made the experience even more enjoyable.

Like all couples, they had their share of disagreements and even a few spats that brought fleeting doubts about the prospects of eventual marriage. However each always realized their love for the other was much stronger than occasional hurt feelings and misunderstandings.

Jack went "home" to Kansas for major holidays and for a month or so between each summer school and fall semester. While he enjoyed those times with Pops and Nana, he greatly missed Clara and their friends.

After Jack left for college, Fred and Susie resumed their 'empty-nest' lives and enjoyed a variety of trips across the country as they took advantage of Fred's military perks for guest housing and commissary privileges at installations from coast to coast. They especially enjoyed re-visiting places where they had lived during their Army days.

They managed to end up in Houston often, but were careful not to overstay their welcome or interfere with Jack's college life. They couldn't have been happier about his budding relationship with Clara.

Graduation was a big event for both families and bittersweet for the young couple as they were aware that this was the end of an era of being with their large group of friends on a daily basis as they pursued shared interests.

But it was also a sweet time of planning the wedding, going through graduation exercises, and enjoying a stream of parties and celebrations.

Gallivanting in Galveston

Their wedding was very special not only to them, but also to Susie and Fred, who proudly officiated the event. Susie enjoyed being the matriarch of the family and continually celebrated the special person her grandson had become. It was also special to Clara's family, and of course, a multitude of friends.

After the wedding they drove to Galveston and spent part of their week-long honeymoon happily recalling the events of their lives that brought them to this exciting start of a life "officially together."

One evening as they walked from their bed and breakfast to dinner at a favorite beachfront restaurant, they continued reminiscing about their time together. Their reservation was for seven, and soon they were seated at a table at the edge of the deck overlooking the serene bay waters. They were close enough to the beach below that they could hear the salt water washing in and out.

"Hi, I'm Zoe and I'll be your server tonight. Can I start you with a drink?"

"Hi, Zoe. We'd each like a mojito and your large bucket of steamed clams with zingy horseradish to start."

"I'll get that put in for you."

As Zoe left to turn in their order, Jack said, "You know what I was most looking forward to as I left Kansas to start college?"

"Being with me?" Clara answered playfully and hopefully.

Jack reached in his pocket and brought out a faded sketch depicting the two of them video chatting each other from four states away. A big heart encompassed the couple and the title read "The Future Mr. and Mrs. Jack Miller."

"Oh, Jack… you're always the romantic! When did you draw that?"

"When we were juniors in high school. I knew then I wanted to spend the rest of my life with you. I didn't show this sketch to anyone, but I kept it, looked at it often, and decided I'd give it to you on our honeymoon!"

"This is better than a million roses or a ton of chocolate… or… it's better than anything. Thanks, Jack!" Her adoring eyes said it all.

Taking the well-worn picture, she carefully folded it and put it in her purse.

They were a handsome couple framed against the calm, blue Gulf waters and its ever-present sail boats slowly moving with a beautiful setting sun and cloudless sky.

Jack, tanned and confident with his easy smile, was comfortable in a stylish, colorful, open-collared shirt, white slacks, and accompanying deck shoes.

Clara was stunningly breath-taking in Jack's eyes as her white sun dress accentuated and complimented her youthful figure, brownish red curls, and always cute freckles. He had been in love with that freckle-faced neighborhood girl since elementary school.

From the start, they had been seemingly able to talk about deep feelings, joys and concerns, God, and most any and everything with each other. Being together was both fun and energizing for them both.

Jack continued, "I really didn't care where I went to school as long as you were gonna be there," he smiled.

"You know I felt the same," she responded.

"Remember our freshman year when we had that fun party at

my house and after everyone left we both fell asleep on the couch in the living room before I was supposed to have you home at one?"

"All I remember was about 2 in the morning, my dad waking me up by pounding on the picture window right behind us and yelling, 'Wake up and come home, girl!' That was about as involved as he got in my life.

"I remember!" Jack said. "I remember that it took several sessions with you talking to your mom before she agreed to you living on campus where she wouldn't know what hours you kept or what you did. Eventually they did trust you. Well…trust us, I guess!"

"I don't remember much about our classes that first year," Clara said. "But I do remember the friends we made and what our life was like– probably because it hasn't changed a lot!"

"Yeah, remember when we found out about being able to get degrees online at our own pace at the Grace Seminary?"

"Boy, do I! We agonized over trying to do that and get our music education degrees too. Deciding to take a light load at the university so we could also do our seminary studies was one of the best decisions we ever made!"

"Yep. Even though it took an extra year at U of H, Jesus worked it all out. We have a pretty good back-up plan now… we can both teach music K-12 if we ever want to, and you have your Counseling degree from our Grace Seminary and I have my Theology of Grace degree."

"Jesus really worked things out for our education, but just think about the relationships He led us to!"

"Yeah, who would ever have thought that Claude and I… us… would become so close– both with he and I starting the Texas Trinity Trio and with Jenny being such a great friend too?"

"Yeah, and with Jesus orchestrating it so that you guys met Rusty– who not only played keyboards, but also was blown away with learning that God was totally different than he'd been taught. And Sheri came along and made a perfect six-some."

"Clara, what are the odds of the six of us getting together five years ago, still being best friends, and doing music and telling people about how good Papa really is?"

"I'd say the odds were one in one– a hundred percent– since Papa obviously put this whole thing together!" She laughed.

Clara became the very rare "girl singer who was also the band leader's girlfriend" who could actually sing! She was the accomplished and winsome face of the group, emceeing and singing with the Texas Trinity Trio as they managed to play club gigs, university functions and events, and developed their very non-traditional ministry.

They used the musical trio setting to help people understand how Jesus, Papa, and Sarayu had always existed in their Divine Triune circle dance of Their unconditional love and everything good that flowed from their Grace (love in action): joy, peace, patience, kindness, goodness, gentleness, the faith of Jesus, compassion, and never-ending mercy.

Sheri and Jenny, who had musical backgrounds but didn't play with the group, enjoyed their valuable part of helping manage the business, logistics, promotion, social media, and other aspects of the ever-widening opportunities the group was enjoying.

"I sure never imagined I'd be involved in starting and leading grace communities when we first did our little grade-school newspaper years ago!" Clara reminisced.

"Yeah, I'm glad we didn't call them 'churches.' You know Pops was right about that… as he was, and is still, about a lot of things."

"You and he really have a special relationship, don't you, honey?"

"Yeah, very special. He not only did his duty by taking me in when I wondered what was gonna happen to me, but he and Nana went way above and beyond. Looking back, I see now that they gave up their whole empty nester golden years to take on the full time responsibility of raising me…"

"Not just raising you, it seems to me that he mentored you and was more involved in your life even than most fathers are." Not only was Clara complimenting Jack's grandfather, but she was also expressing the sadness of her own father being emotionally and physically absent during much of her growing up years.

Like many good men and women, he had let his participation in the corporate world become priority over his family. There was frequently work to do at home, business trips to other cities, evening business dinners with clients, weekend seminars and total allegiance to the company that all-to-easily gave the impression that career came first.

He was a faithful husband and provided well for his family. He was a good, pleasant man, fun to be around… when he was around. Clara didn't have bad memories of her childhood and adolescent years, just a sadness shared with her siblings about missed opportunities.

"Of course Pops and Nana were involved– they were always there, supportive and encouraging. But you know the life-lessons I get from that old man are priceless. Wonder how much longer he'll…"

Clara took Jack's hand across their table, and silently shared their mutual realization that at 83, he and Nana probably wouldn't be there to see their great-grand kids grow up to be very old.

Eventually she spoke, "Priceless is a great description, Jack. What you, and now I, and an ever-growing group of people have learned about God and are experiencing in our new life in Christ is… well, priceless!"

"Sure is. And to think that we'd be able to take that knowledge and experience and develop it into what seems to be like a career with the band… who'd a thunk?"

Zoe reappeared with their Mojitos and clams and asked, "Have you two lovebirds decided on your main course yet?"

"Not quite. Could you give us a few more minutes, please?" Jack told her.

"I love what Sheri and Jenny are doing with the visuals and graphics for our live performances and the recordings. The number of social media followers is really encouraging!" Clara told him.

While the Texas Trinity Trio continued to play secular gigs that paid well enough to provide good incomes for the three couples, that part of their work also supported their spiritual performances that didn't always provide much of a stipend. They managed to sell a good number of DVD's at both types of events.

Spiritual and secular were terms they used to describe the

difference between their two types of performances, but they all believed that everything is spiritual. God is in everyone, at work in everyone, and drawing everyone to the knowledge of God's unconditional love, grace, inclusion, and acceptance of them.

"Yeah, Clara… and the opportunities we get just from hanging out with folks at the clubs and private parties are amazing. Most everyone is excited to hear that God's not angry, keeping a list, and eager to punish them!"

"Most everyone… except the die-hard transactional religious folks," she lamented.

"Let's not ruin our honeymoon with talking about that!" Jack said.

"Yeah, sorry. I know everyone will eventually come to know and enjoy Papa's love for them… it's just so frustrating sometimes with the mean-spirited stuff that happens.

"Let's not ruin our honeymoon…"

"Ok, ok… I won't say anymore!" she smiled.

As their waitress stopped by again, they gave their orders and Jack asked, "Are you from Galveston, or just working here for the summer?"

"Actually, I am from here," she said. But I'm going to college at Baylor and am just working at my old job for the summer. I love coming back to the ocean!"

"What are you studying?" he inquired.

"Science."

"Pre-med?"

"No, I think I want to teach. My parents are both teachers, and I'd like to do that too– maybe at the university level after I get a couple more degrees, if that ever happens," she laughed.

"Baylor, huh?" Clara teased. "We just graduated from U of H, so I guess that makes us rivals."

"You both graduated? Cool! Are those wedding rings?"

"Yep, we tied the knot last Saturday and came here for our honeymoon."

"Sweet! What will you do now?"

"We both teach," Clara smiled.

"Oh, wow! You both teach the same thing?"

"Yep," they said in unison, smiling at each other.

"So, what do you teach?"

"We teach people that God really loves them and isn't mad at them." Clara smiled.

"Come again?"

"We teach people that God really loves them and isn't mad at them." Jack grinned, partly anticipating a fun conversation with Zoe, and at the same time fondly remembering Pops giving that response to a number of unsuspecting people over the years.

"Uh, it would sure be nice if that were true, but that's not what I've heard."

"I know how you feel," Clara offered. "That's where I was for a long time. I was sure happy to learn the truth about the really good God who's for us all."

Looking around to make sure she didn't have other tables that required her attention, Zoe stated, "Actually, I've lived in fear all my life that I can never measure up to God and that He's watching me like a hawk. I didn't tell my folks, but I don't go to church at all when I'm away at school. I just can't stomach any more times of feeling worse when I leave church than when I came in. I'd rather just put it out of my mind."

"Zoe, there's another way to go. A fun, happy, wonderful relationship with God… who's never mad at you, but always madly in love you," Clara joyfully said.

"That would be too good to be true. Oh, I have to turn your order in and get back to my other tables. Excuse me, please."

The newlyweds never grew tired of interactions like they were having with Zoe. They didn't always bear immediate fruit, but sometimes they did. Other times they were able to maintain contact with people and nurture their eventual growing in grace. Sometimes, of course, people just weren't ready.

"Good thing we have a few more days… and that we like the food here!" Jack said.

"Yep, if Zoe's gonna be working, I'm thinking this is our place!"

Soon, she returned with their orders. Careful not to push, Jack talked about the food, commenting on how delicious it smelled and how aesthetically it was plated.

"Hope you enjoy it. Let me know if I can do anything else for you."

"We're good," Jack smiled. "Just ready to enjoy!"

As Zoe left, the newly-married Millers settled in for a savory treat, sharing each other's order and soaking in the beachfront beauty and their delight of each other.

After fifteen minutes passed, their waitress came by and asked, "Is everything all right?"

"Oh man," Jack gushed. "I think I could come back tomorrow and have the same thing again!"

"I can't promise we'll have the same special, but if you come back tomorrow, I'll take good care of you again."

"We may just do that… even if you are from Baylor," Clara teased.

"Do you really teach what you said? Do you have a position at a Christian school somewhere that lets you teach that?"

"Oh, no… not at a school. We play in a band that gives us opportunities to interact with people, and we have little informal groups of ten to fifteen people who hang out at houses or restaurants… whatever. They just get together and encourage each other and we help teach them how much God loves them."

"Are they like bible studies?"

"Not like you're probably thinking a bible study looks like," Jack laughed. "We have food and beer sometimes. We talk about life and what's going on with us and how we're feeling about things. Usually someone gives their take on one of our Facebook posts or short videos I make and they discuss that. Sometimes a group will go to one of our concerts."

"That's not like the bible study I used to go to… and quit," she said somewhat bitterly.

"What happened, Zoe?" Clara asked tenderly.

"I was made to feel so… like I wasn't good enough. Just like at church when I was growing up. At first they said God's love was unconditional. They were excited to get me to come, but when I did then they started telling me all these things I had to do to keep God loving me unconditionally.

"And they really put me down because I'm a science major. They hammered me about the six-day creation and how bad Darwin was. I decided I didn't need that. Never went back."

"I'm so sorry, Zoe. Those were probably good people, they just are misguided and misinformed. They've believed lies all their life and don't know there are other ways to look at God. We've had the privilege of helping lots of people with that background. Once they see the light… boy, are they happy!"

"Uh, got to help some other folks. I'd like to hear more."

After Zoe left their table, Jack said, "Jesus was right when He said 'the harvest is ripe,' wasn't He?"

"Well, yeah. He's like… always right!" Clara smiled.

"Oh, yeah…" Jack grinned as he broke open another crab leg.

"So, we play in Waco again later this summer, don't we?" Clara inquired.

"Let me finish this leg. The melted butter is getting cold."

After checking their schedule on his phone, Jack said, "August 17."

Zoe came back and asked if they needed anything.

"Could you bring some more hot melted butter? I didn't time things right and mine's gotten cold."

"Sure thing. I can bring you a dessert menu if you'd like."

"Please do," He responded.

She quickly returned with the hot butter, which Jack immediately sunk another piece of crab into, and then savored the bite.

"Zoe, we're gonna play in Waco August 17th. I think it's for some kind of welcome back deal. We're part of a concert with some other bands too."

"You in the band?" Zoe asked Clara.

"I sing a little."

"A little!" Jack exclaimed. "You're the star of the group and you know it."

"I sing a little," Clara smiled. "Jack's a great drummer, and we have really cool keyboard and bass players. Sometimes we have some horns. We usually look for local people who might play a few tunes with us."

"My boyfriend plays sax. He's in the Baylor band and plays with a show band. You should hear him."

"I'd like to," Jack said.

"They're actually here on the island all summer. That's another reason I came home! They play outside at 17th and Seawall. They start at 10 tonight. But I doubt it's your kind of music... you're like a Christian group, right?"

"Hardly!" Clara laughed. "We're a jazz group. We just happen to all love Jesus and love telling people about how good He and His Papa are. But we don't do any 'Christian' songs."

"Sometimes we do Amazing Grace," Jack interjected, "but not like you ever heard it in church!"

"Got any CDs?" Zoe asked.

"We have DVDs. But not with us... this is our honeymoon!" Clara laughed. "We might have one back at the B and B."

Seeing the deck fill up with more people, Zoe said, "I'd like to watch it sometime. What would you like for dessert?"

"First, could we take a selfie with you? We're making memories on our honeymoon and we'd like to include you," Clara asked.

"Sure," she said, nervously looking at the other tables beckoning her.

They quickly got a great shot of Zoe leaning down to be in between the honeymooners and Jack said, "Want to split the big chocolate thing, honey?"

"You know I do," Clara said.

"Be back with it in a minute," Zoe promised.

"I wonder what her story is?" Jack pondered.

"She's got one. You taught me that everyone does!"

"Actually, Pops taught me that!"

"Oh, yeah..." Clara reached for her phone and quickly started sending a message.

"Anything I should know about?" Jack asked.

"I sent our picture with Zoe to Pops and Nana."

"Really? What for?"

"Read what I wrote him."

Jack teared up as he read: *Our waitress wants to be a teacher. We told her that we're teachers too. You can guess the rest of the story. Love, Clara.*

Zoe soon brought them a huge, decadent mound of chocolate cake surrounded by vanilla ice cream drizzled with chocolate sauce and topped with cherries and whipped cream.

"It's to die for!" She said. "You guys don't look like you'll have any problem, but I can't have more than one of these a week. I gain a couple of pounds every time, and then I have to work out more to lose it!"

"Well, you're only on your honeymoon once. So we're gonna live it up tonight!" Jack told her.

"Enjoy. I've got a lot of people to take care of, sorry."

By the time they finished, they decided it might be wise to take a long walk on the beach to work off a little of their feast and enjoy the moonlight on the ocean.

When Zoe brought their check, Clara said, "Zoe, you've taken great care of us. Thanks so much! Here's my card for the band and it's got our Facebook info on it and my phone. You can check the band out there and if you like, come and hear us in August."

"Thanks, it's been my pleasure serving you. I'd like to talk more, but…"

"We can see you're slammed," Jack said. "No worries, we might come earlier tomorrow night. What time does your shift start?"

"Five. See you," she smiled and rushed off to a rowdy eight-top who were all enjoying the bubbly like there was no tomorrow.

"Tough job," Jack observed.

"Yeah, I hope they take good care of her. She's been busting her tail for them."

Leaving a generous tip as Pops had taught him, they waved at Zoe as they left.

"What a night!"

"And it's not over yet," Jack smiled.

"Just what were you thinking, my dear?" Clara asked knowingly.

"I was thinking it's 9:15 and if we timed it just right, we could have a nice walk and end up at 17th and Seawall and catch a little bit of Zoe's boyfriend's band."

"That all you were thinking?" She asked impishly.

"Well, that's a start," he grinned, taking her hand and making their way to the beach.

The Next Day

With no alarm set, Jack and Clara slept in way past their usual time and barely made it to breakfast before their bed and breakfast finished serving. Neither was very hungry, but the fare was delicious and they decided this could be both breakfast and lunch.

"Want to take the ferry to Port Bolivar and see some dolphins?"

"Sure! Let me clean up and text Mom. I promised her I'd check in once in a while."

Getting her phone from her purse, Clara remembered she'd put it on the do not disturb mode before they went to bed and she found a text from an unfamiliar number.

"Hmmm, what's this?"

Opening her text she read silently: *This is Zoe. I went to your Facebook site. Could you possibly meet with my boyfriend and me before work tonight, like maybe at 3 at the coffee shop next door to the restaurant?"*

"Ok, it's 10:30 now. Do you think we could do the ferry & get back in time to meet someone at 3?"

"I guess so, but I thought we could go to dinner early, like at 5, so we could maybe visit with Zoe some more. Who would we meet with?" He asked.

Handing her new husband her phone, she smiled as he read the text.

"I think we can make that work… Papa, You're really something! You tell her yes, I'll make the dinner reservation. I need about a half hour to do something. Let's leave for the ferry by 11:30. It should all work out.

He took his ever-present sketch book and excused himself to go to the front porch of their quaint bed and breakfast for thirty minutes.

Afternoon Fun

Feeling the saltwater spray on their faces, delighting in watching the dolphins play, and seeing each other enjoy the fun time they were having together made for a great excursion to Port Bolivar and back.

They enjoyed people watching, especially families where the kids were excited about the ship, the seagulls, the dolphins, and most everything.

They had ample time to retreat to their bed and breakfast, change clothes, freshen up, and get to the coffee shop a few minutes before 3. They each ordered an iced coffee drink and obtained a table for four in a corner area that would facilitate a private conversation.

Soon, Zoe arrived with her sax playing boyfriend. She, a trim, fair-skinned blonde with her hair pulled back in a pony tail that exposed a rose tattoo on her neck, and he, a dark African American with a short-on-the-side, but very high haircut, were a fun looking couple that wouldn't attract attention in most liberal university settings. However, in many other parts of Texas and the rest of the country, things could be different.

"Hey, Zoe!" Clara and Jack said at virtually the same time.

"Hey! This is my boyfriend, LaGerald."

After exchanging hugs with Zoe, their new-found friend, and fist bumps with LaGerald, Jack said, "Man, we really enjoyed hearing your band last night! You had the crowd jumpin' and yellin' and really groovin' with you, especially on those super high endings of some of your solos!

"Oh… you were there?"

"Yeah, Zoe told us about you, so we caught some tunes. It was too crowded to get close to the band, but we enjoyed you from the back of the place. We didn't stay real late cause we'd had a full day."

"And a full meal," Zoe added. "Most folks who have our big bucket of clams, lots of seafood, and the big chocolate dessert can barely walk out of the place. Thanks for the great tip, by the way!"

"We enjoyed it all," Clara responded.

"And thanks for the tip about your Facebook site. I read some posts and listened to the first two videos of your 'Journey to Freedom.' 'Unfulfilled Expectations' and 'Explanations Needed' really spoke to me– that's pretty much where I'm at on my journey, 'cept I didn't know it was a journey… I thought it was a dead end!"

"Me too," added LaGerald. "My grandparent's raised me. They're good people, but Grandad is an old-fashioned, 'hell-fire and brimstone' preacher in San Antonio. I grew up being religious and all that, being at the church all the time, and eventually playing with the worship team. All that was fine with him, but when I started playing with other bands… then at clubs… then dating a white girl… He makes his displeasure very apparent, so does the rest of the church…" he lamented.

"I had the same type of religious background," Zoe added. "But it was a white's only church. My folks are really old school. They still say 'colored people' and while they aren't mean about it, they are not pleased at all with me dating LaGerald. He gets to come to dinner at our house, but it's so stiff and awkward, neither of us even want to be there together. They actually have the curtains drawn over the living room picture windows. They don't want the neighbors to see."

"I'm so sorry, Zoe," Clara said, compassionately taking her hand for a moment.

"Yeah, that sucks. I was raised by my grandparents too. My Pops also was a pastor… different deal though. He wasn't into religion at all. So what prompted this nice invitation to get together with you guys?"

"Zoe called and woke me up early," he smiled. "I know it must have been something important 'cause she knows how tired I am after playing 'til 2 in the morning. She was all excited and said I had to watch your videos about 'Unfulfilled Expectations' and 'Explanations Needed.' She said I'd like your band… which I do! And that I should hear what you had to say.

"It's really cool how you set the deal up, like a teaser, then play a tune, then come back and get to the meat of things. I like that… and the band."

Looking at Clara, he said, "You got some lungs, lady! Nice singin'!"

"Thanks! So, what hit you about Expectation and Explanations?"

"Well, man, it's like in the church somebody's always sayin', 'God is great all the time!' You expect something good to happen, but then bad stuff happens, man. People get cancer, you know, and they die… sometimes they suffer a lot. The church has big prayer meetings praying for Sister Jones to get the healin', then after the prayers, the ladies get together and make plans for who's gonna take which meals to Sister Jones' family… cause they know she's gonna die. What's up with that, man? It's like they go through the motions, but don't really believe.

"It's like they got these religious rituals they got to do to be good church people… but they know they don't work, man!

"And they're always talking about and praying for Johnny Jenkins to come back to the Lord and come back to church, 'cause he ain't been there for years and he used to be so involved.

"But I know Johnny Jenkins, man… and he's a really good dude. He works hard and keeps a job and is nice to his kids and his ol' lady. He coaches his boy's ball teams and goes to all their school things, you know? I see him payin' for other kids uniforms and stuff like that. He ain't got religion, but he lives like Jesus did… seems to me, anyway.

"Then some of these folks prayin' for him to come back to church and saying how he's lost and far from the Lord… they ain't workin', man. They always wanted the church to bail them out. I see 'em yellin' at their kids and backhandin' 'em. They go to the games, but they yell at the kids and tell 'em 'bout all their mistakes… and they yellin' at the umps…

"Seems to me like Johnny Jenkins is closer to God than the church folk, know what I mean?"

Zoe jumped in. "I see the same stuff you guys… not with everyone, but with lots of people. But what gets me is the talk about God's unconditional love and how He love's everyone. But my church people don't love everyone. They don't love African Americans. They don't love Muslims… and they sure don't love gays.

"One of my classmates who I was in Sunday School with for years came out last year. She's a really nice, fun girl. But she came out. She's not welcome at church anymore and the only reason her folks can come is 'cause they all but disowned her. That's not love. They think God is like that, but He can't be… if He's good, can He? How can God's love be unconditional…and have all these conditions?" She was almost pleading for her new friends to tell her God can't be like that.

LaGerald continued, "And the hell thing, man. I mean, you know, if I ever get married and have kids, I sure as hell ain't gonna fix up some torture chamber in the basement before they're born, just so I can fry the ones that don't do what I want.

"I don't know what you think, man… maybe you gonna get up an' leave. But it just don't make sense, man, that if a nice kid or little ol' lady in India or the Congo or the Amazon… if they never heard of Jesus– God's gonna fry them? Can't be!

"I asked Grandad about that once a few years ago and he got real stern and said, 'Boy, God's ways are higher than our ways and if God says He's good, then He's good. The Good Book don't lie, boy, and don't you be questioning it, hear?'

"I pretty much checked out after that. I still went, still played in the band and said the right things and raised my hands at the right time… but you know, I just wasn't there. I'm real grateful for my grandparents raisin' me, and they good people, and I don't want to disrespect them.

"But what I bought before, man, I just can't sell. You know?"

"We know, man. Man, do we know." Jack answered.

"Look, guys," Clara said, "We've just met you guys, and there's no reason for you to believe anything we say. But we're gonna lay some things out there, and you take them and talk about them, and most importantly, ask Jesus if they're true. He will answer you… and you'll know inside you what's right. There's a better way!"

"And we also want you to know that your folks, and your grandparents, and the people in their churches– they're not intentionally lying to you. They're just misinformed and have never heard the truth. Unfortunately, most folks haven't… especially religious folks. They can be the slowest to come around, but they will. They will."

During the next hour and a half, Clara and Jack tenderly and clearly explained how God is love… love in relationship.

Jack said, "Take a look at all that water out there in the Gulf. And the Gulf's massive, you know, and there are all the oceans. That water never runs out!

"Now if I say God 'is' water… that's a different deal than 'God gives you water.' That's what He *is*, and He is eternal… *forever*. See, if I say God 'has' love, which could run out… well, it could be for you but not for me. He could give me some love if I did well… but withhold it if I screw up. But if God *is* love…that's never gonna run out, right, 'cause God never changes!

"When you understand that God *is* love… and everything He says and thinks and does flows from His unconditional love that always does what's best for people– that changes, like, everything!"

They told their new friends that before creation, the Trinity chose them, and everyone, to be in Their Divine Triune circle dance of love and everything that flows from that love: joy, peace, patience, kindness, goodness, gentleness, the faith of Jesus, compassion, mercy, and grace.

They explained that grace is actually love in action– love that continually washes over, in and through everyone.

Jack carefully explained that everyone is included and in God's love, there are only His children… everyone. There's no in and out, us and them, etc. The difference is some people believe and some don't…yet.

Then Clara lovingly showed them how 'hell' is a religious construct; how the word isn't actually in the original language. She explained the fire metaphor– how God's white hot, fiery love is all-consuming, it eventually consumes all that's against us, all that's bad and evil… it's curative and restorative, but it's never punitive.

Zoe and LaGerald hung on every word. Many times they were tempted to say "but what about…" however, they so wanted what they were hearing to be true that they hardly interrupted the newlyweds. They were especially intrigued with what they heard about 'religion.'

"I noticed that you both mentioned 'religion' and being 'religious' when you talked about your churches," Jack said. "Jesus didn't come to start a new religion or to help people keep the law better in the Old Covenant Religion. He came to usher in a whole new, non-religious deal… and He did!

"Religion comes from a Greek word that means bound up, and that's what religion does to you. It binds you up! Religion always lets people down."

Clara continued, "We've learned that religion is mankind's work to gain and maintain a right relationship with God by what we do. Not just the Christian religion, but all religions are like that. But Jesus isn't into that at all!

"Jesus is love…God is love. Grace is God's unconditional love in action. Grace is what God did to bring us to Him!"

What God Requires, God Provides

"Excuse me, but I just have to get some clarification here," Zoe said. "God's holy and righteous and He requires that we work to become holy and righteous… isn't that right?"

"Half right!" Clara replied. "Here's the truth– God is holy and righteous, and He does require that we be holy and righteous… now, here's the really good news! Whatever God requires… He provides! Always. You can take that to the bank!"

"Here's what He did," Jack continued. "Before creation they decided this, then at Jesus's finished work at the cross, God the Father was in Christ Jesus, reconciling everyone forever to Him, not counting anyone's sins against them. This whole deal was God's doing– for us– in advance!

"God worked it out so we all died with Jesus, we all were buried with Jesus, and He raised us all with Jesus to new life in Christ… new creations, with new hearts, pure, holy, right with God and without fault! He did it all! He put you, and everyone, in Christ! He made you holy and righteous in advance! What He requires, He provides!"

"Man, that's totally different than what religion laid on me. I can hear my grandad's voice now… and the elders and revival preachers. 'Your sin separated you from God, you got to get right with Him. Here's what you got to do, boy.' Then they laid it on us– stuff no one could ever do. It never worked."

"I know, man. I was really lucky. My Pops taught me what I'm telling you. Jesus is love– totally and only love. There's nothing bad about Him or His Papa, or the Holy Spirit. He knows that only He can satisfy. Religion can't. Music can't. Money can't. Friends can't… only He can satisfy."

Clara commented, "I didn't grow up religious, but I was always looking for something that would satisfy me. I thought if I hung out with the right friends, that would do it. I thought if I made good grades and got 1's on vocal solos at state contests, that would do it. I thought if I had the right boyfriend, that would do it," she grinned at Jack.

"Those things are great for what they do… they just don't ultimately satisfy. Now, here's the problem, religious folks have been taught… and they think… that religion and church will satisfy. They think if you just do all the right things and be a good person, that will be it.

"But we've all found…that's not it. That doesn't do it!"

"Ok," Zoe said. "But what does do it? What does satisfy? What exactly is it?"

"It's not an 'it,' Zoe." Jack said, gently. "In Jesus' day, the religious people asked Him the same question. They thought it was an 'it'… they called it 'Eternal life.'

"Jesus told His buddies the night before He died, 'This is eternal life, that people actually know the Father'– personally, intimately, like a married couple– as intimate as you can get. That you hang out together, that you share everything, that you talk, you listen, you love, you go through ups and downs together. It's a relationship closer than any human relationship.

"It's… your name, Zoe!"

"What?" she was startled.

Clara continued, "Your name in Greek, the language the New Testament was written in means: a certain kind of life. The most vibrant, alive, pulsating, joyful, joyous, peaceful, strong, energized kind of life possible… life that is empowered and energized by God… by the Holy Spirit in you."

"I've been missing that… I sure don't have that…" she lamented.

"You have it, Zoe. You just don't know it yet. Jack and I can both see Christ in you… and LaGerald. Jesus is there!

Continuing, Clara said, "Jesus showed us that what really satisfies– the only thing that does– is Him… Christ living in you who actually talks to you and listens to you and explains things to you and tells you what He's thinking about things. It's abundant life that has no comparison to anything else! Until you experience it, you can't comprehend it."

Clara literally glowed as she shared what Jesus had revealed to her, and both Zoe and LaGerald felt something inside them resonate, indicating that what she was saying was right and true.

"I've never heard this stuff before, but it feels so... right... even though it doesn't sound right to my religious mind." Zoe said.

"Feels right... that's good, real good! Let me help with this, if I can." Jack interjected. "Do either of you play guitar?"

"Yeah, we both mess around a little on it."

"Do you guys have a piano at home?"

"My parents do," Zoe said.

"We had several at Grandad's church."

"Ok, I don't know if you've ever done this or not, but I want you to try it. Take a guitar and tune it– with the piano. Then stand it up on the piano bench, and then play a low E and let it ring. Do you know what will happen?"

"I do!" LaGerald exclaimed. "I used to do that all the time just 'cause it's so cool!"

"What happens?" Zoe asked.

"When you play that low E, the same string on the piano vibrates, man! You ain't touching it or nothing, it just vibrates. It sings– you can hear it. It's spooky... like magic!"

"Exactly!" Jack said. "In music, they call that sympathetic vibration. The vibration on the guitar string goes through the air, hits the piano string, and it vibrates too! Same thing in life, Jesus's real life... when you hear the truth like we been telling you, that truth resonates with truth inside you...something inside vibrates! It's like you feel something that says, 'That's right! Believe that!'

"That's what I've been feeling today with you?" Zoe queried.

"Yep! Now... listen to the rest of this," Clara said. "The Holy Spirit of Jesus inside of you resonates with your spirit, your heart, what you feel– the real you. But, your mind--that has listened to all the lies of religion, your mind goes--'That's not right. It can't be. Look at this bible verse...remember what you've been taught.'

"See, your mind is gonna fight your heart. So remember to listen to your heart– listen to what you feel deep inside."

"But…" LaGerald interrupted, "what if you guys are not telling the truth. What if what you're into is a cult, man? What if all this stuff ain't right?"

"How's what you've been into before, how's that religion been working for you? You want to go back to that?"

"Hell no. No way! We told you how that didn't work, how we've been hurt by it."

"Trust your heart, man. Give your heart a chance. Give Jesus a chance. Look for His love and peace and joy and acceptance. Listen to him. Just get off by yourself and get quiet and ask Him. Just say, 'Jesus, is this true, I want to know!'"

"I'll do that. I will!"

"Me too," Zoe added.

"Wait a minute," LaGerald said. "Is this brand new… does anyone else believe this stuff?"

Laughing, Jack said, "Get this, man, this is what the first church believed. Those folks knew the Truth. It wasn't till 300 years later that religion messed it up. There have always been people who know this, but religion tries to stop it."

They visited some more, then finally, Clara said, "We really want to be respectful of your time. Zoe, you said you have to be to work at five and we have reservations shortly after that. What time do you go on, LaGerald?"

"Not til 10. I'm good."

"You want to join us for dinner, our treat?" Jack asked.

"Me? Naw… it's your honeymoon, man, you don't want a third wheel buttin' in. I'd spoil your whole romantic evening!"

"We have the whole evening after dinner to be together… we'd love to have you join us," Clara stated.

"I don't know, man."

Jack interrupted, "Zoe, can you change our reservation? Make it for three people– and still make sure we can have a nice table overlooking the Gulf?"

"I think I can make that happen" she smiled.

"Ok then, we're gonna go back to our place and check in with our families. We'll be back at 5:30." Jack told them.

Dinner and an Invitation

It was a bit awkward for LaGerald, at first, having his girlfriend serve him while he was with another couple, but they soon settled in like old friends. Their mutual background broke the ice and provided a great venue for Clara and Jack to show their new friend how they taught about God's unconditional love via the Texas Trinity Trio.

"You know, man, we've been starting little groups on some different campuses around the state. They get together at apartments or clubs or restaurants, wherever, and talk about stuff– sometimes about our videos online, sometimes about whatever. We've had a few people from Baylor come to our concerts in Dallas and ask us about starting a group there.

"I'd be all over that, man! I know Zoe would too!"

"We're gonna be there in August, maybe we could get a little group together then and hang out for a while. We'd like to have you blow a couple of tunes with us too, man."

"Really? I don't know if I know your stuff."

"You got the Blues in Bb?" Jack laughed.

"Yeah, Man, I got that!" he laughed. "Wouldn't be worth much if I didn't!"

"Tell you what, you listen to some of our stuff online, pick out a couple of things you like. If you got a friend or two– horn players, bring them too– long as they play like you do!"

"Really?"

"Yeah, man!"

Then Clara asked, "Jack, don't you have something you wanted to give LaGerald?"

"Oh, yeah! Thanks, Clara!"

As LaGerald wondered what was going on, Jack reached in his pocket and pulled out piece of paper, unfolded it, and gave it to his new friend.

"Where did that come from... a promo brochure?"

"Nope. I drew it this morning after we found out we were gonna meet you."

"Man! You captured the whole thing last night! Me wailin', the whole band, the crowd, the gulf– you got that all in this one picture and I can feel the energy that was there. Shoot, man...

thanks, this means a lot to me."

"Me too" Jack said.

For the rest of the evening, every time Zoe came to serve them, LaGerald told her how excited he was to get to play with them back at Baylor.

When Zoe brought their check, Clara took a selfie of the four of them, later sending it to Pops saying: 'possible new group in Waco!'

As always, Jack left a very generous tip along with presents for their new friends.

Two copies of "Grace Is" contained identical handwritten notes inside the cover, the only difference were the names: To Sweet Zoe was on one, To My Man, LaGerald on the other. They each said:

"This is a copy of the book my dad wrote for me before he died. It sums up what he and we believe really well. I look forward to hanging out with you and talking more about Grace: God's unconditional love in perpetual action for everyone! Til we meet again -- Jack"

Zoe and LaGerald were genuinely excited to get their gifts, and the evening ended with everyone exchanging email and cell numbers and agreeing to friend each other on Facebook.

As they left, Clara said to their new friends, "Til we meet again!"

Walking out of the restaurant, the honeymooners looked back to wave and they saw LaGerald excitedly showing Zoe Jack's sketch.

"I just love it when Jesus asks me to do something and I get to see the fruit right away."

"Me too, honey." Clara squeezed his hand and they made their way to their B and B.

The Honeymoon's Over

Jack and Clara saw their new friends briefly a few more times before their honeymoon was over and they left to settle into married life back home in Houston.

However, they stayed in touch with their Baylor buddies. Both LaGerald and Zoe were like sponges... reading and liking Jack's blog posts and devouring the videos– especially the Texas Trinity Trio doing tunes sandwiched in between Jack, Clara, or other group member's talking about their new life in Christ. They ordered several copies of "Grace Is" to give to their friends.

They listened eagerly to all of the group's videos. They especially liked one called "Reconciliation."

On that session, before the band played, Jack did a little monologue. Zoe and LaGerald were mesmerized as he said, "When I was 10-years-old, my mom and dad died while rescuing flood people in Houston. For a long time, we didn't find out what caused it. I left Texas and went to Kansas to live with my grandparents.

"Then, eight years later, a guy we'd never met showed up at our house in Kansas and told us that my folks were washed away in strong high waters because he didn't follow protocol with a safety rope they had. He dove in to save a little girl instead of going after them.

"At first I was filled with rage and I wanted to choke him to death... I wanted him to pay for the hurt he caused me and my grandparents. But Jesus in me kept talking to me. He took that hurt away. He told me it wasn't the guy's fault. He helped me see that guy the way Jesus saw him. He showed me that Jesus loved him just like He loved me... and that Jesus reconciled that guy to Himself, just like He did me.

"I was able to forgive him, accept him, and reconcile with him. Jesus did all that. You know what happened to that guy? He's one of my best friends. He's standing next to me right now. We're gonna feature Claude Montgomery on bass right now on this tune called Amazing Grace."

As LaGerald and Zoe watched the video, tears were streaming down their faces. The Holy Spirit of Christ was speaking to each of them. They both had been hurt by people.

LeGerald often said that all he got from his folks was his name. Lavita and Geraldo combined theirs to name their son. Confusion over his name was the least of the troubles in life they bestowed on him.

LaGerald's dad left him and his mom before he was a year old. He never saw him again. He and his mom moved in with her folks – his grandparents. But she was a free spirit and couldn't live with their heavy-handed, religious ways... especially the shame she felt from them and their church.

One day she went to work in the morning, leaving LaGerald with his grandmother, and she never came back. The last he heard, she was in prison in Louisiana. Christ in him was moving him to forgiveness and reconciliation.

After the great rendition of Amazing Grace ended, which included Clara's poignant vocal solo, they heard Claude Montgomery's tearful testimony of how Jesus changed his life through the forgiveness and acceptance that Jack and his grandparents gave him.

"That's the real thing, LaGerald."

"Yeah, man, I feel it too."

Bearing Down at Baylor

The foursome got together again when the Texas Trinity Trio played at Baylor. LaGerald and a trombone playing buddy sat in with the group and played a couple of blues tunes that brought the house down when they ended with the band playing four bars, then Jack would take a drum solo for four bars... and they repeated that pattern with ever-increasing velocity and energy to a wild climatic final chord with high, screeching sax notes and Jack wildly flailing at the drums.

The audience gave them a standing ovation and clamored for more. Expecting him to announce an encore, the audience, instead, raptly listened as LaGerald said a few words.

"Me and my girlfriend, Zoe," he said as he pointed her out in the crowd, "we're gonna start a little group here at Baylor and stay in touch with these guys. They got something that's real and we're gonna talk about that and learn together. If anybody's interested in hanging out with us... go over and talk to Zoe."

Jack took the mic to thank the crowd, introduced their encore, and finished with his signature, "Til We Meet Again."

Then they did, indeed, play another rockin' tune, and as the musicians played, they watched happily as a number of people surrounded Zoe. Jenny and Sheri helped her get people's info and give them a flyer about an upcoming get-together.

They videoed the concert and sent it to Pops and Nana.

That evening was similar to many others the group experienced around Texas. It was becoming a major deal for the group to keep up with their Online Community Church friends who now represented little grace communities in almost two dozen college towns.

Jack was drawing heavily on Pops' continuing advice as he mentored friends to facilitate those various groups.

Fred, of course, was elated to still be involved, and was especially grateful for video chatting capabilities. However, he was aware that at his age, his time in this life was inevitably coming to an end. Soon he would not have to contend with attacks from The 'Hellish Darkness' ever again, but instead would be eternally surrounded by the Source of Light.

Part 10
The Last Convertible Conversation

Jack really cherished these trips back to Kansas, especially now that he could bring Clara with him. He worked the band's schedule to be off for Thanksgiving week so that everyone could be with family. Thanksgiving was always special with Nana and Pops. He was also anticipating their next trip at Christmas when they expected to have their newborn son with them.

It was an unseasonably warm, late November day, so Jack put the top down on Pops' convertible– which replaced his cherished Really Is that Jack totaled while in high school.

It was about 73 degrees and there were no clouds in the bright Kansas sky as the 25-year-old opened the door for his 85-year-old Grandfather, who remained in good health, albeit with weakened legs that prevented him from being as active as he would like. He chose not to drive anymore due to deteriorating eyesight.

As they drove away from their comfortable and familiar home, Pops burst into singing Home on the Range and gave special emphasis to, "and the skies were not cloudy all day!"

Pops could still see well enough to point out their special, familiar landmarks as they made their way through the town and out into the country. Jack drove slowly, savoring every moment with his surrogate father, mentor, and friend. Memories of spending every day with him from the age of 10 until he left for college formed a beautiful collage ranging from special events to the everyday assurance that Pops was always there.

Even after he left home for college, Jack remained very close to his Pops. They often video chatted where conversations first ranged from mundane check-ins to Jack seeking advice and counsel for his music degree or his online courses with the Grace Seminary. Later, he often conferred with his grandfather about relationship situations with Clara and with other band members. Financial decisions and opportunities also occasionally entered their conversations.

In addition, now that their grace communities were springing up all over the Midwest, he drew more and more on Fred's advice from his experience leading a church and subsequent grace community in Lawrence.

He was very grateful for Pops' sage advice. Fred was equally grateful to be able to help and was genuinely blessed to know that his grandson valued his advice. However, he always made sure to remind Jack that the most important thing was for him to ask Jesus what He was thinking about a situation or circumstance, and to then go with what He said.

Nana was often involved in these long-distance conversations and Jack would occasionally call her individually. For Susie, Clara was filling the void of the daughter-she-never-had, which Rachel enjoyed being for some time years ago.

Jack still remembered the combination to the lock on the four-generations-old gate that served as a private entrance to their special hidden lake, still preserved on the family's original homestead. As with many things that started in their unique relationship fifteen years ago, the roles were now reversed. Jack opened the gate, drove them through, stopped, and went back to fasten the lock and ensure their privacy.

Fred had fond memories of that baton being passed to him in his own father's later years.

Parking at the foot of the abandoned railroad trestle, Jack said, "Remember the times we were here when Mikey was with us."

"Yep," the old man replied. "He was a good friend… but age eventually took its toll…"

Silently, the two men slowly made their way to what had become their accustomed place to sit and marvel at nature's beauty. Jack had to help His grandfather, who was now a little unsteady and used a cane.

As they sat, they noticed the symmetry of the lake's border reflected in the clear, still water. It seemed that nothing ever changed here except for nature's seasonal adjustments.

On this day, the trees were mostly bare as the last remnants of fall's foliage had dropped to the ground a few weeks ago. Squirrels scampered up and down trees storing nuts for the winter. Crows filled the air with loud blasts, and the ever-present geese occasionally trumpeted their own communication to the soundscape. In between the loud fowl emissions, beautiful tunes from songbirds created nature's melodious contrast.

"When we first came here with you, Mikey was all over those ducks and geese, wasn't he?"

"Yep. He never caught one though. I think he just liked messing with them," Pops smiled.

While savoring their special time together, Jack was also grateful that at this same time, Clara and Nana could have their own private time as well. Both grandparents shared their excitement over the approaching due date of their first great-grandchild, a boy, who was expected in a month.

After a bit of reflective silence, Fred asked, "When you're in Texas and you think of this place, what comes to your mind?"

Thinking for a minute, Jack replied, "Peace. Trust. Assurance. Knowing everything's right with the world."

"Yeah, me too. You know I came here with my dad and grandfather, whom we'll both enjoy together one day. It was fun to catch fish, but I realized after I left home, fishing was just an excuse for an opportunity to be together. This is where I learned a lot of life-lessons that stood me well through the years.

"You never wanted to fish, though, did you?"

"No… I couldn't stand the thought of pulling something up out of the water after my folks…"

"Oh… yeah…"

They both enjoyed being lost in their own thoughts for a while… neither feeling the need to 'keep the conversation going.'

"I'm sure looking forward to bringing my son, and other kids if we have them, here one day."

"Yeah, I wanted to talk to you about something Nana and I have been thinking about concerning this stage in our lives."

"What's that, Pops?" He asked, with a touch of anxiety.

"Well, I'm getting more unsteady and we don't know how many more years we'll be able to keep up our big house, yard, the barn and everything. We've been looking into a retirement center where we'd have a nice apartment, but a lot less responsibilities. We'd also have instant care available if we'd need medical help or something like that."

"Sounds like you've been doing your homework. How do you feel about all that?"

"Oh, I think every older person would like to stay in their home where they're comfortable and have memories. Moving to a retirement center in some ways is like making final plans. In other ways, though, it removes a lot of worry about how we're gonna keep up with all the responsibilities of keeping a large home going. We're ok with it. We're actually looking forward to making new friends and letting them know that I'm a teacher!" He smiled.

"That line has worked well for us, hasn't it?" Jack laughed.

"You too! So, we've found a place that we really like. We've had dinner there a couple of times and made friends with the activities director. She's interested in having a pastor there who could lead weakly bible studies!

"Wow! That's wonderful. I look forward to seeing it. So, Pops, will you sell the house..." he asked wistfully.

"Financially, we don't have to. We were thinking about giving it to a ministry where it could be used well... and we'd get the tax deduction from the transaction which would benefit us as well."

"What ministry are you thinking of?"

"Oh, I don't know... some group that's very legalistic and focuses on sin, hell, judgment, exclusion, right moral living... working hard to please God...that kind of group..."

"Still got your roguish sense of humor, don't you?" Jack laughed.

"Actually, now that you officially have a 501 (c) (3) non-profit ministry with your Grace Community, and since you're starting groups in college towns all over Texas, we thought maybe you'd like to have a furnished place where you could do retreats and training meetings for your leaders, that could also maybe be a hub for starting a group in Lawrence and maybe other places in this area."

"You've given this a lot of thought, haven't you?"

"No, actually we didn't know what to do, so we asked Jesus to tell us what He was thinking. He told Nana and me both this was what He wanted. So Jesus did all the thinking."

"Seems to me like He probably thought this up before

creation!"

"You think!"

They both laughed and shared their mutual joy in the intimate relationship they each had with their Creator and Friend.

"How's that sound to you, son?"

"I ain't gonna argue with Jesus… or you! I'm honored, of course, that you, Nana, and Jesus would want to do that with our ministry. It will be a real blessing to a lot of people, I know.

"So, what's your time-table for this, Pops?"

"Sometime next year. We'd like to have you all here for Christmas and have some memories of your son at the old place, then we'll see how the timing goes.

"Wow… well, that will give us time to do some planning with the group in Houston. Maybe we can work something out for the band to come and play at something for KU and have the opportunity to meet some students who might be interested.

"Can you come the last week of March, right after spring break?"

"You got something in mind?" Jack smiled.

"Oh, I know this guy… we've got something all set up if you can do it. It will pay pretty well, there are always a lot of students there, and we've actually got some friends who will convert the workshop and man-cave into living areas. I think there's room for the other two couples in the trio to stay there.

"Oh, and I've got a trumpet player I want you to meet who's been watching your stuff on YouTube. He'd like to bring a friend and play with the Texas Trinity Trio. Real nice young guy and he can play too."

"Do you have a seating chart for the guest dignitaries and confirmation on Perrier and oranges for the dressing room too?" He laughed.

"I haven't got that far yet… but we have the main things already lined up… if you can come."

"When we get back to the house, I'll get right on that and make sure the group is available."

"You are."

"What do you mean?"

"Nana checked your calendar on your website. You don't have

anything scheduled then."

"Well, I guess I'd better let the rest of the group know! You're a hoot, you know that?"

"I've been called other things too, you know!"

"Any other surprises you got for me while we're out here?"

"No, but I've got a question. I've been thinking a lot about what people have to look forward to, in this life, once they get the revelation of Jesus's finished work at the cross, unconditional love expressed as grace, and Christ in them. What would you say is the biggest difference in your life since you started to see these things?"

"That's a no-brainer for me. We talk a lot about that with our groups. It's when we start to see Christ in everyone else. When we realize there's no us/them, no in/out, no saved/unsaved. Once you realize the Holy Spirit of Christ is in every single person, and you start to actually see Christ in them– the hope of glory… that's a game-changer, you know?"

"Yep, that's exactly what I've experienced and seen in others over the years. What would you say that realization brings about in you?"

"Uh, well… peace. I don't have to worry if someone is saved or not. I don't have any pressure of thinking if I don't present the gospel exactly right, it will be my fault if they go to hell."

"Anything else?"

"Sure, the joy of knowing that all other people are included… the joy of knowing that God really is good and that He– They– really do love everyone… unconditionally."

"Love. Joy. Peace. I've come to realize that the things we call the fruit of the Spirit that all flow from Their unconditional agape love that always does what's best for the other person… those things seem to each come as the result of the one before them."

"How's that, Pops?"

"Well, once a person gets the revelation that God's love really is unconditional and for everyone, that immediately produces joy! Out of that love and joy comes the peace that you just described. Then, because we know the Trinity has already included them in Their Divine Triune circle dance, we can be patient… we don't have to worry or get uptight that someone's net yet where they will be.

"That then means we can be kind, good, and gentle with them. We have the faith of Jesus that they're right in God's timing… just like we always have been. It takes all the pressure off, don't you think?"

"That's a great analysis, Pops… I totally agree."

After a few moments of grateful reflection for what Christ has done in both their lives, the two Miller men decided to call it a day for their time at their special retreat place.

Fred took a last glance at the lake and softly said, "Til we meet again…"

Eventually Jack helped his Pops back into the convertible and as they slowly drove through the field back to the gate, each had a sense that the next time Jack came here, it would be with his new son instead of with his Pops, and a generation would pass. It wasn't a bad feeling… just a recognizing of what really is.

Section 11
Remembering Pops

Hearing the special ring tone of Amazing Grace sound on his cell phone rang during breakfast, Jack happily answered "Hi Pops! How you doin'?

"Jack, it's Nana. I can't find my phone. Pops will never experience The 'Hellish Darkness' again. He's dancing with Jesus, Papa and Sarayu now."

"Oh, Nana! What happened?"

As Susie Miller told her only grandchild about waking up and finding that her husband of over 6 decades was no longer living, Jack fought off his own emotions to comfort her. Finally being assured that a friend was on the way and that Nana had planned in advance what to do, He told his Nana how much he loved her, then broke the news to Clara.

He very much appreciated his wife's shared love for his Pops and Nana, and was grateful to be able to experience this time together. However he also needed some time by himself.

After a while he left to jog and shared his thoughts with His ever-present companion, Jesus. Their conversation included memories of the great sadness of losing his parents and his emotional roller coaster in the ensuing days, months and years.

They talked about the memorable Convertible Conversations he had with his grandfather and about the life lessons he learned. His heart swelled as they recalled their involvement with the Kelly family and others.

Fun memories of shared musical experiences washed through his thoughts.

He chuckled as he remembered Pops interrupting him right in the middle of his message at their wedding with "Hey! You're not listening to me at all! You're thinking about Clara!" How right the old man was! They shared that story often.

Jack was thankful that The 'Hellish Darkness' didn't come. He knew that was because of his strong awareness of Jesus. Finally it was time to go home and start making travel plans and arrangements for what would happen in Kansas.

Celebration of Life

It seemed very appropriate to Jack (and probably most everyone else who was there) to have Frederick Jackson Miller Sr.'s celebration of life in a country club ballroom with high glass windows on two sides overlooking a beautiful golf course.

Remembering Pops in a staid funeral home or in a formal church with pews, organ music, and stained glass windows just wouldn't convey the essence of Fred Miller.

From her experience of being with her husband as he officiated weddings, funerals, church services and other events, Susie thought she would be able to easily handle this event without him. However it was much harder than she anticipated. Clara's help made all the difference.

As they greeted the guests at the entryway to the ballroom, Susie, now occasionally using a walker, but still spry and full of life, stood between Jack and Clara with their toddler, Freddie, at her side. They had a college friend who was part of their new group at KU whom little Freddie loved, available to take him to a separate room when he got tired of the proceedings.

"Pardon me boy, is that the Chattanooga Choo Choo? Track twenty-nine, boy you can give me a shine," wafted through the air as it and several of the Glenn Miller Band's hits from the 40's played over the sound system. Most all the guests smiled and seemed to have a livelier step as they heard "In The Mood," "Little Brown Jug," and "Moonlight Serenade."

While there were just a few of Fred and Susie's high school and college classmates still around and in good health, those who lived in the Lawrence area, as well as several who flew in from around the country, arrived early... as octogenarians usually do. Former servicemen and women who played in Fred's army bands were there. While they were thinking of Fred before they arrived, the Big Band music brought back even more memories.

A myriad of friends and associates from music, education, church, and the general public came to honor their friend.

After the room was full and the hour arrived, Jack made sure that his grandmother was ok, checked his lavalier mic, and made his way to the portable stage, and set a notebook on a black music stand. Since that was the medium that his grandfather employed to direct bands and teach the Good News from, it seemed more appropriate than a podium.

"Welcome, everyone. I have the privilege of telling you all about my Pops, Frederick Jackson Miller, Sr. I'm Frederick Jackson Miller the third, so I have a little insight into what this man was like. I'm certainly aware that most of you knew him longer than I, and know him in different ways than I have. He touched many of your lives in a variety of good ways."

"I want to call your attention to the front of the program, which is a sketch I drew at a particularly hard time in my life where my Pops helped me in ways that mere words couldn't convey.

Jack then read the obituary listing the accomplishments of his grandfather's life, his relatives and the request that any memorials go to the Texas Trinity Trio's expanding ministry of college groups across the Lone Star state, Kansas and beyond.

He continued, "Those are the usual things you read about someone's life when they graduate to the next life. However, those things don't even come close to showing you what my grandfather was all about.

"Other than my Nana," he said as he nodded at Susie, "there's no one I've ever known that embodies unconditional love like Fred Miller. As some of you know, they became my surrogate parents when my mom and dad graduated to the life-after 17 years ago."

Claude Montgomery, sitting with the family in the front row, looked at Jack with tears streaming down his face. They were tears of joy and sorrow produced by the unconditional love the Millers lavished on him... not only the day nine years previous when he told them about being involved in Freddie and Rachel's untimely death...but then as they became friends and literally welcomed him into their lives.

"Many of you know Fred Miller as a talented musician... which he is. By the way, I'm using the present tense today, because Fred Miller is more alive today than he ever was in his life before!

"He was very talented, successful, and productive at his profession… but whatever profession he had chosen would have been nothing more than a useful means to encourage, lift up, and motivate people to enjoy and experience life to the fullest.

"As he progressed in his life, he came to experience an ever-expanding understanding of what real living was all about.

"His friend, Jesus, said that He– God– came to earth, so that we all might enjoy and experience abundant life… life to the full! Jesus came to reveal what the Forgotten Father, as Pops called Him, was really like.

"To Pops, every day was another opportunity to experience that God was even better than he believed the day before.

"Jesus revealed to Pops that God's very essence is love. Love is not something God does because He has to. Love is not something God gives or measures out to certain people who 'get it right' and please Him.

"Love is not something people can earn or deserve from God. Love is not something God will do only after people say the right prayer, confess the right way, and produce the right kind of living according to the religious group they belong to.

"Love is who God is… His very essence. Everything God says, thinks, and does flows from His perfect love!

"Jesus's closest friend during their three-year ministry time wrote in 1 John 4:16: MB

> We have come to know and believe the love that God has unveiled within us. God is love; love is who God is; to live in this place of conscious, constant love, is to live immersed in God and to feel perfectly at home in his indwelling. So now, with us awakening to our full inclusion in this love union, everything is perfect! Its completeness is not compromised in contradiction. Our confident conversation echoes this fellowship even in the face of crisis; because as he is, so are we in this world – our lives are mirrored in him. Fear cannot co-exist in this love realm. The perfect love union that we are talking about expels fear. Fear

holds on to an expectation of crisis and judgment. (which brings separation) and interprets it as due punishment (a form of karma!) It echoes torment and only registers in someone who does not realize the completeness of their love union (with the Father, Son and Spirit and with one another.) We love because he loved us first. (We did not invent this fellowship, we are invited into the fellowship of the Father and the son!)

"Many times, at events like this, a scripture is read and some of us zone out. Some of us go, 'Oh, that's a nice verse.' Some of us give it a little thought but that's about it.

"That's not my intent today. I'm not preaching you a sermon– my intent is to honor my Pops and the best way to honor him, in my opinion, is not to elaborate on his many accomplishments, but rather to tell you who he really is… what the essence of Frederick Miller, Sr. really is.

"I learned in the first few days when I came to live with Pops and Nana that the phrase 'the really is' was all-important to them! Pop's hardtop convertible was named the Really Is.

"He showed me that we all need to be convertible– able and willing to change– like his car did when we put the top down. Only then, after we changed, could we see what really is.

"Pops saw what really is! He understood that God is love. I don't mean that he knew the theological implications of that or a religious doctrine of love. I mean he abided in God's love. 'Abide' is an old scripture word that no one uses any more… but Pops knew what it meant, because he did it. 'Abide' means to dwell in seamless union…to continually be present with someone… to listen to them and talk to them and be with them all the time. Pops did that. Today we would say that he 'hung out' with God 24-7.

"That doesn't mean to hole up in a secluded place with your bible and prayer book and a library of books about God. It doesn't mean to have a long list of things you want God to do and you repeat them over and over to God every day. Far from it.

"Pops hung out with God. He heard God. He related to God. He saw and heard God in nature, in music, in art, and most of all... in other people... *all people.* He laughed with God and cried with God and joked with God. Pops knew that God has the best sense of humor there is.

"Until I started hanging out with my Pops, I didn't know you could hear from God. I've found out over the years that most people are afraid of hearing from God because they think all they will hear will be condemnation, guilt, shame, rules, regulations, and a continual list of all their wrongdoing and where they don't measure up– which they think is pretty much everywhere with God.

"Pops found out that none of that is true. He found out there is no condemnation from God. Period.

"Pops found out that God loves everyone unconditionally. Unconditionally means 'without any conditions' period, as he used to say. He taught me that religion says that God's love is unconditional, but then it starts listing religion's conditions, which are not God's conditions.

"Lots of people over the years questioned Pops about hearing from God. A lot of people don't believe that is possible. He used to say that you hear God from your inner ear... that's tuned in to God.

"Early on, I asked him what you did to hear from God. He said, 'You just ask Jesus if He's there... say 'Jesus, if you're there, I'd like to hear from you... what do You want to say to me?'

"As usual, Pops was right! I, and many of you, have been listening to the Living Word of God, Jesus, speak to us daily.

"Pops really learned how to communicate with... listen to, talk to, and relate to Jesus... who lives in Pops and who lives in every human being whether we know it or not.

"He especially internalized and appropriated the old version of the verse I read earlier that says, 'There is no fear in love; but perfect love casts out fear, because fear involves punishment, and the one who fears is not perfected in love.'

"He knew, and passed on to everyone with whom he had the opportunity, that when you absolutely know that God loves you and everyone unconditionally– without conditions– then you need never fear punishment or judgment! He studied and learned what scripture says, and the early church believed, that at His finished work at the cross, Jesus judged us all perfect!

"The fact that Pops came to know God personally, and know that God is love and not be worried about judgment or punishment...that affected Pop's life... as it did my Nana, whom you know as Susie. They came to see all people differently than they did before.

"Pops saw Christ in every person he encountered. Young/old, black/white, rich/poor, religious/non-religious, grumpy/pleasant, scoundrel/saint... Pops actually saw Christ in everyone! You think that won't change your life?

"Here's what I want you to know about Fred Miller, Sr. – He modeled God's unconditional love. There was never any question in my mind that Pops loved me unconditionally... without condition. And I sure gave him reason not to love me sometimes...like when I totaled his prize possession, his convertible: the Really Is.

"Once he was assured that I wasn't hurt, he simply said, 'there are other convertibles' but there's only one you. Now, let's go help the other person whose car hit you.'

"That's called grace... which is unconditional love in action.

"I have to be truthful and say that he did get a little upset and swear at me later that night. That woke my grandmother up and I had to lie to cover up for him" he laughed. "The last thing we heard her say before she went to bed was "Liars and Cussers. What's a pastor's wife to do!"

"That's exactly what happened!" Susie said from the front row and the entire crowd burst into laughter.

"Over and over I saw him love me unconditionally, and over and over I saw him love other people unconditionally. One of the prime examples of that is my close friend Claude Montgomery, whom many of you have heard play with the Texas Trinity Trio. You've heard his testimony on videos or in person.

"When Claude came unannounced from Houston and showed up at our house here in Lawrence to tell us that he thought he was responsible for the deaths of Pops's son and daughter-in-law, my parents– I saw unconditional love put in action. That was grace.

"Pops used to use this illustration... he said if you're speeding and a cop pulls you over and you deserve a ticket and you get one, that's life. That's the way the world works. But if the cop lets you off, that's mercy. You don't get what you deserve. God is like that.

"If you deserve a ticket, but the cop doesn't give you one and instead, he gives you a hundred dollar bill and says, 'have a nice dinner with your wife tonight,' that's grace. You get something really good that you don't deserve and didn't earn. That's God's unconditional love in action.

He paused a moment, smiled, and then said, "If you deserve a ticket and *you* give the cop a hundred dollar bill– that's a bribe."

After the laughter subsided, he continued, "Pops taught me that, and unfortunately, that's what many of us do with God. We say, 'God, if you'll just let me off, I'll never do it again. I'll devote my life to you. I'll quit doing whatever. I'll throw $100 in the offering plate.' We try to bribe God. That's not what God wants.

"Mercy and grace describe my Pops perfectly. Over and over he didn't give me what I deserved, and instead, he gave me grace. And he did that with you all... and with everyone he was with.

"I know he wasn't perfect in his life here. Sometimes he didn't listen to God just like the rest of us. But that was never his intent. The longer he walked with Jesus, the less he reverted to his old ways. He wanted to give mercy, grace, and unconditional love to every single person he came in contact with.

"Of course, that wasn't always the way he was. He told me about the way he used to power up and control and intimidate the soldiers in his first army bands. He said that when God demonstrated and revealed His unconditional love to Pops then Pops started giving grace and unconditional love to his band members.

"That can be extremely hard in a strict military environment. I've heard some of you who knew him before and after relate that Pop's concept of military regimen was often different that the Army's concept!" Jack smiled and enjoyed the chuckles, Amen's, and Hooah's from the military people in attendance.

"Pops lack of interest in rules, regulations and traditions was never more apparent than with organized religion. After becoming a pastor, in a few years, he and Nana left organized religion. In fact, he was often accused of promoting disorganized religion. That really bothered him. He was okay with being called disorganized, but he didn't want to have anything to do with religion!

"He loved helping people who had been judged, chastised, condemned, and excluded by organized transactional religion… because he knew those were the very people Jesus came to help. He knew that any attempt to convince people that they had to do some transaction to get right with Jesus was an affront to Christ's finished work at the cross.

"Pops didn't angrily crusade against Transactional Religion. He learned that the best criticism of the bad is the continual practice of the best. He wanted to show people what really is… God's unconditional love for all, so he practiced doing that so often that when his friends would encounter counterfeit religion, they'd easily discount it.

"There are a few more attributes my grandfather had that are important for you to know about. Most of you experienced them.

"Pops understood scripture differently than a lot of people. He believed that God was love and that everything God says and does flows from His unconditional love. Once that became his foundation, he then evaluated scripture differently.

"Anytime he saw a passage that seemed to indicate that God was harsh, vindictive, punitive, judgmental in a legal sense… any time he saw a passage that said God was keeping a record of our wrongs, couldn't stand to be around sinners and had to be appeased somehow… he decided that either that was a mistranslation of the original, or the context was misrepresented, or there was something he just didn't understand yet.

"He learned that God is only good… there is nothing bad in God, and all good things come from God. He taught me that scripture tells us that some of those things, or attributes, that describe God include joy, peace, patience, kindness, goodness, gentleness, the faith of Christ, living under the Spirit's control, compassion, mercy, and grace.

"Pops learned that whatever was true of God, was actually true of each of us, because Christ lives in us. He knew that was a mystery to most people and he delighted in explaining it to folks… as he did with many of you. He loved Colossians 1:27, NKJ "This is the mystery… Christ is in you all, the hope of glory!"

"I could talk about how my Pops lived and demonstrated all of the attributes of Jesus. I won't elaborate, but I'll just say that he was able to be at peace in situations that really rattled me. Even when rotten things happened, like my parents dying suddenly, his initial reaction was anger and questioning God, doubting, all that, but real soon He listened to Jesus and he had an inner confidence that I would now describe as joy.

"He experienced attacks from what he calls The 'Hellish Darkness' just like the rest of us. Sometimes he got angry and questioned God. Sometimes he cussed and threw rocks. Sometimes he pounded on the side of the house til his knuckles were bleeding. All that happened when my folks died.

"He didn't put on a fake smile and say that they're in a better place. Not at all. He, like Nana and me, was devastated. He was sad. He grieved. He questioned God. He got really angry when his imagination wondered about some person who may have caused the accident.

"However, he quickly turned to His friend, Jesus. He might let his mind go to dark places for a moment or a little while, but he always remembered to go back to God and say something like, 'God, I don't understand this. This is what I'm feeling but I want to know what you want me to know. I know you work all things out for the good, so I thank you for that. I want to see what really is.

"Then he'd listen to God. And pretty soon his whole attitude and countenance would change. He still felt sad or whatever, but he regained that quiet confidence of trusting God.

"He helped me through the loss of my parents in a way you could never imagine… unless you knew my Pops.

"Pops told me that patience surely wasn't a human virtue of his. But he loved the fact that when he was tempted to be impatient, quick to judge, and quick to castigate– he learned to stop, tell Jesus that he was starting to overheat, and ask Jesus what He wanted him to know about the situation.

"Often, Pops would hear something from Jesus that really came out of left field but turned out to be true.

"One time I was part of an unfortunate, or so I thought, incident one of the first days at my new school, where another boy was dared to smear my white shirt with ketchup at lunch. That boy got in trouble and got a two-day suspension.

"But he got in way more trouble at home. That night his parents brought him to our house to apologize and Pops listened to Jesus. He understood that the boy's father, like Pops, really struggled in life because of unrealistic expectations their fathers had on them. He learned that the boy was really gonna be in for it with his dad, who was a rather stern and harsh military officer.

"Pops took the boy's dad aside that night, using a little military ingenuity, if I remember right! He listened, heard, and talked to that man. Then they became friends and regularly came to our Grace Community that met Sunday evenings. Jesus changed that man in a dramatic way, over time, which was wonderful for him and for his family.

"Rather than my incident being unfortunate, because of Pops listening to Jesus, I got to become lifelong friends with Major, now Major General Boyd Frye, Annaliese, and Robby, who came here today from Washington D.C. where General Frye works at the Pentagon." As Jack motioned towards the Frye's, there was a spontaneous round of applause, and a chorus of hooah's accompanied by tears of joy.

"Another time as school was getting out, I witnessed a beating administered by a classmate's father who ended up being convicted of second degree murder and was sent to prison. Pops helped him tremendously. Today, William Kelly is involved in prison ministry with his son, Pat. Stand up, please, Will and Pat." More applause…more tears of joy.

"I could tell lots of stories like that about people all over this room, but time doesn't permit.

"I want to also tell you that everything I said about my Pops is equally true about Nana. They are both the real deal!" As he clapped for her, the room exploded into a standing ovation, which, of course, greatly embarrassed Susie Miller.

"Nana, Clara, little Freddie Jackson Miller the 3rd, and I look forward to visiting with anyone who can join us in the room next door where we'll have drinks and sandwiches in a few minutes. Actually, Little Freddie really likes situations like that. He might be the most social person you've ever met. Don't be surprised if he asks you to play with him!

"In closing, I want to share with you another of Pop's favorite and most meaningful scriptures. This is from John 14:20 NKJV where Jesus said, 'In that day you will know that just as I am in my Father, you are in me and I am in you!'

"More than anything, Frederick Jackson Miller, Sr. wants each of you, his friends, to know to the core of your being that Jesus, His Father, and The Holy Spirit are in you… and they love you unconditionally. Their total desire is for you to enjoy and experience Their love… as Pops and Nana do.

"Now, some of you thought you were coming here to pay your respects and say goodbye to Fred Miller. He would want you to know that we're not saying goodbye, we're saying, 'Til we meet again.'"

A Note from The Author

If something about the unconditional love of God for everyone–as taught by Fred and Susie Miller to their grandson Jack, and to others, resonated with your spirit, you will be encouraged through the following resources. Also note that in the novel, scripture verses were annotated 'NKJV' meaning New King James Version and "MB' indicating the Mirror Bible. Unmarked verses were the author's translation.

Future Resources from Paul Gray

In the Chapter "Turning Eleven" of Convertible Conversations, you learned about a book that Jack's father wrote for him before he died. It's titled "Grace Is." This book, written in a "page-a-day" format that can be used for daily reading or as a workbook or group study book, explains Fred Miller's understanding of God and the Bible, will be released in the spring of 2018.

In the chapter "New Old Clothes and Freddie's Last Letter" of Convertible Conversations, Jack received a book that his deceased father had written 8 years previous. The author has taken actual "Notes From Papa" that he has journaled while conversing with "Papa" and compiled them in a book, titled "Notes From Papa" (a 365 day devotional book) which will be available in the fall of 2018.

About Paul Gray

Paul and his wife of 48 years, Kitsy, live in Lawrence, Kansas where they continue to facilitate growing in grace at the church they founded in 1991, New Life in Christ. They have three wonderful grown children and 6 amazing grandchildren! *Convertible Conversations*, a short week-day video series on a wide range of topics, are posted by Paul at *Online Community Church* on Facebook.

Before starting New Life in Christ, beginning in 1969, Paul was involved in a variety of businesses ranging from retail music stores to a long-distance telephone company, including Paul Gray's Jazz Place, a popular Lawrence, Kansas jazz venue where he performed with his group, The Gaslite Gang. Concurrently, he served in the United States Army National Guard and Reserves for 24 years as a bandmaster.

In 1999, his church started a medical clinic for homeless individuals, The Heartland Medical Clinic, which continues to serve the medical needs of thousands of patients each year.

Paul Gray holds an education degree from the University of Kansas and a degree in theology from Global Grace Seminary.

More information about Paul, videos and musical recordings can be found at www.gracewithpaulgray.com

Spiritual articles/videos can be found at: www.godisforme.org.

You may contact Paul Gray at: convertibleconversations@gmail.com.

Books by Paul Gray

Grace Is and *Notes From Papa* (a 365 day devotional book) are scheduled to be released in 2018.

Fishnet Experience

Paul Gray is co-author of *Godly Men Make Godly Fathers!* (15 Christian fathers have contributed to this book which was released in October, 2017. Paul's chapter is titled "Parenting Help From THE Helper!" It is published by Motivation Champs Publishing.)

Paul Gray's Suggested Resources

Paul Gray's Top Ten Recommended Books
(In No Particular Order)

- *Patmos* by Baxter Kruger
- *Beyond an Angry God* by Steve McVey
- *God's Astounding Opinion of You* by Ralph Harris
- *The Shack* by William Paul Young
- *The Shack Revisited* by Baxter Kruger
- *Parable of the Dancing God* by C. Baxter Kruger
- *Saints in the Arms of a Happy God* by Jeff Turner
- *The Mirror Bible Paraphrase* by Francois Du Toit
- *Grace Walk* by Steve McVey
- *The Divine Dance* by Richard Rohr

Other Great Books

- By Andre Rabe
  Adventures in Christ
  The Secret of Contentment
  Metanoia
  Desire
  Imagine
- *It is Finished* by Blaise Foret
- By John Crowder
  Cosmos Reborn
  Mystical Union
- By Paul Ellis
  Hyper-Grace Gospel
  The Gospel in Twenty Questions
- *Heavens Doors* by George. W. Sarris
- By Wm. Paul Young
  Cross Roads
  Eve
  Lies We Believe About God
- *We Make the Road By Walking* by Brian D. McLaren
- *The Rest of the Gospel* by Dan Stone & Greg Smith

- By Bill Gillham
  What God Wishes Christians Knew About Christianity
  Lifetime Guarantee
- By Steve McVey
  The Secret of Grace
  Grace Rules
  52 Lies Heard in Church Every Sunday
  A Divine Invitation
  Unlock Your Bible
  When Wives Walk in Grace
- By Preston Gillham
  No Mercy
  Battle for the Round Tower
- *Helping Others Overcome Addiction* by Steve McVey & Mike Quarles
- *A Woman's Walk in Grace* by Catherine Martin
- *Bo's Café* by John Lynch, Bruce McNicol & Bill Thrall
- By C. Baxter Kruger
  The Great Dance
  God is For You
  Across All Worlds
  Jesus and the Undoing of Adam
- By John Eldredge
  Beautiful Outlaw
  Waking the Dead
- *He Loves Me!* by Wayne Jacobsen
- By Jody Marie White
  Chosen by God
  Scarlet White
- By Richard Rohr
  The Naked Now
  Falling Upward
  Everything Belongs
  Yes And
- By Peter Enns
  The Sin of Certainty
  The Gospel in Ten Words

- *One Way Love* by Tullian Tchividjian
- *The Fish Net Experience* by Paul Gray
- *Been There, Done That* by Mike Miller
- *The Inescapable Love of God* by Thomas Talbott
- By Bradly Jersak
  A More Christlike God
  Here Gates Will Never Be Shut
- By Ivan A. Rogers
  Dropping Hell and Embracing Grace
  Grace Nuggets Uncovered
- By Brain Zahnd
  Unconditional
  Beauty Will Save The World
  Sinners in the Arms of a Loving God
  Farewell to Mars
- By Francois Du Toit
  God Believes in You
  The Logic of His Love
- By Peter Enns
  The Sin of Certainty
  The Bible Tells Me So
- *The Unspoken Sermons* by George MacDonald

Devotional Books

- *The Grace Walk Devotional* by Steve McVey
- *Grace Walk Moments* by Steve McVey
- *Face to Face – Praying the Scriptures for Intimate Worship* by Kenneth Boa
- *My Utmost for His Highest* by Oswald Chambers
- *Jesus Calling* by Sarah Young

Recommended Grace Websites:

www.newlifeinchrist.com
www.perichoresis.com
www.gracewalk.org
www.lifecourse.org

www.ingramcontent.com/pod-product-compliance
Lightning Source LLC
Chambersburg PA
CBHW060453090426
42735CB00011B/1974